W9-CHS-619

The Online Journ@list

The Online Journ@list

Using the Internet and Other Electronic Resources

Second Edition

Randy Reddick

FACS Los Angeles & London

Elliot King

Loyola College

Harcourt Brace College Publishers

*Fort Worth Philadelphia San Diego New York Orlando Austin San Antonio
Toronto Montreal London Sydney Tokyo*

Publisher	Christopher P. Klein
Senior Acquisitions Editor	Carol Wada
Product Manager	Ilsa Wolfe-West
Senior Project Editor	Charles J. Dierker
Art Director	Garry Harman
Production Manager	Serena Manning

ISBN: 0-15-505222-5

Library of Congress Catalog Card Number: 96-80011

Address for Editorial Correspondence: Harcourt Brace College Publishers, 301 Commerce Street, Suite 3700, Fort Worth, TX 76102.

Address for Orders: Harcourt Brace & Company, 6277 Sea Harbor Drive, Orlando, FL 32887-6777. 1-800-782-4479.

Website address: http://www.hbcollege.com

Harcourt Brace & Company will provide complimentary supplements or supplement packages to those adopters qualified under our adoption policy. Please contact your sales representative to learn how you qualify. If as an adopter or potential user you receive supplements you do not need, please return them to your sales representative or send them to: Attn: Returns Department, Troy Warehouse, 465 South Lincoln Drive, Troy, MO 63379.

Printed in the United States of America

6 7 8 9 0 1 2 3 4 5   066   10 9 8 7 6 5 4 3 2 1

Preface

In the 1830s the high-speed steam printing press was invented, changing journalism forever. First radio in the 1920s, and then television in the 1950s, became mass consumer media.

In the 1990s, widespread computer-based communications networks, most prominently the Internet, came online. Once again, the practice of journalism has been changed forever.

Pat Stith, Pultizer Prize winner and computer-assisted reporting specialist for *The* (Raleigh, N.C.) *News and Observer* has said, "Those who use these tools will be ahead. Those who don't will be left behind—and may not survive."

Nora Paul of the Poynter Institute has told journalists, "By taking advantage of the access to information and people available to you by using a computer, your research and interviewing can have a range and immediacy that is simply impossible without a computer's assistance."

Since the first edition of *The Online Journalist* appeared, the Internet and other computer-based communications networks have emerged as dynamic, widespread, accessible new channels of communication. The World Wide Web, which was still an insiders' secret when we began the first edition of this book in 1993, is now used by most major companies in the United States to communicate to audiences large and small. Many government agencies, corporations and nonprofit organizations are making vast amounts of information available online.

Moreover, nearly all students have access to the Web, and newsrooms are slowly providing reporters with Internet access at their desks. This edition of the book reflects and incorporates those changes.

The Online Journalist describes and demonstrates how reporters can use the Internet and other online resources to do their jobs more efficiently and effectively. It also discusses the impact that this still-new technology will have on journalism, the pitfalls that reporters and editors must avoid as they enter cyberspace, and the legal and ethical issues that are raised by online journalism. Finally, it reviews some of the pioneering efforts at publishing online.

Jargon-free and intended for both students and professional journalists, this book has value for everybody from those first tentatively dipping their toes into the online world to experienced Net surfers. It guides readers from making the initial connections needed to utilize online resources to applying those resources on enterprise reporting projects.

In addition to introducing the range of online resources and clearly explaining how to use all the major applications on the Internet, *The Online Journalist* includes appendixes that point out useful online resources for journalists, a glossary of terms, and guidance for selecting an Internet provider.

As we did in the first edition, we feel grateful to many people. We would like to thank our families—our wives Anita and Nancy; our children, Aliza and Marcie, Laura, Ben, Roxanne, Jennifer, Heather, and Jacob.

We continue to be grateful to many journalists, educators, colleges and media companies for the help and encouragement that they have provided in the development of this second edition. Among them are e-mail discussion list owners Elliott Parker of CARR-L, George Frajkor of JOURNET, and Rosemary Armao of IRE-L. Tom Johnson challenged journalism educators in a 1992 *Quill* magazine article to get digital. This book is in part a by-product of the discussion that he started.

This book has built upon the work of others who deserve recognition. "Zen Artist" Brendan Kehoe, "NorthWest Netter" Ed Kockner, and "Internet Hitchhiker" Ed Krol generously made available online their guidelines to the network before the 1992–1994 flood of Internet books. Others who did likewise: Odd de Presno, "Big Dummy" Adam Gaffin, and the EARN Association. John Makulowich and John December have created and maintained resource lists of interest to journalists and journalism educators.

We were helped by many other generous contributors to relevant e-mail discussion lists, including: Joe Abernathy, Jack Lail, Peter Weiss, Steve Doig, Tom Boyer, Russell Clemings, Steve Outing, Bruce Siceloff, Steve Yelvington, and Dan Gillmor.

People in the academic community who have encouraged this work include Sue O'Brien, Judy Solberg, Dolores Jenkins, Nancy Green, Lillian Kopenhaver, Ralph Izard, Guido Stempel, Hugh Culbertson, Pat Washburn, Tom Hodges, Carolin Cline, and Milverton Wallace.

We would also like to thank the following professors for their reviews and feedback on the first edition: Mike Cowling, University of Wisconsin–Oshkosh; Nancy Roberts, University of Minnesota; Paul Adams, California State University–Fresno; Kim Walsh-Childers, University of Florida; and Jim Ross, Northeastern University.

Scientific Computing & Automation magazine continues to be the publication in which many of the reporting techniques and online publishing ideas described in this book were experienced in action. We thank Jack Martin, Terry McCoy, Jr., and Dave Esola for their support and vision in this effort. We thank Aimee Kalnoskas for being a delightful comrade-in-arms. John Joyce, *Scientific Computing & Automation's* Internet columnist, has also taught us some tricks for which we are grateful.

Loyola College provided Internet access and other resources. We appreciate the support and encouragement provided by Neil Alperstein and Andy Ciofalo for this project and for seeing the contribution that the Internet can make to the Department of Writing & Media.

FACS and the FACS trustees have encouraged continued development of *The Online Journalist*.

Randy Reddick, reddick@facsnet.org
Elliot King, king@loyola.edu

Contents

Chapter 5   Gopher Jewels   85

Chapter 6   Telnet & FTP: Internet Core   107

Chapter 7   Groupspeak: Lists & News   135

Chapter 8   Chat Zones, MUDs, and BBSes   161

Chapter 9   Search Strategies & Case Studies   185

Chapter 10   Law, Ethics, and the Internet   203

About the Authors

Randy Reddick is Editor and Director of FACSNET, an online research service for journalists operated by the Foundation for American Communications (FACS). He served as managing editor of *The Daily Press* and as vice president for Paso Robles (Calif.) Newspapers, Inc. from 1973 to 1988. He earned a Ph.D. in mass communication from Ohio University and has taught at Ohio University, Texas Tech University, and the University of Southern California. Reddick is a frequent speaker at professional conventions and seminars.

Elliot King is an assistant professor of media studies at Loyola College in Maryland and editor in chief of *Scientific Computing & Automation* magazine. He has co-authored or co-edited six books, including *The Online Student: Making the Grade on the Internet,* also published by Harcourt Brace College Publishers. He holds a Ph.D. in sociology with an emphasis in mass communication from the University of California–San Diego and an M.S. in journalism from Columbia University.

Chapter 1

An Introduction

Tom Regan of the Halifax *Daily News* was doing a story on Canada's troubling national debt. "Several politicians and right-wing business groups were running around yelling 'The sky is falling!' and demanding that the government make enormous cuts in Canada's social programs," Regan wrote. "I wanted to find out if there was any substance to these dire predictions."

What Regan did was to post some messages to Usenet news groups and to electronic listservs related to Canadian politics. In his postings he asked "for anyone with real information to reply to my query." Then he used an Internet program named Gopher to find static documents on the Canadian economy. All this took him about a half hour, he reported.

"When I checked an hour later, responses to my queries abounded," he wrote. He had notes from a professor in Montreal and the names of "three international economists from major U.S. financial firms who said Canada's debt crisis was being overblown." Another note led him to an expert on Canadian economics living in Australia.

"Without the Internet, it would have taken weeks to research the story, and I would have been limited to 'experts' in and around Nova Scotia," Regan concluded.

Regan is among a growing number of journalists who have discovered tools new to the trade. These tools enable reporters to use computers as a means of communicating with other people and of accessing information stored throughout the world.

Sergio Charlab, special projects editor at *Jornal do Brasil*, had a challenging assignment. An important book about computers and the human mind had been translated into Portuguese. Charlab said that *The Emperor's New Mind* by British mathematician Roger Penrose "is interesting, but it was not easy for a non-technical person to analyze its thesis." By posting messages to what he felt were appropriate Usenet news groups, Charlab found others who had not only read the book but had written papers critical of some shortcomings in Professor Penrose's theory. Ultimately, Charlab obtained the e-mail address of Professor Penrose and "interviewed" him. All this without one telephone call.

In the fall of 1996, Silicon Graphics, a major computer manufacturer released a new line of equipment ranging from workstations to supercomputers. The announcement revealed the technological direction of the company for the next several years. For months, company officials had stumped the country, alerting key journalists and analysts of their plans.

But for the announcement itself, Silicon Graphics organized a real-time press conference on the World Wide Web. Journalists and others accessed the Silicon Graphics Web site, where they obtained background briefing papers, biographies of senior executives and press releases describing the new products in detail. They also could listen to a live audio feed of company officials outlining their plans. And they could submit questions via e-mail to which the executives could respond.

For its last set of major announcements the year before, Silicon Graphics had asked about 75 journalists to fly to company headquarters in northern California. By moving their press conference to the Web, they were able to attract more participants at less cost. And the journalists themselves received a superior briefing about the key issues.

This chapter will:

- describe the mission of the book.
- discuss the relationship of technology, access and journalism.
- characterize the target audience for the book.
- point out the differences between the first and second editions of *The Online Journalist*.
- suggest a sequence for using the book to master online skills.

The Mission of this Book

This book is about empowerment. It is about the empowerment of individual journalists, the empowerment of entire organizations, and the empowerment of other information providers.

This book describes a group of information-gathering tools that make some types of high-level reporting less dependent on company resources than on a journalist's initiative. The objective of this book is to teach good journalists how to practice better journalism.

In the past, elite media with enormous news budgets have sent out correspondents to centers of power and to locations of history-making events at home and abroad. They have had access to the inaccessible.

Today, "ordinary" reporters and student reporters using global computer network resources have instant electronic access to important documents, government data, privately held information, the world's greatest libraries, and expert sources and government officials without ever leaving their desks. Instead of going to Washington, Ottawa, London, or Cairo, New Delhi, Beijing, Taipei, Tokyo, or Cape Town, today's journalists may bring to their own desks resources from important centers of the world. And the same tools that reach around the world work down the block and around the corner.

Moreover, a reporter "fishing" for people who have firsthand knowledge of newsworthy events can reach tens of thousands of potential sources in just a couple of hours. A carefully worded query posted in the proper news groups, entered into online forums, and sent out to the right electronic mail lists can quickly net a bountiful harvest of eyewitnesses to some event, of victims to some plot or oversight, or of people with other firsthand knowledge that qualifies them as a news source.

Finally, every reporter who has held a beat has had to interview somebody on topics about which the reporter had little background or expertise. Aside from being uncomfortable, the reporter is likely to ask ill-informed questions. Such questions elicit answers that do little to inform readers or audience members. Many news sources make it policy not to waste time with poorly informed journalists.

Again, through network resources the journalist can quickly locate and download "white papers" on just about any topic imaginable. Tucked away on sites on the World Wide Web, in news-group cubby holes, listserv archives, and various specialized computer directories are storehouses of information that can provide journalists with answers to basic questions. More important, with that information in hand, journalists can ask more penetrating and probing questions than they could in the past.

Technology, Access, and Journalism

Interesting, timely, and accurate information is fundamental fodder for good journalism. For the last century, access to information has primarily defined the work that reporters do. Beats and specialization revolve around access. Police reporters work with information from the police. Court reporters become experts in understanding legal information. Sports reporters traffic in batting averages and zone defenses.

For years, the White House beat was considered the most prestigious in journalism. At the bottom line, the role of a White House reporter was defined by access to information from the White House. The first White House reporters hovered close outside the Executive Mansion itself, monitoring who entered and left for meetings with the chief executive. In the early 1900s, Theodore Roosevelt began meeting formally with reporters on a regular basis. His actions granted a certain status to those reporters. From then on, White House reporters were privy to information that reporters working in Philadelphia, Chicago, or Los Angeles just could not get on a timely basis.

That situation is rapidly changing. With the development of commercial databases, computer bulletin boards, and the Internet, journalists working anywhere can have the same access to much of the information once restricted to White House reporters. Today, any reporter with access to the Internet can visit the White House briefing room at http:// www.whitehouse.gov/ and obtain White House press releases, transcripts of press conferences and speeches, summaries of reports generated by Federal agencies, and a host of other material.

Along the same lines, business reporters can now obtain Securities and Exchange Commission filings electronically. Science reporters can explore the databases of the National Institute of Health, the National Science Foundation and the National Library of Medicine among other resources. Court reporters can access court filings and decisions. In almost every area of interest to journalists, reporters dramatically increase their access to information through electronic communications networks.

In the same way that telephones allowed reporters to interview people around the country, electronic communications networks allow people to locate and obtain information from locations around the world. In short, online information allows reporters to do their jobs better no matter where they are physically located.

The Payoff of Increased Access

The question is, "Do reporters need access to more information?" After all, isn't there already a glut of information? Moreover, with so much information available, will reporters be reduced to simply sifting through information produced by others to pass on to busy readers?

The answer is complex but clear. The more access to information reporters have, the better reporters will be able to fulfill their mission to inform the public about key issues and interests of the day. More access to more information can only lead to better journalism.

The late investigative reporter I.F. Stone demonstrated in the1960s and early 1970s the power of exploring public sources of information ignored by other people. Relying exclusively on not-so-obscure, but little-publicized public documents, he revealed how the U.S. government misled the American people about its policies in Vietnam. To review most of those documents, Stone had to be in Washington. Increasingly, a reporter anywhere in the country has that ability.

Increased access to documents can also reduce reporters' reliance on specific sources, allowing them to be more independent and objective and making it more difficult for politicians and handlers to put a specific "spin" on events. For example, in the summer of 1994, the Clinton administration pushed for passage of a $30 billion crime bill. Some Republican senators charged that the bill was filled with pork-barrel projects. Most of the reporting about the bill consisted of charges being hurled back and forth in Washington and the potential political repercussions for President Clinton if the bill was defeated.

But with that bill accessible online, reporters from Altoona to Anchorage could have downloaded and analyzed what kind of impact the proposals would have had in their communities. They could have then interviewed local sources to get their readings on the measures. Local officials could have reflected on the impact of the bill—not on inside-the-beltway politics but in their own communities. Using online access, reporters can make national and international news more relevant to their own communities. Should they wish, reporters anywhere can now analyze the federal budget according to their own criteria rather than the criteria of politicians in Washington.

Far from reducing reporters to sifters of information, the explosion of access to a wider range of sources of information will make the role of reporters much more valuable. Reporters will be able to develop more authoritative stories more quickly. More important, reporters will be the only ones in position to synthesize information from disparate sources into stories that are relevant to their readers.

For example, let's say a legal reporter wants to investigate the performance of the local court system. Among the key questions: "How long does it take civil suits to be resolved?"; "How many judges does the civil court have and what is the total budget?"; and "How satisfied are the litigants who use civil court to resolve their dispute?"

In addition to surveying local court records and interviewing local, self-interested participants, the reporter with online access could compare the local court performance to court performance in other similar cities. The reporter could identify experts, key players and knowledgeable observers around the country to provide insight and perspective. If there were appropriate federal information, that could be identified and located as well. The reporter could network with other reporters working on like topics, drawing on their expertise and experience. And all this research could be conducted without traveling and within the normal daily work routine.

Reporters craft useful, interesting stories. Online access to wider sources of information means that more reporters can pursue more stories of greater interest to specific readers or viewers. More fact-filled and broader in scope, those stories should be of greater value than ever before.

For Whom this Book Is Intended

You do not have to be a Macintosh Maven, a Windows Whiz, a UNIX Virtuoso, or any other kind of computer guru to be proficient at harvesting online information. This book tells journalists what buttons to push to find the information they are seeking. It does so using plain English. *The Online Journalist* assumes that most journalists have little desire to become computer programmers or to learn computer languages.

Instead, *The Online Journalist* assumes that most reporters have in mind certain information they need and that they want the information in a hurry. If they get the information quickly, they can spend their deadline time crafting the best story possible rather than wrestling with inflexible machines. Not only will journalists proficient with these tools have more time to write, their reports can be more thorough and comprehensive. It is the aim of this book to enable journalists to get quickly and easily the information they need in their work.

Other books about the Internet are more general and diffuse, aimed at less specific audiences. Journalists who develop keen interest in the Internet may want to read some of the other books, but, generally, all the information you need to use the Internet and these tools is included here.

Of course, to use online sources of information, journalists have to have online access. Although there are several levels of online access, to fully use the tools described in this book, you need to have access to the Internet and the World Wide Web.

There are several different ways to get access to the Web. Almost all colleges and universities in America are now connected to the Internet and the Web. Students and faculty should consult their information-services support team to arrange e-mail accounts and get an overview of the online services on campus.

Off campus, many media companies provide, or plan to provide, online access to all of their reporters. Many already have at least a couple of computers networked to the Internet. In the not too distant future, Internet access in media companies should be as ubiquitous as telephone access.

Moreover, millions of people have arranged their own Internet access either through commercial services such as CompuServe and America Online or through Internet service providers. AT&T, MCI and other major companies provide Internet access as do many small providers around the country. Although many people use Internet service providers primarily to gain access to the World Wide Web, in most cases these providers also offer the full range of Internet tools such as e-mail, Telnet, and FTP, all included in the same monthly service charge. Appendix B offers a more in-depth look at access issues.

In addition to having online access, this book assumes that the reader has some familiarity with computers and uses a computer for word processing. This book describes the process of finding information online and bringing that information to your computer. The assumption is that at least in terms of text files you find online, you will be incorporating material from those files into your work on computer.

Although this book describes how to make use of computer-based tools to do better research for stories and projects, this book is NOT a computer book. It is written in English, generally speaking, the "newsroom variety" of English, cleaned up a little.

There is no attempt in this book to be all-inclusive or encyclopedic. Instead, we have focused on a limited selection of network tools that are

- easily accessible through the Internet or, if commercially based, priced for the common person.
- either indispensable tools (like e-mail) or ones that provide a high rate of return for the time invested in learning to use them.

We have thus intentionally avoided some network facilities altogether. And we have intentionally refrained from providing exhaustive discussions of those tools we do describe.

Instead, *The Online Journalist* teaches how to use online tools and how to get further help for each tool. This is especially important when we are describing a moving target like the Internet, which changes shape from week to week. Each tool is described in a setting that illustrates how the tool may be (or has been) used by journalists.

As with other tools, the user becomes more proficient and skilled with frequent use. *The Online Journalist* describes the tools and provides electronic addresses of computer sites housing information or providing services of particular value to journalists. It is hoped that you will test the tools and hone your skills by employing them at many sites. Appendix A contains an extensive list of electronic addresses for online resources that will serve as starting points for online journalists.

Although *The Online Journalist* occasionally describes commands unique to VMS or UNIX systems, it generally assumes that most readers will be accessing online resources from a personal computer of the Macintosh or IBM compatible variety. With some more basic tools, you may connect to distant computers and talk to those computers through a program with a plain, text-based, command-line interface. But most often, particularly using the World Wide Web, you will enjoy the benefits of the graphical user interface associated with Windows and the Macintosh.

Between the First and Second Editions

As noted in the first edition of *The Online Journalist* (and noted again in this edition), the Internet is a moving target. New services are coming online and existing services are improving rapidly. Moreover, the use of the Internet is exploding.

Perhaps the most significant development since the publication of the first edition of this book has been the growth of the World Wide Web. When this book first appeared, there were only a few thousand Web sites worldwide. One of the most popular sites was at a community college in Hawaii—because it was one of the only sites available to visit.

Now there may be 100 Web sites on the campus of Loyola College itself and many more Web home pages there. Most large companies have extensive presences on the Web that they advertise routinely on television. Government agencies are scrambling to make information available on the Web. Small companies, nonprofit agencies, local governments and untold numbers of others who provide information to the public either have Web sites or are considering their use.

But the proliferation of information on the Web is only one aspect of the change. Driven by the competition between Netscape and Microsoft, Web browsers (the software used for navigating the Web) are emerging as the umbrella tool for all of the Internet. In addition to navigating Web sites, Web browsers often can be used to survey Usenet news groups, connect to Telnet servers, manage File Transfer Protocol operations and stand in as the interface for other Internet tools.

The new importance of the Web is reflected in Chapter 4, which is devoted to that aspect of the Internet.

The second major change is that the Internet is less of a novelty in journalism and society at large. At the time of the first edition, it seemed that only pioneering journalists and those with an affinity for computers were using the Internet. Like database reporting, the Internet was the domain of a few specialists in newsrooms or on campuses.

That is no longer the case. Although still far from routine or commonplace, the Internet has now become more familiar to thousands of journalists and millions of people.

The increasing, regular use of the Internet has raised the stakes for journalists. Being the first to use the Net is no longer enough. The goal now is to use these resources effectively.

How to Use this Book

The best advice about how to use this book depends largely on what you know already, your comfort level with computers, your courage or determination, or whether you are otherwise motivated to learn what's available online. The sequence of chapters follows the sequence most people follow as they become familiar with the Internet. Chapter 2 offers an introduction to cyberspace and an overview of the tools available. Chapters 3 through 8 describe the Internet tools available to journalists, starting with the most common and useful.

Chapter 3 looks at electronic mail (e-mail). E-mail remains the most heavily used Internet service. You can have e-mail access without access to other Internet services. For many people, e-mail is as frequently used as the telephone and the fax machine for one-to-one communication.

Chapter 4 provides an in-depth survey of the World Wide Web. The Web clearly is the most dynamic new medium to emerge since television. Indeed, many see it as the starting point for the long-promised "Information Superhighway."

Chapter 5 demonstrates how journalists can use Gopher, an older Internet browser than the Web browsers of today, but still useful. Chapter Six is concerned with Telnet and File Transfer Protocol, two basic tools that help form the foundation of the Internet.

Chapters 7 and 8 teach about programs in which the Internet is used for many-to-many communication. Chapter 7 looks at Usenet news groups and electronic mailing lists, in which individuals can have their messages read and sent to many readers. Chapter 8 looks at ways that people can communicate in real time on the Internet using Internet Relay Chat, MUDs and MOOs.

Chapters 9 and 10 look at larger issues involved with journalism and cyberspace. Chapter 9 lays out strategies for journalists to effectively use this new access. Chapter 10 explores legal responsibilities, implications and ramifications of the growth in the use of online resources.

The World Wide Web, in particular, is not just a means for reporters to access information. It is a new medium to distribute information. Chapter 11 briefly looks at some of the first efforts using this new channel of communication.

Finally, the book has a Glossary and two appendixes. Appendix A is a directory of starting points of interest for journalists on the World Wide Web. Appendix B gives advice about gaining online access.

When Something Doesn't Work

Neither the Internet nor other online resources described in *The Online Journalist* is yet an "Information Superhighway." But, like other heavily traveled highways, portions of the Internet seem perpetually under construction. You will encounter delays. You will find roads closed.

When you do, move on to other resources. You will find some delays are only temporary; try them again some other time. Some sources of information will be no longer available. Some will not look like what you expected. Changes and facelifts are a daily occurrence on the Internet.

Often, you will have to be patient and persistent. But patience and persistence are keys to good journalism.

A Last Word

This is a hands-on book. You will be introduced to a new set of tools. The only way to become skillful with them is to use them as often as possible. We suggest that you read this book with a net-connected computer at your side, trying out the tools and tips that the book describes as you go.

But a hammer and a saw and a nail do not make a great carpenter. As you master these tools, you will also want to think about the way you practice journalism. Even if you are familiar with the Internet, this book should help you figure out how to best apply the Internet to the tasks of journalism.

The Internet potentially allows journalists to practice their craft in new ways. The real payoff comes when you realize that potential.

Chapter 2

The World Online

In January 1994, Albert Gore, Jr., vice president of the United States, subjected himself to a question and answer session in which more than 300 people participated. In the space of 90 minutes, Gore faced a battery of questions about problems ranging from educating children with special needs to ending the civil war in Bosnia.

This was not a press conference nor a speaking engagement organized by a specific organization. It was the first live, online conference with a United States vice president. The questions were provided by people who had signed up to participate in a forum on CompuServe, a commercial information service. Gore was stationed at a personal computer in the West Wing of the White House. The questioners and the questions were completely unscreened. The people who asked their questions first received answers. Others watched the interaction on screen. (See Figure 2-1).

Once the domain of journalists from elite media companies, the questioning of prominent people is now an everyday occurrence online. In a typical week in 1996, journalists and journalism students online could quiz everybody from hip hop artist Smoothe Da Hustler to race car driver Janet Guthrie. Business reporters could question executives at Bell & Howell's annual corporate meeting via the Internet.

In 1995, Kristin Leutwyler, senior editor at *Scientific American*, was writing a personality profile. She needed to interview Nicholas Negroponte, director of the Media Lab at the Massachusetts Institute of Technology and author of the book *Being Digital*. Told by the press office at MIT that Negroponte was too busy for telephone calls, faxes or face-to-face meetings with journalists, she asked for weekly electronic mail exchanges, and met her deadline.

In 1996, Douglas Brown, a junior at Loyola College in Maryland, was assigned to do an in-depth report on environmental problems and proposed solutions for the Chesapeake Bay region. Using the World Wide Web, he could access every piece of legislation pending in the U.S. Congress concerning the Chesapeake Bay.

The use of the Internet and other online information resources has become an important tool for journalists for a simple reason—it allows journalists to do their jobs better. Using the Internet, reporters can find information quickly, information that was once quite difficult to obtain. They can also communicate with people in new and convenient ways.

As with all tools, however, online resources are used more skillfully by some than by others. In this chapter, you will

- learn the basics of the computer infrastructure which makes the online world possible.
- receive an overview of the Internet.
- be introduced to several common Internet applications.
- review other online information services.
- survey some of the diverse information available online.

Fig. 2-1: Part of the transcript from Vice President Al Gore's first online conference on CompuServe.

```
% Moderator recognizes question #6
  glen Falkenstein (102)


(#102,glen Falkenstein) What do you think is goiong to end the problem in
bosnia?
(#196,Vice President Gore) We (the US) have believed for some time
(#196,Vice President Gore)  that the Bosnian government forces should
(#196,Vice President Gore) not be subject to the internation
(#196,Vice President Gore) embargo on the arms they
(#196,Vice President Gore) need to even the odds. And we have proposed
airstrikes
(#196,Vice President Gore) to prevent the agressors form taking
(#196,Vice President Gore)  advantage of the situation
(#196,Vice President Gore) while the arms are delivered.
(#196,Vice President Gore) But our allies, whose votes we need in
(#196,Vice President Gore) the Security Council, don't
(#196,Vice President Gore) agree. We will continue to work for peace, though,
(#196,Vice President Gore) in other ways — including maintenance of the
toughest sanctions against
(#196,Vice President Gore) Serbia in history. And the biggest airlift of
(#196,Vice President Gore) humanitarian supplies since the Berlin
(#196,Vice President Gore) airlift. And if a real agreement
(#196,Vice President Gore) can be reached, we will help enforce it.


% Moderator recognizes question #8
  David Rogers (26)


(#26,David Rogers) Mr. Vice President...
(#26,David Rogers) Hello from a Houston, Texas student...
(#26,David Rogers) What effect will the information highway...
(#26,David Rogers) have on our health care system...
(#26,David Rogers) in our future?
(#196,Vice President Gore) It will make it possible to conduct remote
(#196,Vice President Gore) diagnostics with much higher accuracy,
(#196,Vice President Gore) and to link patients to the right specialist
(#196,Vice President Gore) regardless of geographic location...
(#196,Vice President Gore) And by making the transfer of large
```

The Emergence of Computer Networks

Negotiating the online world is as important a skill for journalists as good interviewing techniques and a smooth style of writing. But the world online is complex. Not only is it relatively new, it is still under development. It is changing rapidly.

To be able to understand those changes, it is important both to be familiar with key terms and to have a basic understanding of the infrastructure itself. In the same way that it is important to understand generally what happens when you dial a telephone, it is important to understand generally what is happening when you send and retrieve information via computers.

The key technology underpinning all computer-based communication has been the development of computer networks, the physical linking of two or more computers. The computers can be linked through telephone lines, through other types of cables (including high speed fiber optic cable), and, potentially, through wireless technology as well.

The number of computers in a network can vary considerably. At one level, all the computers in a work group can be linked. The workgroup-level network can then be attached to a department-wide network and then to a company-wide network. The company-wide network can then be joined to other company networks and so on.

As companies, government agencies, and universities have expanded the number of computers they operate, they have created networks to allow people to easily share information and application programs. These networks are known as local area networks (LANs). In a local area network, one or more computers may function as a central resource for several other computers. The central computer is known as a server and frequently contains files that many people on the network use. It also contains the software that allows each of the computers on the network to share information with each other. One type of computer network design is called client-server computing.

Understanding Client-Server Computing

With client-server computing, one computer does not perform every task that is needed to complete a given activity. Instead, different computers on the network perform different parts of the job. In this way, the job can be completed more efficiently and computer resources are used more economically.

Most client-server tasks—particularly Internet applications—consist of at least two steps. In the first, you request a specific piece of information or a specific job to be completed. In the second step, the request is fulfilled and the results are returned to you for display.

The software which makes the request or issues the instructions as to what is to be done is called the "client." The software which fulfills the request and returns the results is called the "server." The same client-server terms apply to the computers on which the respective software resides.

To put it in more familiar terms, think about a client and an accountant. The client asks the accountant to prepare her income tax return. The accountant performs the work and returns the results.

With the Internet, which is a network of computer networks and will be more fully described shortly, you use the client software to make requests to a server. For example, World Wide Web browsers (client software, Chapter 4) makes requests to Web servers for information. So, in order to surf the Web, you need access to a Web client and a Web server.

This client-server relationship is crucial to understanding the Internet and what happens among computers on the Internet. If you understand this client-server relationship and two other network concepts, you will be better able to understand the capabilities of the Internet. You will understand why some things work on the network under one set of circumstances and not under others. When the unexpected occurs on the Net, you will have at your disposal the principles to explain the event. You will understand whether the problem is with the client, which is under your control, or the server, which usually is not.

Host, Client, and Server

Beyond the client-server relationship, the other two critical concepts are those of the network-host and of the different ways of connecting to the network. In simple terms, a computer is performing host duties when it controls computer terminals (or other computers emulating terminals) which are attached to it by some form of cabling.

In addition to personal computers, many universities and large businesses allow their students, faculty, or employees to have an account on a central computing facility. When you get the account, you are given a user name and a password. With your account comes an e-mail address. You may be allocated a certain amount of disk storage space on the central computer. That computer, which is a host, runs all day and all night. It receives mail for you and stores it until you read the mail and dispose of it. You interact with the host computer through the use of a terminal or a computer that is acting like a terminal. All the action, however, takes place through the host.

For people who access the online world through commercial service providers such as America Online or one of the hundreds of Internet access companies, the service provider's computer acts as the host. The service provider's computer will, for example, send, receive and store mail for you. Your personal computer acts primarily as a way for you to send commands via your keyboard or mouse to the service provider's computer.

Host computers are also connected to the network and can have client software residing on them. When we use that client software, the host computer becomes a client to some other computer, which is the server. For example, you may use your computer at home to dial into your university or news room system, which is host to your e-mail account and provides you with access to the Internet. Once you are connected and logged in, you might type "gopher" to launch Internet Gopher client software (see Chapter 5) that resides on your host. As you make menu selections, the host computer then establishes connection with another computer, perhaps several hundred miles away, and asks the distant computer to serve up some files. Thus the host computer has also become a client to the distant computer.

At the same time it is possible that other people are also accessing the host, asking it for files. The host then can perform server duties as well. It is easy to see how confusion can result when one computer may be in turn client, server, and host. Indeed, one of the strengths of client-server computing and the Internet is that any computer on the network can be a client or a server, depending on the task it performs.

But just because a computer can serve as a client does not necessarily mean it can serve as a host, controlling the activity of a terminal or a computer emulating a terminal. One way to remember the difference between a server and a host is that a server provides documents (text, program, or data files) while a host computer provides network access, disk space, and/or software access.

One parting word about hosts. To this point we have described what is called a local host, a host that physically resides on your campus or in your office building and upon which you have an account giving you limited disk space. But let's say your local host does not offer an Internet Relay Chat client (Chapter 8) and you want to participate in a chat. Using Telnet (Chapter 6), you can log into a computer that does have an IRC client you can use. This distant computer becomes a remote host because it is distant and yet it is providing you access to network facilities and controlling the activity of your computer.

Client Location Governs Functionality

The distinction between local and remote hosts has an important impact on the functionality of the client software to which you have access. All files and information on the Internet are maintained and communicated in client-server relationships. The server makes files available to other machines (clients) in a format recognized by client software running on the client machine. Where the client software is located and how it is accessed determines what features of the client are available to you as a user and how efficiently the client software operates from the user's point of view.

In terms of where the software resides, a client may be said to be local or remote, just as a host is local or remote. You have a local client if the client software you are using to go out and get information resides either on the host computer where you have disk space or resides on a computer at your desk and you have disk space available on it. With remote clients, you sit at a "dumb" terminal—or an intelligent computer running terminal emulation software—connected to a distant host computer on which you have no disk space allotted.

Because you do not have access to disk space when you are working with a remote client—you may be logged on as a public or anonymous user—you may not be able to use all of the client's features. For example, you will not be able to keep "bookmark" or "hot list" files used by World Wide Web and Gopher clients (Chapter 4 and Chapter 5). Nor will you be able to keep the "news.rc" file Usenet news readers employ to keep track of subscriptions and what has been read (Chapter 7).

Network Connection Type Affects Functionality

Basically, you connect to the rest of the world on the Net in one of two ways. In the first scenario, your computer has a network card and network wires coming into your computer through the card. This is known as a "hard wired" connection or a "direct" connection. Such a connection is desirable because it frees the user from reliance on host computers for client software and, to some extent, for access. Instead, one is free to select one's own client software for Internet access and avoid slowdowns brought on by overworked, bogged down hosts. Data files move quickly across the network, free from slow modem bottlenecks.

In the second scenario, you use telephone lines and a modem to reach a host computer that then gives you Internet access. This is known as a "dial-up" connection. Many dial-up services offer SLIP (Serial Line Internet Protocol) or PPP (Point-to-Point Protocol) access. Such access permits the network navigator (you) to use local clients specially configured for such access. Although you still must go through a modem to access the network, SLIP and PPP connections provide many of the benefits of direct connections. If you must go through a dial-up connection, try to get one with SLIP or PPP access. Most commercial service providers offer full SLIP or PPP connects. If you can't get a SLIP or PPP connect, you will have to use the provider's client software residing on the provider's host.

Cyberspace Is the Networking of Networks

Over time, servers in different locations have been connected to one another, often using dedicated data lines and specialized computers called routers. In addition, computers are sometimes networked using fiber optic lines and other technology that allows digital information to move at much higher speed than it does on voice telephone lines. The development and implementation of high-speed data transmission lines has made the "Information Superhighway" possible.

Internetworking represents the connecting of smaller computer networks to form yet larger networks. The development of large networks of networks has depended on two factors. First, physical links among computers had to be installed. Second, computers had to "speak the same language"—to use similar rules or communication protocols for identifying, transmitting and handling information.

In practice, internetworking currently functions in the following way. A university or private concern provides individuals with personal computers. The personal computers are then networked with other personal computers, work stations, minicomputers and mainframe computers, depending on the specific location. The network is then connected with other networks. Using a personal computer working through a server (called a gateway, in this text), individuals can access information residing on computers in more distant networks. The key is having a computer that can access a network, which can, in turn, access information on other computers on other networks. Computers in the internetwork are usually linked by higher speed, dedicated data transmission lines rather than voice telephone lines.

Conceptually, accessing information in this way can be compared with entering a large building with many rooms. Each room you enter has several other doors. You keep opening doors until you find the information you want. High-speed lines allow you to move from room to room quite quickly.

The most famous collection of internetworked computers is the Internet. However, the clearest example of the way an internetworked system functions to allow users to access information in remote locations may be the library system put together by the Colorado Alliance of Research Libraries, or CARL. CARL has developed software that allows libraries scattered throughout the nation to be linked with each other. For example, users at Loyola College in Maryland can access the library system through terminals in the library itself, through Loyola's campus local area network server, or by dialing in using a personal computer.

After accessing the system, users can survey the holdings of the Loyola/Notre Dame library, which are rather limited. But, by selecting Item 3 from the main menu, users can survey the holdings of the University of Maryland, Montgomery County Public Library and Maryland Interlibrary Consortium. Users can also use the public access catalogs from colleges from Florida to Hawaii, including the Lane Medical Library at Stanford University, the Los Angeles Public Library and the Atlanta/Fulton County Public Library.

```
                        Welcome to ORACLE
                      the online system of the
                      Loyola/Notre Dame Library
                             serving the
      College of Notre Dame of Maryland and Loyola College in Maryland

    ^^^^^^^^^^^^^^^^^^^^^^^^^^^^^^^^^^^^^^^^^^^^^^^^^^^^^^^^^^^^^^^^^^^^

            1.  ORACLE (Loyola/Notre Dame Library)


                     2. Library News
                     3. Maryland Libraries
                     4. Out-of-State Libraries
                     5. Document Delivery Services
                     6. Informational Databases



         Enter the NUMBER of your choice, and press <RETURN>
```

Fig. 2-2: Libraries have internetworked with each other for years. This screen from the Loyola College system provides access to several outside libraries.

Being able to access those additional libraries is only the first step. Let's say you decide to see what is available at Morgan State University, which is just down the street from Loyola. From Morgan State University, you can also access libraries throughout the country, including Arizona State University. From Arizona State, you can access yet more colleges and universities that participate in the CARL network.

Each time you select the public access catalog at a different university, your personal computer or terminal functions as if it were a terminal connected directly to the computer on which that information is stored. What is most significant, however, is that the menu or user interface for each system is exactly the same. If it is part of the CARL system, it is as easy for you to find information on a public access catalog halfway across the world as it is to access information in the library you use every day. More important, once you access the CARL library system, you have access to the information on the catalogs in many parts of the network, depending on the specific arrangements made by your local librarians. The material that can be accessed through internetworks represents the portion of information generated at a specific location which the developers or owners have decided to share with or open to the public. Journalists should be aware that many universities and public libraries are now affiliated with CARL.

What Is the Internet?

While the CARL system is an effective way to search for information in libraries across the country, it has been the rapid development of the Internet which has made online skills indispensable for journalists. Some veteran users of the Internet like to argue that it defies definition. One old timer once defined the Internet by describing what it wasn't. Quickly others shortened his definition to "The Internet—not."

The Internet is not an organization. It is not an institution. It is not a club. You cannot become a member. Nobody owns the Internet; and strictly speaking, nobody controls it, governs it, or takes responsibility for it. Still, the Internet can be defined in terms of a physical structure as well as a set of rules.

Physical Structure like a Highway System

While complex, the structure of the Internet is understandable. "Internet" is a term used to describe the interconnection of many computer networks in a way that allows them to communicate with each other. Although the popular term "Information Superhighway" is misleading, the Internet is like a road and highway system for information and conceptually functions in much the same way. Consider this extended metaphor. In the United States, you can drive a car from Los Angeles to New York. You can do this for two reasons. First, there are physical links called roads. These roads take many different forms from single lane neighborhood streets to twelve-lane, limited access interstate highways. If you were to take a cross country trip, you would be likely to travel on many types of roads.

In addition to the physical links, however, to make the trip from Los Angeles to New York safely, you need to have a set of rules that govern the way all the travelers use the roads. You must know that you cannot cross a double line in the middle of a road; that you must stop at red lights; and that you must travel within certain speed limits, depending on the type of road and weather conditions.

The Internet is the same kind of network as the road and highway system, but instead of moving vehicles occupied by people, it moves packets filled with information. The Internet is composed of physical links, but in the same sense that no one road connects a home in Los Angeles directly to a home in New York, no single link connects all the computers on the Internet. In the automotive world, different neighborhoods are linked by larger streets. In the Internet world, these larger streets create regional networks. Regional (mid-level) networks connect the computers at different universities, companies, and other institutions. Like larger streets, these mid-level networks enable data to travel faster than data on local area networks.

The specialized computers that control the flow of information on the mid-level networks are also physically linked to what are termed national backbones. The national backbones use lines that transmit data at yet higher speeds and use higher capacity computers to handle information traffic. In the United States there are several national backbones for the Internet. The largest and most influential backbone—and the one which has enabled the Internet to be used by a wider community of people—was the high speed network initiated by the National Science Foundation, named NSFNet. That backbone has now been privatized and is operated by AT&T and MCI. Telephone companies, cable television operations, and other communication specialists are vigorously competing to install high speed networks throughout the country. The same process is underway in countries around the world.

"Internet" is the word used to describe the interconnection of these successive levels of networks. As such, the Internet is the series of physical links that serves as the road system for computer-based information sharing. It encompasses the local networks within organizations through which information moves slowly, but only for short distances; the mid-level networks linking universities, companies, and other organizations; and the national backbones, which allow a lot of information to travel long distances at very high speeds.

A Set of Rules: The Internet as Agreement

The physical links are only one aspect of the Internet. One way to define the Internet is that it is an agreement. This agreement encompasses sets of rules or protocols that allow the information to travel from computer to computer on the Internet "highway system." If a computer or computer network does not support that set of rules, it is not part of the Internet. In other words, to send and receive information via the Internet, computers must package information in the same way. If a computer cannot do that, even if it has a physical link to a network, it is not part of the Internet.

Think of it this way. Motor vehicles and airplanes are both forms of transportation but airplanes cannot use the road system. There are many types of networks and ways to send information between computers. But only computers that follow the specific rules associated with the Internet can use the Internet.

The over-arching protocol or set of rules used on the Internet is called the Transmission Control Protocol/Internet Protocol (TCP/IP). The IP part of the protocol is the address for every computer that is physically linked to the Internet. Each computer has a unique address. The IP part of the protocol identifies the sender and destination of information.

The TCP element of the protocol controls the way information is sent through the Internet network. It is according to the TCP protocol requirements that the ability to log onto remote computers, transfer files and perform other operations on the Internet have been developed. At one level, TCP serves as a quasi operating system for Internet applications, allowing Internet applications to interact on computers that, themselves, have different operating systems such as UNIX, VMS, DOS or Macintosh OS. Many companies are now using the TCP/IP protocols to send and receive information internally. Internal computer networks using Internet technology but not open to the public are called Intranets.

In summary, the growth of the Internet has stemmed from two factors. Physical links consisting of high-speed data lines have been established connecting the computer networks—or internetworking—of universities, governments agencies, businesses, and other organizations. These links have created a de facto national network. Second, the widespread acceptance of TCP/IP protocols allows information to travel transparently through the linked networks which comprise the Internet, even though different computers have different hardware architectures and different operating systems.

Network Control

Understanding the structure of the Internet sheds light on several important questions. Foremost is, "Who controls the Internet?" The answer is that no one entity controls the Internet. Instead, there is a layer of control at every network level. For example, the people responsible for the administration of your local network may choose not to develop a complete link to the Internet but only to support electronic mail. They can decide how much information on the central computers at your site will be available to other people on the Internet. Most important, they decide who gets an Internet account and the rules governing that account. For example, Chinese authorities have decided to block information they deem inappropriate from entering China via the Internet. Some commercial Internet providers screen out pornographic material. And some providers do not support the full range of Internet services described below. Many companies and some colleges and universities, for example, do not support Usenet news groups (Chapter 7).

Cost Structure

The lack of a centralized management organization has also had an impact on the cost of using the Internet. Building, maintaining and developing the Internet is an ambitious and costly undertaking. Currently, universities, business enterprises and organizations generally pay a flat monthly or annual fee to connect either to a regional network or a national backbone. Once connected, however, organizations are usually not charged on a usage basis. Consequently, most do not charge individual users for using the Internet. Some commercial service providers, however, do charge by the hour for usage.

Viewed another way, the cost of accessing the Internet is similar to the cost of cable television. With cable, you pay a monthly fee and then you can watch as many programs on as many different channels as you like. With the Internet, once the monthly charge is paid, users can employ as many services as often as they like without additional charges.

This current pricing structure is significant for journalists. It means that you can search the Internet as diligently as you like for relevant information and can communicate with as many people as you can identify via e-mail without worrying about receiving a huge bill at the end of the month. Moreover, it means the Internet can open sources of information—both archival and human—that would be too expensive or difficult to access in any other way.

For example, an editor of a specialized science magazine was looking for someone to write articles about new developments in laboratory automation. Working through the Internet, he came in contact with scientists in St. Petersburg, Russia, who were active in that topic area. Over the course of several months, the editor and the scientists collaborated to develop two articles. At one point in the editing process, the editor was exchanging information with the scientists on an almost daily basis. He did not have to worry about accruing huge costs. Also, the time differential between the U.S. and Russia was not a problem.

Some people would like to change the pricing mechanism for the Internet. They would like to see users charged for the time they are actually online or for the specific services they use. If the pricing mechanism is changed, it could have a dramatic impact on the functionality of the Internet for journalists, particularly those working for smaller organizations.

A History of the Internet

While the Internet is clearly the largest computer network of its kind, it is not the only one. There are other similar networks such as Bitnet, which links universities, and FidoNet, which links thousands of bulletin boards, and Usenet, which was created to facilitate online discussions. Nevertheless, the Internet is by far the dominant network of its type. Moreover, many of the alternative networks are beginning to meld themselves into the World Wide Web (Chapter 4). Nearly all have electronic mail links (Chapter 3).

The growth of the Internet can be measured in three ways: the number of host computers connected to the Internet, the number of users connected to those host computers, and the amount of information or traffic carried on the Internet. Because of its decentralized structure, precise usage figures are hard to determine. But, by all measures, the Internet is rapidly growing. Some people project that by the late 1990s, more than 100 million people will have access to the Internet. In 1996, officials at Sun Microsystems, a leading provider of World Wide Web servers and creator of the Java programming language, predicted that, eventually, all people will have a Web server. If those projections prove accurate, and it is impossible to say with certainty that they will, the Internet will eventually represent a communications network that will rival, or perhaps surpass, the telephone system in its importance and usefulness to journalists.

Military Origins

Ironically, the Internet was not originally conceived as a global communications system. Like some other useful technologies, the Internet has its roots in the need for military preparedness. In the 1960s, the Advanced Research Projects Agency of the United States Department of Defense began funding projects to develop an experimental computer network to support military research by allowing people spread across the country to more easily share their computer files and send messages to each other.

The Department of Defense wanted the network to be able to function even if parts of it had been disrupted, presumably in a war. The researchers decided that by using an addressing system, which they called the Internet Protocol (IP), the communicating computers themselves could ensure that the information was successfully transmitted or received and every computer on the network would be able to communicate with every other computer on the network. In other words, they wanted a peer-to-peer network.

In 1969, an experimental network called ARPAnet was launched with four nodes. The participants were University of California at Los Angeles, the Stanford Research Institute, University of California at Santa Barbara, and the University of Utah. By 1971, there were 19 nodes shared by 30 universities. Developing ARPAnet was complicated because different sites used different types of computers, and the protocols that were developed had to work on many different computer architectures and operating systems. The challenge was to develop rules of communication that would allow information to be sent over many different kinds of networks without regard to the underlying network technology. These protocols began to appear in the mid-1970s and were known as the Transmission Control Protocol, or TCP. By the early 1980s all the systems associated with ARPAnet standardized on TCP/IP.

Supercomputing Centers Established

The next impetus for the Internet came in 1987, when the National Science Foundation decided to establish five supercomputing centers around the country and link them through its own high-speed network known as NSFnet. Since the cost to connect researchers directly to the supercomputing centers with dedicated high-speed data lines would have been prohibitive, NSF encouraged research institutions to form regional networks, which, in turn, were linked to the supercomputing centers. That strategy has led to the basic structure of the Internet, with its multiple layers of networks.

The exponential growth in the use of the Internet began with the launch of NSFnet in the late 1980s as researchers in academic and governmental settings took advantage of the new opportunity to collaborate. In 1990, an effort was undertaken to include commercial and non-profit organizations as well. By the middle of 1993, by some estimates there were more than three million commercial Internet users and that number was growing at a rate of 10 to 20 percent a month. Commercial organizations have the fastest rate of connection to the Internet of any single type of user community. In 1994, the number of Internet sites registered with commercial domains surpassed the number of educational institutions. Since the mid-1990s, most major companies and tens of thousands of smaller ones have connected to the Internet.

The final technological breakthrough also came in the early 1990s. First, researchers led by Tim Berners Lee at CERN, the European particle physics laboratory, created a protocol for hyperlinking information residing on different computers. They called the system the World Wide Web. Shortly thereafter, students and researchers led by Marc Andreesen at the National Center for Supercomputer Application at the University of Illinois developed a client program named Mosaic which is characterized by a graphical user interface. And the online revolution moved into full gear.

Internet Applications

Describing the programs associated with the Internet and applying them to the tasks of journalism will be explored in depth in the next several chapters. This section will provide a brief overview of the different types of software tools available and briefly describe their differences. In a sense, it will survey what's available in your Internet toolbox before you go to work and choose the ones to use.

Internet software applications combine the client-server and host-terminal models of computing for nearly all the applications described in the pages that follow. When you use an Internet software application, the client software will be either on your personal computer, the computer you log onto for access to the Internet (your host), or on yet another computer to which you connect in order to use client software you may not have yourself. As you navigate through the Internet, you will find yourself logged onto different host computers, sometimes gaining access to different client programs and also accessing different servers. It can be complicated. Fortunately, the purpose of advanced Internet software is to hide this complexity from you; and to a large degree it succeeds.

The Internet has six basic application protocols: Electronic Mail (e-mail), World Wide Web (Hypertext Transfer Protocol or HTTP), Gopher, Telnet, File Transfer Protocol (FTP), and Usenet (news). Each has specialty client software, and many Web browsers, such as Netscape from Netscape Communications and the Internet Explorer from Microsoft, are capable of reading and displaying data from all the applications.

Electronic Mail

Electronic mail is one of the most useful features of the Internet and is often the application with which people begin. Electronic mail is a method to send messages back and forth among people with Internet addresses as well as people on other networks with mail connections to the Internet.

The Internet supports both person-to-person communication that is delivered to the electronic address of the intended recipient and one-to-many transmissions in which information is automatically sent to lists of people. Electronic mail and ways to locate people's e-mail addresses will be discussed in Chapter 3. E-mail discussion groups, a method of communicating with many people at once using e-mail, will be discussed in Chapter 7.

World Wide Web

World Wide Web is the most exciting new tool for the Internet and is the reason for the hoopla which has engulfed the Internet since the mid-1990s. It is based on a technology called hypermedia. With hypermedia, information in one document can be linked to other, related documents. For example, let's say you have found a bill in the U.S. Senate in which you are interested. The names of each of the authors of the bill can be linked to brief biographical sketches that are actually stored on a completely different computer. Let's say the biographical sketches include the amount of money senators raised for their reelection campaigns. That information could be linked to a document that lists all of their campaign contributors.

Moreover, linked information can consist of not only text and graphics, but audio and video information as well. The World Wide Web is an ambitious, exciting and powerful attempt to link connected information wherever it may be located on the Internet, allowing the user to easily access and retrieve related files. The Web will be discussed in Chapter 4.

Gopher

Gopher was the first program to integrate the information search and retrieval process on the Internet. Like other Internet applications, Gopher consists of servers and client software. More than 2,000 Gopher servers have been linked. When you find something you want, the Gopher client software retrieves it for you through menu-based commands. With Gopher it does not matter exactly where the information you want is located. It does not matter what kind of information you want to retrieve. Nor does it matter what tool you need to use to retrieve that information. You use tools from a menu to perform each operation. Gopher will be fully discussed in Chapter 5.

Telnet

Telnet allows you to log onto another computer on the Internet. That computer is known as the remote computer. Once you are logged onto a remote computer, it is as if your keyboard were attached to that computer, which then serves as your host. You can do what the people who regularly use that computer can do. Frequently, if the computer you use to access the Internet does not have specific client software with which you want to work, you can use Telnet to connect to another computer that does have the right tools. For example, the law library at Washington and Lee University provides access to a wide range of other databases and client programs. Hytelnet incorporates extensive guides to Telnet sites around the world. Once you locate a site, Hytelnet hands you off—with instructions— to Telnet so you can log onto and to explore other sites. Telnet and Hytelnet will be explored in Chapter 6.

FTP

FTP stands for "File Transfer Protocol." As the name implies, it facilitates moving files from one computer to another. It has become the common language for sharing data. Unlike Telnet, in which you often must know a specific password to successfully log onto the remote computer, anonymous FTP has become commonplace. With anonymous FTP, anyone on the Internet may transfer files from (and sometimes to) a remote system using the word anonymous as the user identification. Archie is a program that locates files that can be transferred via FTP. The Archie program reads an index of more than 1,000 FTP sites. It is updated constantly and its "what is" command describes the files you have found. Once you have located files via Archie, you can transfer them via FTP. FTP and Archie will be discussed in Chapter 6.

Usenet News

Usenet is a network of several thousand online bulletin boards organized into topic-oriented "news groups." Within these news groups, people read and post (as if to a paper bulletin board) messages related to the topic for which the news group site is home. There are already more than 10,000 news groups with participants ranging from Elvis Presley fans to political activists, from computer enthusiasts to music composers. Usenet is one of many networks connected to and accessible via the Internet. Usenet news is described in Chapter 7.

Other Applications

Internet Rely Chat (IRC) turns the Internet into something like an international CB radio network. IRC is organized into different channels with different themes. When you log onto an IRC server, you see a list of channels, select a channel, then join the conversation. You can also establish private channels of communication using IRC, allowing you to interview individuals privately online. IRC will be discussed in Chapter 8.

MUDs and MOOs, designed as entertainment, are specialty programs that manage role-playing games acted out on a global scale. Because MUDs and MOOs provide real-time interaction across networks, they also offer potential in distance education settings and other situations where conferencing is valuable. They are described in Chapter 8.

As sophisticated as the application tools get, the basic operation and purpose of the Internet remains the same. At its core, the Internet is a communications network among computers. It allows you to locate and retrieve information on other computers linked to the Internet as well as send and receive messages electronically to and from other people on the Internet and elsewhere.

Other Online Information Sources

Although the Internet is, by far, the most significant vehicle for accessing online information, other sources do exist, many of which predate the explosive increase in the use of the Internet. They include computer bulletin boards and commercial information providers.

Computer Bulletin Boards

Long-distance bicycle racing is not as popular in the United States as it is in Europe. So when the Tour de France was run in the past, enthusiasts in the U.S. had to settle for short, outdated articles in the back pages of the sports section of the newspaper.

No longer. During the 1994 event, people could log into the Bicycle Bulletin Board, a computer bulletin board service for cyclists in Carlsbad, California, and enjoy fresh coverage. Observers from the course itself, as well as people watching the race on the BBC in London, posted reports and impressions regularly. Journalists who wished to report on the event but could not attend in person could still communicate with many people on the scene. Furthermore, they could interview people in the U.S. and elsewhere who were interested.

Though not as fanatic as many soccer fans during the World Cup, cycling aficionados take their sport very seriously. The Bicycle Bulletin Board gave reporters a mechanism for increasing the number of sources with whom they could communicate as well as opening up the possibility of new story angles.

Electronic bulletin board systems, often called BBSes or bulletin boards, are computerized information services that can be accessed using a computer, modem and telephone line. When somebody dials in, the bulletin board's computer serves as the host computer. By some estimates, there are more than 40,000 bulletin boards in operation today.

With such an array, their structure and content vary greatly. In fact, many computer bulletin boards are run by entrepreneurial individuals using rudimentary technology. They may have one or two telephones attached to an old computer. There are several inexpensive software packages that allow people to set up their own bulletin board systems. Computer bulletin boards operated by an individual contain information of interest to the person who sets up and maintains the system—the system operator or "sysop."

At the other end of the spectrum, the federal government operates several bulletin boards from which people can access information the U.S. government has collected. These computer bulletin boards contain huge amounts of information and are enormously useful to reporters.

Generally, bulletin boards will have some or all of the following features. They may have electronic mail; that is, users can send and receive private messages to and from the system operator or other people who are registered with the system. They may have forums or conferences to which people who are connected to the bulletin board send public messages that can be read by everyone who accesses the system. Some allow for live interactive communication—the ability to chat—with other people who are logged into the system at the same time.

Many bulletin boards have searchable databases. The system operator has stored (or has allowed others to store) files that can be downloaded from the bulletin board to the user's computer. Sometimes bulletin boards can be efficient means of obtaining specific information such as bibliographic references, full text articles, and information about organizations. Text files of information can be downloaded from most BBSes, then later edited and/or printed at the user's computer. Many bulletin board operators also store shareware and public domain software that users can also download.

Some bulletin board operators charge people for access to the board. In those cases, users must register in advance and are billed in a variety of different ways. But many bulletin boards, perhaps the majority, are free. They are operated as a hobby, a service by a larger company (such as a magazine publisher or other type of information provider), or they are a service of a government agency trying to disseminate information to interested parties.

Commercial Information Services

In concept, commercial information services such as America Online (AOL), CompuServe, Dow Jones News Retrieval and others are similar to BBS systems. Both BBSes and commercial information sources provide all the same services (including private electronic mail, live interactive communication, conferences and forums, and information and software that you can download to your computer).

Commercial services, however, provide a much broader range of information than most bulletin boards and are supplied with information from many of the major providers of information. You can book airline tickets; buy, sell and track stocks; or access online malls to buy gifts, books, flowers and candy. The commercial services also provide a range of tools that help people find and use the information they need. Commercial services often charge an hourly rate for access and a premium for specialized services.

Perhaps most important for journalists, commercial information services develop relationships with other information companies to offer their products online. For example, many offer users access to reports from the

Associated Press, UPI, Agence France Press, Reuters, and other wire services, including the wire services "day book," which lists potentially newsworthy events occurring in a specific city.

Providing wire service reports is a vivid example of the way computer-based communication networks expand access to information. In the past, very small newspapers, magazine publications, and colleges and universities could not justify or afford the expense of receiving wire service information. Although publications cannot republish the wire service reports they receive from online services, they can use those reports to stay up to date with breaking news. Also, using a clipping service, reporters can save articles on topics of interest to them as background for longer reports.

The gamut of information available from online services is extremely wide and potentially very useful for journalists. The drawback is that the more you use a commercial database, the more expensive it becomes. Indeed, there are two classes of commercial information services. The first type, such as the Lexis/Nexis system, is directed primarily to corporate users. Lexis provides computerized access to legal information while Nexis provides access to newspaper articles. The price for these services puts them beyond the reach of many smaller companies and most individuals. And while some universities do have subscriptions, most do not.

Other services such as Prodigy and CompuServe are aimed directly at consumers. If heavily used, they become expensive. Still, they can be affordable to freelance writers and students and are certainly affordable even for small companies. Conceptually, electronic bulletin boards and commercial databases can be considered alike because of the way they are accessed and used. Generally, using a personal computer, you directly call the bulletin board or commercial service you want, and then, using commands on the host system, you access information available on that host system. They can be thought of as a branch of a library or a store.

The Convergence of Cyberspace

Reacting to the explosive growth of the World Wide Web, commercial service providers are rapidly integrating their services with the Web. Microsoft, for example, is repositioning the Microsoft Network, which it originally launched in 1995 as a new commercial information service, a super-Web site. America Online, CompuServe and Prodigy act as access providers or gateways to the Web for their subscribers. For example, once you dial into AOL, with just a few clicks of the mouse you can access information on the Web.

Conversely, large Internet access providers such as AT&T and Pacific Bell have indicated they will allow users dialing into the Internet to automatically connect to AOL or CompuServe directly. Of course, to access the information stored on the CompuServe or AOL computers, you will still need to be a subscriber to those services.

Within a short period of time, the Web will also be the home for commercial information providers, at least those who wish to reach a wide, consumer-oriented market. There will still be a fee required to access those sites—but that will be true for other sites on the Web as well.

What's Available Online

Asking what kind of information is available online is a little like asking what's in the Library of Congress. One might as well ask what's available from agencies of the federal government; from leading universities, research centers and think tanks; from large companies, publishing houses and organizations in the business of collecting and disseminating information; or from tens of thousands of entrepreneurs who collect and offer information in areas of their own interests. What's available also comes from hundreds of thousands of people who use computer networks to communicate with each other every day through discussion lists, news groups, postings to bulletin boards, and in a variety of different ways.

And remember, the sources are not limited only to the United States. International information links are strong in many areas. Clearly, there is a lot of information out there—too much to catalog. In fact, nobody knows exactly what is available on line and where it is. The growth represents both an opportunity and a hazard for journalists. The opportunity is that, sitting at your desk, you can access information that you may not have even known existed. The hazard is that you will waste a lot of time looking at information that is not relevant to the projects on which you are working.

With that in mind, the following is a partial list of information and services accessible online through computer bulletin boards, commercial databases, and networks such as the Internet that are relevant to journalism. All of these categories of information will be more fully explored in subsequent chapters and a catalog of these sources is in Appendix A.

Government Information

The federal, state and local governments are the largest producers of public information, and reporting on the activities of government is the biggest single area of concern to journalists. At the federal level, nearly all executive branch agencies, including the White House, the Food and Drug Administration, the National Institutes of Health, Department of Agriculture, National Science Foundation, Environmental Protection Agency,

Social Security Administration, National Archives, Securities and Exchange Commission, Department of Defense, military bases around the world, and scores of others now provide access to their information via computer bulletin boards or through the Internet. One federal BBS system (FedWorld) provides access to more than 130 other federal BBS systems. Many state court systems have begun to offer electronic access to some of their records. U.S. Supreme Court decisions are available online.

The range of information these agencies provides varies. Some, such as the National Archives, primarily offer access to their catalogs and directories, allowing users to identify information they will then have to get using more traditional methods. More important to journalists, many agencies now distribute their press releases and major reports online. Online access represents a vehicle to get both timely information and background material quickly.

Human Sources

In general, most people develop online techniques to access documents. For journalists, however, electronic communication also offers a new way to identify and communicate with people. Communicating with people who have relevant information will continue to be one of the fundamental ways journalism distinguishes itself from other types of fact-finding activities.

Online access to people is provided in several different ways. First, there is electronic mail in which individuals can send private messages back and forth to each other. Sometimes people who refuse to accept a telephone call from a journalist may be willing to respond to an electronic mail message. Electronic mail is a very convenient and efficient method of communication.

Beyond e-mail are news groups and discussion lists. Although technologically they operate differently, in practice, both discussion lists and news groups are like conversations among hundreds or even thousands of people who are interested in a specific topic. For reporters, these online conversations can serve as windows into the concerns of the people involved in those issues as well a source of e-mail addresses to communicate directly with individuals later. There currently are thousands of discussion lists and news groups operating covering topics from United Nations activities concerning global warming to sado-masochism.

Third, public relations agencies and others now frequently use online communications specifically to reach reporters with potential sources for their stories. For example, public information officers in colleges and universities have assembled lists of university-based experts in different fields, which they forward to reporters upon request.

Many computer bulletin boards, commercial computer databases and the Internet have what is called "chat." Chat is the functional equivalent of the telephone. People who are online at the same time can communicate with each other simultaneously. At times, chat conversations can appear like telephone calls on a party line. A lot of people can participate at the same time.

Finally, many people have created personal home pages on the World Wide Web. These pages are often filled with solid information about the person.

Libraries and Special Depositories

The revolution in electronic communication has transformed the image of librarians from that of custodians of dusty monuments to learning to that of front-line warriors in the information age. Librarians have played a leading role in making information accessible to journalists and others. In one dramatic example, the catalogs of the Library of Congress are now accessible online. The Library of Congress is a powerful tool for journalists.

In addition to the Library of Congress, major public libraries, including federal depository libraries in many cities, college and university libraries, and many specialized libraries are now online as well. For example, the catalog of the French National Institute for Research in Information and Automation (INRIA) is accessible online, as is the U.S. Environmental Protection Agency Library, the Columbia University Law Library, and the Australian Asian Religions Bibliography. Clearly, the range of special repository and library-based information is enormous. In addition to the libraries themselves, very helpful reference material can be found as well. The *CIA World Factbook,* which contains dossiers on 249 nations, can be accessed online, as well as the CIA World Map and the USGS Geological Fault Maps.

Books and Magazines

Increasingly, publishers are experimenting with online versions of their publications. Many magazines now offer online editions, which often consist of a scaled-down version of the entire magazine. Moreover, magazines such as the New Republic and others are offering electronic access. From time to time, drafts of books (particularly books about the Internet) circulate electronically before they are published.

In addition to current publications, newspaper and magazine archives are available online. Often, receiving the full text of an article involves a cost; however, several places permit you to identify useful articles online for free. For example, the Montgomery County Public Library has an index of *The New York Times, The Washington Post* and *The Wall Street Journal.*

Other Good Stuff

While government data, access to human sources of information, libraries, special collections, and other publications are probably the types of information available online most useful to journalists, there is a wealth of additional information as well. Public domain software and shareware is readily available online. Public domain software is software for which the copyright is no longer enforced (or doesn't exist), so anybody can legally use it. A lot of software developed at research laboratories and other government-funded sites is released directly to the public domain. Shareware is a way to distribute software in which a user pays a license fee only after he or she has tried the program and decided he or she is actually going to use it. Some of this software can help journalists become more productive.

In addition to software, there is an ever-expanding array of information available online. Most commercial computer databases offer a range of financial services including tracking and trading on the stock market as well as access to the Official Airline Guide, Zagat's Restaurant Guide and much more. Hobbyists reflecting a wide range of human interests have set up shop online. Basically, if you look long enough and hard enough, you can probably find information on just about any topic you could imagine as well as the e-mail addresses of people with expertise in those areas.

Finally, people like to play games with computers and there are many different types of games available. One of the more interesting aspects of the Internet is the ability to play elaborate fantasy role-playing games in virtual locations called Multiple User Dungeons, or MUDs.

The Future of the Infrastructure

Distinctions among the different components of the online infrastructure should continue to blur over time. Nevertheless, for the foreseeable future, the online world will be segmented in several different ways. The first is cost. Large amounts of information, particularly information developed by libraries and universities, will continue to be free. But companies will charge for many other kinds of information.

One of the most important questions for journalists that is currently being debated is whether government information should be available electronically without cost or at low cost. In the past, from time to time, the federal government has sold its information to a third-party supplier, which then resold that information to the public at a fairly high cost. In 1994, the Securities and Exchange Commission, however, backed off a plan to sell exclusive rights to the electronic records of the information it gathers to a commercial information service, which would then resell that information. Instead, it began to test electronic access to the public at a nominal cost.

Maintaining low-cost public access to government records in an electronic form will be a key priority for reporters and editors. Ironically, media companies, including newspapers, can find themselves in a complex situation concerning the low-cost availability of government-generated information in electronic formats. Some consider adding value to government information and then reselling it as a potential new source of revenue.

Cost of access is a significant issue as well. Currently, companies pay a monthly flat fee for a connection to the Internet, the most important internetworked system. After the fee is paid, you can use the Internet as often as you like without additional charges. You can send electronic mail to Russia or Israel at no additional charge. This makes the Internet extremely cost effective for journalists and others with limited budgets. There are those who believe, however, that there should be a usage charge for the Internet. And as responsibility for developing and maintaining the information infrastructure shifts primarily from the government to private corporations such as telephone companies and cable operators, the cost to access specific networks could go up.

The third area in which the different components of the online infrastructure will continue to be distinguished will be the speed at which the lines themselves can carry information. As high-speed lines are installed, new kinds of information, particularly audio, video and graphics-based information, will move freely from computer to computer. Despite all the hype in the press, installing the necessary high-speed lines is a costly, time-consuming, ongoing process. Consequently, for the foreseeable future, certain kinds of information will be available only through specific providers and to specific recipients who are connected to the high-speed lines.

In the early 1900s, Lincoln Steffens traveled from city to city documenting municipal corruption. His book *Shame of the Cities* is a classic of muckraking. Its power came from the information he collected. The online infrastructure will give you access to more information more efficiently than ever before in the history of journalism. The result should be better stories with more information which better serve the needs of readers and viewers. The challenge for journalists is twofold. They need to learn how to access the necessary information. And they have to be able to fashion that information into compelling stories.

Chapter 3

Contacting People by E-mail

The Johns Hopkins University is the intellectual crown jewel of Baltimore. Birthplace of the modern research university, Hopkins is the home of one of the most prestigious medical schools in the country. It is the leading academic recipient of federal funding for scientific research. Its students have earned well-deserved reputations as academic grinds.

The Johns Hopkins University is not a usual venue for shootings. But on April 10, 1996, a student pulled a .357 Magnum from a bag and shot sophomore Rex Chao in the back of the head and then again in the chest. Chao, an honor student and member of the Hopkins Symphony Orchestra died shortly thereafter. Tobert Harwood, Jr., who had been chairman of the College Republicans club, was charged in the crime.

The campus and the city were shocked. How could this happen among the cream of the crop? To answer that question, a team of reporters from *The Baltimore Sun* interviewed the people who knew the men. They also examined the e-mail correspondence the two men had, printing excerpts of their electronic exchanges on April 21.

The material was moving, revealing an intensely personal relationship between the two men which had gone horribly wrong. It provided insight into the incident which probably could have been gained in no other way.

Since the early 1990s, the use of electronic mail, or e-mail as it is generally known, has exploded. As far back as 1992, a survey of corporate management information and telecommunications managers indicated that electronic mail was among the most important technologies in meeting their companies' messaging needs. As more and more companies have connected to the Internet, e-mail has become even more important. When Lou Gerstner, chief executive officer of IBM wants to send a message to his troops, he often uses e-mail.

Along the same lines, the use of electronic mail as a tool for journalists has steadily increased as well. Once the private domain of early adapters, now thousands of journalists routinely use e-mail for internal and external communication. Many include their e-mail addresses at the end of their articles.

Journalists can use e-mail to communicate with their colleagues and with sources. They can use e-mail to check facts and quotes. They can use e-mail to gather ideas and insights not available in other ways. Finally, they can also use e-mail to subscribe to discussion lists in which like-minded people communicate about specific topics. During the next few years, e-mail may become as important as the telephone as a means of communicating for journalists.

This chapter will:

- Explore the basics of e-mail, including how to get started, how to understand the anatomy of an e-mail address, and a short exploration of the structure of the e-mail network.
- Describe how to construct an e-mail message and manage your e-mail account.
- Review some of the rules of etiquette which have emerged in relation to the use of e-mail.
- Point out some of the legal ramifications of using e-mail.
- Suggest ways to effectively use e-mail in reporting.

Subscribing to and using e-mail discussion lists in journalism will be discussed in Chapter 7.

The Basics of E-mail

Conceptually, e-mail is not much different from regular mail (affectionately known to the initiated as "snail mail"). You create a message. You address the message to the intended recipient. You deposit the letter into the transmission system, which carries it to its intended destination.

There are differences, however. First, e-mail arrives at its destination much more quickly than regular mail. This aids communications considerably. For example, a reporter for a science journal needed leads to scientists and engineers who were using Microsoft Windows technology for a story she was doing. She sent e-mail to three contacts she had at software companies publishing technical packages under Windows for scientists and engineers. Within a half hour, she received the names of six scientists working at prestigious organizations such as Sandia National Laboratory and the National Weather Service.

E-mail is also more convenient than regular mail. Generally speaking, when you reply to an e-mail "letter," you don't have to find a piece of paper, locate an envelope, remember the person's address, buy a stamp, and put the letter in the mailbox. Instead, you can reply to the message with just a few keystrokes. Most e-mail programs will automatically address the reply to the sender of the initial message. Moreover, most e-mail programs allow you to copy all or part of the original message with just a few keystrokes; therefore, you can respond point by point. For example, when one of the public relations people sent the names of people working with the Macintosh instead of Windows, the reporter copied that part of the message and sent it back, reiterating the request for Windows users.

Finally, e-mail is still more informal than regular mail. In many circumstances, a formal salutation is unnecessary. And you can create a signature which will be automatically attached to all your e-mail correspondence.

But, as powerful and convenient as e-mail can be, it is also fairly complicated to master completely. Indeed, it requires you to have some understanding of the way the computer network you use works as well as the way the Internet functions. Finally, you will have to master client software as well.

Getting Started

The first step in using e-mail is establishing an account on a computer connected to the Internet and setting up a mailbox. An electronic mailbox has two elements. The first is a place in the computer's storage area for the messages you receive. When you access your electronic mailbox, you will see a directory of the messages which have arrived since the last time you checked—your new mail, so to speak. You will be able to

---

Fig. 3-1: E-mail addresses use the syntax of a user's name (or ID) followed by an @ sign, an optional host name, and the host computer's Internet domain. Below the generic address above are two addresses that have been used by one of the authors.

username@host.domain

reddick@facsnet.org

wurlr@ttacs1.ttu.edu

read through the messages one by one, responding to and discarding them as appropriate.

The second element is the address to which others can send you mail, including the storage area for the mail received. The address has two parts consisting of the user name (in this case the name you use to sign onto the computer on which you have the mailbox) and the Internet name of the computer. As you learned in Chapter 2, every computer attached to the Internet has a unique identification number. Most system administrators then associate a name with that number to make it easier for people to use and remember. By convention, the two parts of electronic addresses are separated by the @ symbol.

For example, in 1996 Bill Dedman was the director of computer-assisted reporting for the Associated Press. His e-mail address was bdedman@ap.org. His user name, which was assigned by the system administrator when Dedman had his mailbox set up, is bdedman. AP.org is the domain name for the Associated Press. The .org top level domain reflects that the Associated Press is officially chartered as a non-profit organization.

For computers located in the United States, the last three letters of the address indicate the type of setting, or top level domain as it is termed, in which the computer is located. In addition to the .org domain for not-for-profit organizations, there are six other primary domains: .gov for governmental computers; .edu for computers in educational institutions; .mil for computers associated with military organizations; .com for computers in commercial organizations; .int for international organizations; and .net for computers in companies that provide direct access to the Internet.

Fig 3-2: The Internet addressing scheme tells what type of organization is associated with an internet address. In nations outside the United States, a two character suffix is added. For example .uk = United Kingdom; .au = Australia; .be = belgium; .ca = Canada; .de = Germany; .se = Sweden; .mx = Mexico; .es = Spain; .fr = France.

Top Level U.S. Internet Domains

.edu = Educational
.gov = Government
.com = Commercial
.org = Nonprofit organizations
.mil = U.S. Military
.net = Network providers
.int = International organizations.

The e-mail addresses for computers located outside the United States end in a two letter country code. For example, the address for computers in Canada end in .ca; in France, with .fr.

For the purposes of e-mail and the part of the address which follows the @ sign, different organizations organize their computer networks differently. Some include the exact name of the computer on which the account is located. For example, Cahners Publishing is a $450 million a year publisher of trade magazines and other information products. It publishes *Reseller Management* magazine which serves the computer marketplace. The addresses for the editors at *Reseller Management* are username@rs.cahners.com. RS represents the specific computer on which the editors' accounts reside. Cahners is the name for the computer which serves as the gateway out of the company to the rest of the Internet.

Other companies, organizations, and many college campuses use the name of the computer which serves as the main gateway between the organization and the Internet for the address. For example, an e-mail address at the University of California, San Diego is: username@ucsd.edu. Once a message arrives at the computer ucsd.edu, it is internally routed to the specific computer on which the user has an account.

Knowing how to decipher an electronic mail address will give you some insight into the people with whom you may be corresponding. For example, a person with an e-mail address that includes upenn.edu has an account at the University of Pennsylvania. People with accounts at America Online have e-mail addresses which end aol.com. The e-mail addresses of reporters at the *Seattle Times* are username@seatimes.com. The e-mail account of the President of the United State's ends with whitehouse.gov.

Establishing an Account

To get an e-mail account and mailbox on your computer network, you will have to talk to your system administrator, network operations center or another office serving that purpose. Many organizations routinely give e-mail accounts without charge to all students or employees who request them.

When you set up an electronic mailbox, in addition to being assigned a user name, you will receive a password which only you will know. That means that other people without authorization will not be able to access your e-mail without your permission. A certain amount of computer storage space will also be reserved for your use. Finally, you will be given a procedure describing how to log onto the computer on which your account resides.

Nevertheless, your e-mail account is not private. It resides on your college's or company's computer and can be accessed by the system

```
        To:
      From: reddick@facsnet.org (Randy Reddick)
   Subject:
        Cc:
       Bcc:
Attachments:
```

Fig. 3-3: When you compose e-mail, typically your mail program fills in the "From:" field for you, and you must fill in the "To:" line. Although the "Subject:" line is optional, it is good practice to describe the content of your mail message here.

administrator and others who are authorized to manage the system. Legal issues associated with e-mail will be discussed later in this chapter.

E-mail Software Comes in Different Flavors

Establishing an account is only the first step in the process of getting started. Next, you will have to familiarize yourself with the software you need to read, create, send, delete, and manage your mail. As with other Internet applications, e-mail is a client-server application as described in Chapter 2. The client software issues requests to the server, which actually performs the task. In addition, with e-mail, the client software may also help you manage and manipulate files on the computer on which your account is located. You will have to locate where the mail client you can use is running.

In many cases in the academic world, the software you will need for e-mail will be running on the same computer as your e-mail account. For example, if your e-mail account is on a Digital Equipment VAX computer, you will probably be using a mail program which runs on the Digital Equipment VMS operating system. If your account is on a workstation running the operating system UNIX, you will use a mail program which runs under UNIX.

A common arrangement is for many of the personal computer networks on campus to run an Internet program named Telnet, which will be fully described in Chapter 6. Students telnet to the central computer on which they have their mail accounts, log on, then use the mail software there.

Be forewarned. Software that runs under UNIX and VMS is sometimes harder to use than software that runs on personal computers under
Windows or the Macintosh operating system.

You may have another option, however. Some universities now offer
the PPP or SLIP connections described in Chapter 2 and routinely provided by Internet Service Providers of the type described in Appendix B. If
you have such access, you can have an e-mail client running on your personal computer and call the computer on which your electronic mailbox is
located via a telephone line. Alternatively, a number of schools now allow
students living in the dorms to attach their personal computers directly to
the university's local area network. This arrangement is also being echoed
in select newsrooms throughout North America.

If either of these options is available to you—you will have to talk to
your computing specialists to learn your specific setup—then you can use
Internet client software which was specifically designed to operate on a
Macintosh or under Windows and is much simpler to use than VMS or
UNIX programs. One widespread mail client for Macintosh and Windows
environments is named Eudora. Once you feel comfortable using the
Internet, it will be easy to locate copies of a public domain version of Eudora
("public domain" means the program is free). You will learn how to access
software via the Internet in Chapter 6, which covers FTP, the file transfer
protocol.

People working for news organizations will probably encounter a different scenario. In that setting, most likely you will be attached to a local
area network (LAN). The mail program you will use, often cc:mail from
Lotus Development Corp., Microsoft Mail, or Groupwise from Novell, will
be on your computer already.

If your company does not yet provide Internet mail or you are a free-
lancer, you can subscribe to one of the many Internet service providers.
These providers offer SLIP or PPP connections to the Internet. As part
of their service they provide you all the client software you need, including a mail client such as Eudora. Web browsers can also function
as mail clients.

Another alternative is to subscribe to a commercial online service such
as CompuServe. If you take that route, services such as CompuServe have
their own mail programs. Be warned that browsing the Net through one of
these services can be very costly. After you have used your first five hours
each month, you are charged connect time by the minute!

Given the diversity of ways to set up e-mail accounts, we will describe
the basic mail commands for composing, sending, reading, replying to,
deleting, and managing mail for those of you who have to log onto the
central computer where your e-mail account is located. Moreover, even if
you can use Eudora or other personal computer software as your main
e-mail client, you may still have to know some basic commands in software running under UNIX or VMS to effectively manage the account. The

underlying mail functions are the same in all the mail programs. But Eudora, cc:mail, and Groupwise have Windows or Macintosh interfaces which make them very easy to use.

Creating and Sending an E-mail Message

Creating and sending short e-mail messages is very easy regardless of the computer system you are using. The steps generally will be the same regardless of the system you use; however, the specific commands needed to complete each step will vary from system to system. Currently, even VMS and UNIX have fairly easy-to-use mail programs such as Pine. You will have to consult your e-mail access provider to learn the exact set of commands for completing the following steps.

To create and send a short mail message, first open the mail program. If the mail program resides on a central computer, you must log on first. For example, when you log onto a VMS system, the first thing you see is the system prompt, often "$." At the system prompt, type in the command "mail." This changes the system prompt to what is called the mail prompt, which often is "Mail>." If Pine is available, type "Pine" at the system prompt, and press the Enter key.

Once you are into your mail program, you will signal the system that you want to send a message. In VMS Mail, which is an older program, type the command "send." In other mail programs you can use your mouse to click on the send command.

The computer responds with "To:" then you enter the address of the person to whom you wish to send mail. After you enter the address, which will be discussed later in this chapter, the computer responds with the line "Subject:" If you are using Pine on a remote host, you start the process by hitting the "c" key, which brings up the "compose message" dialog box. You then fill in the "To:" and "Subject:" lines.

After entering the subject in either environment, begin composing the message. When you compose the message, you will be using a text editor. The text editor probably will not work exactly like your word processor so, depending on how user-friendly it is, you may want to obtain a list of commands from your computer resource contact.

Often, text editing in the mail program is awkward. For example, it may be hard to move between lines to correct mistakes. In those cases, you may want to compose longer messages using your regular word processor, then upload that message to send it. Once again, the exact process of uploading files from a personal computer to a central computer varies greatly depending on the exact setup, so you will have to ask someone for a set of instructions for doing that.

And, there is another hazard to guard against if you choose to compose your message on a word processor. The computer on the receiving end may not be able to read documents formatted by your particular word processing software. For example, although CompuServe users can pass messages written in Word Perfect among themselves, they cannot send and receive Word Perfect files to and from other places on the Internet. The safest options are to either use the e-mail software or to send the word processor documents as e-mail attachments in ASCII format. ASCII is the most generic format for character-based information and can be read by nearly all word processing software.

When you finish composing the note, exit the text editor to send the message to its intended destination. To exit in VMS Mail, press ctrl-z (^Z). That is, hold down the control key while you also press the z key. If, after typing your message, you decide that you do not want to send it, you can press ctrl-c (^C) to cancel the message. In Pine, type ctrl-x to send the message or ctrl-c to cancel.

If you use a computer running UNIX instead of VMS, when you log onto the computer, the system prompt is often "%." Using UNIX mail, you can send a mail message either from the system prompt or the mail prompt (the prompt appearing after you begin running the mail program). From the system prompt %, type "mail" and the address of the person to whom you wish to send the message.

More commonly, you will first open the mail program to read your mail and then want to send messages. To open the mail program, type "mail" at the system prompt. This will bring up the mail prompt, which in UNIX is "&." Type "m" then the recipient's address. Again, a more friendly Pine client may be available to you.

In any case, once you have started the send procedure, you will receive the "Subject:" prompt. After entering the subject, press return and begin typing the message. If you want to use a text editor to compose the message, type ~vi on a blank line. When you are finished composing the message, type <esc>:wq to quit the text editor. To send the message after you finish writing it, press <return> to go to new line, then type control/d. If you want to cancel the message before you send it, type ~q on a separate line.

Sending relatively short e-mail messages is easy, even if you must use software such as the basic UNIX or VMS mail utilities. Programs such as Pine for UNIX and VMS make it even more efficient. Instead of having to remember commands, Pine provides menus from which you can select what you want to do. Clients such as Eudora and cc:mail make it as easy to compose and send a message as it is to use your word processor.

Most mail programs allow you to send copies of a message to several people at the same time. Let's say you are working with several colleagues on an investigative project and you want to send the same message to everyone in the group. If you are working with a UNIX mailer, you will see a cc: prompt after you have finished writing your message. Simply type in the addresses of the other people to whom you wish to send the information. To keep a copy for yourself, type in your own address as well.

Commercial Server Domain Names

@aol.com	America Online
@applelink.apple.com	AppleLink
@attmail.com	AT&T Mail
@compuserve.com	CompuServe
@genie.geis.com	GEnie
@mcimail.com	MCIMail
@geis.plink.com	PressLink
@prodigy.com	Prodigy
@well.sf.ca.us	WELL
@world.std.com	World

Fig. 3-4: E-mail is sent to commercial services' subscribers by appending these "@host.domain" designations to the subscriber's user name.

In VMS mail, to get a cc: prompt, at the mail prompt MAIL> you must first type "set cc_prompt" then press return. To automatically make yourself a copy of any messages or replies you send, type "set copy_self send, reply" then press return.

When e-mail arrives at its destination, the message will have a header in the following format:

```
TO      : Recipient's e-mail address
FROM    : Sender's e-mail address
SUBJECT : Subject of the message
```

There are ways to include your personal name in the "From:" line, if you choose. Nevertheless, you should always include your e-mail address as well, either in the "From:" line or in the body of the message, to ensure that the recipient knows how to respond to you via e-mail. Usually, the header also indicates the date the message was sent.

Many people like to create what is called a signature file. A signature file, which usually includes your name, contact information (such as address, telephone and fax numbers, and e-mail address), as well as personalizing information such as a saying or graphic, is automatically appended to the end of every message you send. In programs such as Pine and Eudora, signature files are extremely easy to create and edit. In Eudora, for example, just click on the signature file menu command to create or edit one. In programs such as VMS Mail, a signature file may require three or four lines of programming. A signature file still can be created, but you may have to consult a veteran user.

Addressing Your Mail

As you know, the first step in sending e-mail is filling in the recipient's address. As described earlier, e-mail addresses generally adhere to the following structure: username@computername.domain. Username is the name of the recipient's e-mailbox. Computername is the name of the computer on which the mailbox is located. Domain describes the type of network the computer is on.

The exact form of the address you need to use, however, depends on where the recipient's electronic mailbox is located in relationship to your own. If the recipient's electronic mailbox is on the same network as yours, you usually only have to fill in the username part of the address. If the recipient's electronic mailbox is not at your school or business, you will need to use the full Internet address: username@computername.domain.

For example, assume you are a reporter at *The Los Angeles Times*. If you wish to send a message to another Times staffer, you would only use their user name. But, to send mail to people outside the *Times*, you will have to use the full Internet address.

Some mail programs also require that you signal when you are using a full Internet address. For example, in VMS mail, if you wish to send mail through the Internet, you must begin the address with IN% and enclose the address in quotation marks. The address for the message to someone on CompuServe would appear as IN%"username@compuserve.com."

Once you begin to communicate with people electronically, you will want to save their e-mail addresses. The easiest method is to add e-mail addresses to your standard address/telephone directory entries. Many mail programs support their own electronic directories as well. Often, those directories allow you to associate the e-mail address with the person's name. Once you have made the appropriate entry into the directory, to send mail, enter the person's name at the "To:" prompt.

Getting to the Destination

Although widely used, the e-mail network is not as well developed as the telephone network. As you know, the Internet is actually a network of many different networks. Sometimes the individual networks do not communicate with each other as smoothly as we would like.

Consequently, when you send electronic mail, you can never be sure exactly how long it will take to arrive. While many messages will be delivered to their destinations within a matter of seconds, others can take hours or more. Furthermore, if the network has problems delivering the message, it may try for some time before returning the message to the sender.

From time to time you will have messages returned to you. When mail is returned, you will also receive a message from what is called the postmaster, which is the software handling your message at different points in the network. If you closely read the message, you should be able to determine the source of your problem—frequently a mistake you have made in the address. If you have made a mistake in the part of the address which follows the @ sign, the message from the postmaster will read "host unknown." If you made a mistake in the part of the address preceding the @ sign, the message will read "user unknown." In that case, you know the part of the address which follows the @ symbol is, in fact, connected to the Internet.

Receiving E-mail

Of course, correspondence is a two-way street. When you start writing to people, they will write back. If you are working with programs like Novell Groupwise and you leave your computer on all day, the software will signal you when you receive new mail. With Eudora, you can ask the program to check for new mail at regular intervals and signal when it finds some.

If you do not keep your computer on all day, you must log onto a central computer to access your account or if you are using a certain commercial service provider, you generally will not know if you have mail unless you check your electronic mailbox. In those cases, once you start using e-mail, you must make a commitment to check your mailbox regularly. If you do not, not only are you sure to miss messages, but you give up two of the main advantages of e-mail—the timeliness of the delivery of information and the ability to immediately respond.

A sound strategy is to incorporate checking your e-mailbox into your daily routine. For example, you may want to check your e-mail after you open your mail in the morning, at mid-day, and before you leave for the evening. Or you may want to check your e-mail each time you check for voice messages. If you check your mailbox regularly, reading, responding to, and managing your e-mail is easy.

Once you log onto the computer that handles your e-mail, you will receive a notice if you have any mail. If you do have messages, start your mail client program using the procedure described in the previous section. Once the mail software is running, you will receive a list of messages. In some systems, such as those with VAX computers, you may have to use a directory command (often DIR) to view the directory of new mail messages. The directory listing will indicate the e-mail address (or name, if the sender has personalized this line) of the person who sent you the message and also the subject line of the message.

At that point, you can read the full text of a specific message by typing its number. Once you have read the message, you can delete it, file it electronically, respond to it, or forward it to another person at another address. The commands for performing each of those tasks vary from mail program to mail program, but nearly all mail programs include each of those functions.

Responding to E-mail

In general, responding to and deleting messages is simple, requiring only one-command operations. In VMS mail, for example, to reply to a message, simply type the word "Reply" at the mail prompt when you are reading the message to which you wish to respond. The address to which the response will be sent and the subject line will be filled in automatically. Type your response, then follow the same procedures as you did for sending mail. In UNIX mail, to start the reply process, type "R" and the number of the message to which you wish to reply at the mail (&) prompt.

After you read and/or reply to a message you will probably want to delete it. It is extremely important to regularly delete your messages from your mailbox. Remember, your electronic mailbox is actually storage space on a computer. In most cases, you will have only a limited amount of space reserved for your mail. In some systems, the amount of space reserved for your use is called your disk quota. If that space or quota is filled, your messages may be automatically returned to the sender. If you are using e-mail for personal correspondence, you will miss messages if your mailbox is filled. If you belong to a discussion list, not only will you miss messages, you will create a problem for the person responsible for maintaining the discussion list.

Deleting mail is a two-part process. After you have read a message, you can mark it to be deleted by typing "del" in VMS Mail or "d" and the message number in UNIX mail. The message, however, will not actually be deleted until you exit from the mail program. In VMS Mail it goes to a file called "wastebasket" until you exit the program. In Eudora, after you "delete" a message it goes to the "trash" file. You can "empty the trash" at any time.

If you read a message and do not mark it to be deleted, it will be saved in a special file automatically set up for old mail. To read the messages in that file in VMS Mail, type "select mail" at the mail prompt (Mail>). In UNIX Mail, type "mail -f" at the system prompt (%). In Eudora, it remains on the directory of all your messages. Remember, all the messages you do not delete continue to fill up the storage space on the computer reserved for you. In most cases, you should delete messages after you have read them and responded.

Saving Your Information

Of course, from time to time, you may receive information via e-mail that you wish to save. For example, let's say you have asked a source for clarification of some remarks he made in a telephone interview. When he responds, undoubtedly you will want to save that information for the time when you are ready to write the story.

If you are logging onto a central computer for e-mail, you have three options for saving information you receive. The first is to store information on the same computer on which you have your electronic mailbox, either in the file for old mail described above or in another file.

A second option is to download the file to the personal computer you are using to log onto the central computer where your electronic mailbox is located. This may not be a good idea if you are using a computer in a public access computer lab unless you are careful to transfer the information to a floppy disk which you can take with you. On the other hand, if you are using your own personal computer, transferring information you wish to save from the central computer to your personal computer is appropriate.

There are several different ways to transfer information from a central computer to a personal computer. The first is to download the entire file as a unit. If you are working in VMS, you must first copy the e-mail message to a separate file by typing the word "extract" after you have read the message. You then download the file to your computer. The exact procedure for this varies according to the communications software you use. In UNIX, you can download files by entering "sz" and the exact file name at the system prompt. Although it can be complicated, if you have received some lengthy messages, dozens of pages long, transferring a message in this fashion may be the best route to go. But to learn the exact sequence of steps for your specific situation, you will have to work with your local computer support personnel.

There is another, more straight-forward, but also more time consuming, method for transferring a message from your electronic mailbox to the personal computer on which you are working. You can use the "log" or "capture" feature of your telecommunications program. The log feature allows you to capture an electronic record of everything that appears on your screen directly to a file on your personal computer.

Consequently, as you read a message, you can save it directly on your personal computer, bypassing the potentially complicated procedures of transferring files from a central computer to your personal computer.

Using the "log" feature has its disadvantages, however. First, to capture a file, you must scroll through it entirely. If the message is long or you are under pressure, that could be too time consuming. Moreover, the file may be littered with extraneous information. Generally, as you read your mail, a message at the bottom of the screen will tell you to press the Return key for more information. That message will be included with every screen full of information captured by using the "log" feature.

Nonetheless, the "log" feature is very simple to use. In the telecommunications program ProComm Plus, for example, you hit Alt-F1 to open a log file. In MacKermit for the Macintosh, "log on" is under the File commands. In NCSA/BYU Telnet, the "log on" command is also under the File commands. The file in which the information is captured is under the NCSA/BYU Telnet directory.

In most cases, you can turn the log feature on and off and you can effectively "pause" the log feature, allowing you to pick and choose the information you wish to save. Once you have successfully transferred the information you want from your mailbox to the personal computer you are using, you can easily call it up in a word processor and read it or print it out.

If you are working with programs like cc:mail, you won't have a problem. The program automatically transfers the mail to your personal computer. The information can be cut and pasted into any appropriate document, or you may use the "Save As" command to extract an e-mail message to a text file.

Hard Copy May Be Better

For shorter messages, you may wish to immediately print the messages you want to save, rather than store them electronically. You can do that in several ways. First, the communications software on the personal computer you are using may have a "print screen" command which automatically prints the text on your screen. Let's assume your editor has sent an assignment to you via e-mail which is only two paragraphs long. You read the assignment and want to save a copy on paper. You can simply select "print screen" and the text will be printed on the printer which serves that personal computer.

A second option is to automatically print everything that appears on the screen. Many communication software programs have a feature that turns on a local printer. In ProComm Plus, for example, the command is Alt-L.

Alternatively, with Eudora and the LAN mail programs, you can just select the print command and the message will print on your regular printer.

Still another option, if you are using a Macintosh or Windows personal computer, is to open your word processor, copy the information you want to save from the e-mail, and paste it into a word processing document.

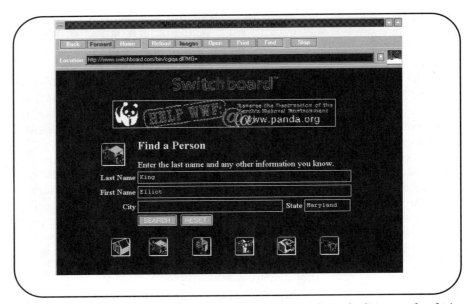

Fig. 3-5: Switchboard is one of several services that help in finding people, their e-mail addresses, and physical locations.

Finally, you can also print messages directly from VMS mail or UNIX. In VMS, enter the command "print filename queuename." The queue name is the network location of the printer you wish to use. Remember, if you are logged onto a central computer, the printer automatically associated with that computer may not be the printer closest to the personal computer you are using. Consequently, unless you understand how to use the queue command and know how to direct the central computer to use a printer close to you, this method for printing will be very inconvenient.

E-mail Basic Functions Reviewed

As a quick review, there are several operations you may perform with your e-mail software. First, if you compose a message, you may send it to an individual. By filling in multiple addresses on the "To:" line and/or adding addresses to the "cc:" line you can electronically copy your message to many people. You may also send your message to an e-mail discussion list by using the same method (Chapter 7).

When receiving an e-mail message, you may reply to it, forward it to someone else with your comments added, or redirect the message, depending on your software capabilities. You may delete the message, and you may save it to a file of your designation.

Finding People

For several reasons, the best way to determine someone's e-mail address is to ask that person directly. Just because people have e-mail addresses does not mean they actually use e-mail regularly. If you access an address from a directory and send an e-mail message, you have no idea whether the intended recipient actually checks the mailbox or, if so, how often.

For example, a reporter once sent a note to a professor who she knew was an active e-mail user asking for advice about a complicated story she was preparing. What she didn't know was that the professor had two electronic addresses and that he only periodically looked at the one to which she sent her message. Indeed, her message was only one of 300 waiting for him at that address. By the time she called on the telephone, he had left town for a conference. She had to look elsewhere for guidance.

Despite the dangers of just sending e-mail cold to somebody and sitting back for a reply, several directories have been established that make it easy to try to find a person's e-mail address. Still, actually finding a specific person's address is a hit-and-miss adventure. Most of these directories are on the World Wide Web, which will be explained more fully in Chapter 4.

Among the larger e-mail directories on the Web are the World Email Directory at http://www.worldemail.com/, which claims to have more than 12 million e-mail addresses; WhoWhere at http://www.whowhere.com which returns not only the address for the name you requested, if it can find it, but other similar names, which can be useful if you are unsure of the exact spelling of the name for which you are looking; and Four11 at http://www.four11.com.

Some other sites that offer e-mail directories include: Switchboard at http://www.switchboard.com; OKRA Database at http://okra.ucr.edu/okra; and Ph Gateway at http://flaker.ncsa.uiuc.edu:8080.

Many of these directories provide telephone numbers and addresses as well as e-mail accounts. Switchboard, for example, has nearly 100 million telephone numbers in its database and is much more convenient to use than the telephone company's directory assistance. One advantage — you don't have to know the area code to find a person.

But the services are not nearly as effective for e-mail. There is a good chance that even heavy e-mail users will not be listed.

The directories are growing rapidly, however, and they are trying hard to get people to register with them. They offer some interesting options for people who do register. People who register with Switchboard, for example, can use its "Knock-Knock" feature. Only people you want to reach can get your e-mail address. When Knock-Knock is on, you will be sent e-mail telling you who wants your address before it is given away. Four11 has what it calls "Sleeper Service." You can be notified when friends of yours register.

In addition to directories, many people now have personal home pages on the World Wide Web. Sources or potential sources with home pages invariably provide their e-mail addresses as well.

The Law and E-mail

In 1995, a person lodged a complaint after seeing obscene words on the Web site of Master Sergeant Jeffrey Delzer of the United States Air Force. Air Force investigators then examined Delzer's e-mail and found that he had been exchanging sexually explicit stories and jokes with other consenting adults using his Air Force computer.

Delzer, a 19-year veteran of the service, was convicted of misuse of a government computer; distribution of obscene writing; and other violations of the law. He was sentenced to three years in jail and demoted to Staff Sergeant, a reduction of two ranks, which cost him $300 per month in retirement pay.

In that same year, Pillsbury fired sales manager Michael Smyth after it was learned that he had e-mailed his boss that the boss' superior was a "backstabbing bastard." Smyth filed a wrongful discharge suit. He lost.

In both cases, the judges ruled that individuals gave up any reasonable expectation of privacy when they use a company network, even if the message was only intended for one person. Through these cases and others, it has been well established that the enterprise which owns the computers on which an electronic mail account is lodged can, under the right circumstances, read the messages in so-called private mailboxes. Companies can read the e-mail of their employees, and presumably universities can read the e-mail of their faculty and students.

It is also important to keep in mind that the same rules of speech which govern regular communication also apply to electronic communication. It is illegal to libel someone online by spreading false information which will damage their reputation. It is unlawful to threaten them. It is illegal to send or store obscene material. (The definition of "obscene" as applied to the Internet is still being argued in United States courts.)

If you act in a way which violates the law, you can be prosecuted. Indeed, the way you behave online can put your organization at risk as well. For example, in 1995, Prodigy, which is a commercial information service, was the subject of a lawsuit because of information one of its subscribers had distributed electronically. In another case, a person was arrested for having illegal telephone credit card numbers stored on his computer. He said that he had received the numbers via e-mail and didn't even know they were there. Nevertheless, he was prosecuted.

Netiquette and E-mail

In addition to the legal constraints concerning online communication, a code of etiquette, termed netiquette, has evolved for e-mail as well. First, messages you send may be forwarded to others, and security in some systems is not what it should be. Consequently, you would not want to say anything via e-mail that you would not face-to-face or that would make you feel uncomfortable if others heard secondhand. Moreover, because your files are accessible to people who have system privileges, you will not want to store private information.

You want to make your e-mail messages as easy as possible for others to read and for them to respond to. Consequently, try to keep e-mail relatively short and to the point. Not only is it difficult to read long messages, the people to whom you send e-mail may not always be experts in operating their own mail utility programs. They may have problems negotiating back and forth through a long message.

The objective of e-mail is to communicate. So, don't forget to include your name, affiliation, e-mail address, and other ways to get in touch with you at the bottom of the message.

Because in many ways e-mail is similar to other public behavior, many media organizations are now establishing codes to govern its use. Among the tenets of the Associated Press guidelines for the use of electronic service is the admonition that accounts are for business use only; people should conduct business on line as if they were appearing at a public meeting representing the AP; people should abide by the mores of the electronic community; and, since the AP's internal server has limited capacity, people should empty their mailboxes and clean out their home directory regularly.

E-mail Is a Tool for Reporters

There was a time when much of journalism was conducted via the mail. Indeed, the word "correspondent" was not a misnomer. Reporters corresponded with their sources, their readers, and their newspapers.

For the last 100 years, however, the interview has been the mainstay of reporting. Face-to-face and telephone interviews are the primary vehicles most journalists use to obtain the quotes they need to produce articles as opposed to research reports or some other form of writing. E-mail has added another technique for journalists to use.

For example, Sally Squires joined the *Washington Post* in 1984. As a staff writer for the health section, she has used e-mail to contact sources, interview experts, query people about studies of interest, and to clarify information. Christine Gorman, an associate editor for the science section of *Time* magazine used e-mail when sources were not easily available or in a different time zone. In 1996, she told a reporter writing for *Merck Media Minutes* that "We can't live without e-mail any more."

Person-to-person e-mail can be a valuable tool for reporters in several ways. First, it can enhance the interaction they have with their sources. Second, it can be a channel via which readers can funnel their ideas to reporters. Finally, in some cases, e-mail correspondence is considered part of the public record. Therefore, journalists can access the e-mail of government officials to learn what is going on behind the scenes.

The most common way for reporters to use e-mail is as an enhancement for personal interaction. For example, e-mail is an effective way for reporters to lay the groundwork for face-to-face interviews. A message can be sent to a potential source who is a stranger, introducing the reporter and letting the source know the reporter plans to call and why. It is a good ice breaker.

From time to time, it may be appropriate to send a source a list of potential questions in advance. It may relax the person and give them time to prepare. Many public affairs officers for the military request that reporters submit questions in advance before interviewing a senior officer. They do this for two reasons: To be sure that the officer has the necessary information to answer the questions and to see how well-informed the reporter is.

E-mail can be used to follow up interviews as well. After a long telephone conversation, you may find that your notes are unclear at certain points. You can then e-mail your source for clarification and amplification. Sources can respond to the questions in a timely fashion without disrupting the rest of their schedules. Checking quotes is a controversial practice among reporters. Those covering government, politics and business are loathe to allow their sources to see their quotes before they appear in print. They fear that official may try to "edit" a quote to make it appear better in print.

E-mail also allows reporters to approach sources in a new way and sometimes get information which they could not otherwise obtain. For example, a reporter for a communications newsletter in Washington, D.C., got wind of shoddy bookkeeping at the National Science Foundation concerning a very high profile project. He repeatedly called the administrator in charge of the project, but the administrator never responded. Then the reporter sent e-mail, laying out the facts as he currently knew them and asking some pointed questions. To his surprise, he soon received a detailed response. Over the next several days, he was able to clarify several issues and write a detailed, informed and balanced story.

E-mail Produces Story Leads

In the same way that e-mail enhances the interaction among reporters and sources, e-mail can enable readers and others interested to more conveniently reach reporters. For at least the past 50 years, news media have basically provided one-way channels of communication. Journalists produce stories; viewers and readers see and read them.

It has been very difficult for viewers and readers to interact with reporters. Newspapers and television news broadcasts don't even make their addresses readily available for their audiences. Calling a busy reporter on the telephone can be an even more unpleasant experience.

Some journalists have begun to make their e-mail addresses more readily available. The results can be dramatic. For example, the e-mail address for Scott Adams, the creator of the comic strip Dilbert (a chronicle of the lives of the employees in the cubicles of a typical high tech company, which runs in 1000 companies in 30 countries), is readily available. Adams has reported that he receives nearly 1000 messages a day and those messages are the source of many of his ideas.

E-mail and the Public Record

As more public officials use e-mail to communicate, reporters and others have argued that their electronic correspondence is part of the record and should be available for review. The National Security Archives in Washington, D.C., which gathers and makes available official documents concerning national security issues, successfully sued to obtain 5000 e-mail messages generated during the Bush Administration.

In January 1996, a journalism student at Metropolitan State University in Denver, Colorado, used the Open Records Act to request the e-mail messages of Governor Roy Romer and top state lawmakers for a two week period. The correspondence included such important morsels as the leftover food available to the governor and his staff.

On the other hand, some local officials may try to use e-mail to avoid state sunshine laws requiring official government meetings to be held in public. For example, after reviewing 70 messages in one month, the executive director of the Arizona Center for Law in the Public Interest has argued that members of the Phoenix city council were violating the state's open meetings laws.

Documentary material has long been an important element in journalism. E-mail creates a new type of document for reporters to survey.

Conclusion

In 1995, two school girls in Massachusetts decided to do an experiment for their school's science fair. If they sent two e-mail messages on the Internet, how many responses would they get in two weeks? The girls guessed 53; one of their moms thought the figure would reach 1,000. After 50,000 replies, the girls had to pull the plug on the experiment, which clearly had mushroomed beyond their wildest expectations. After a year, people were still receiving mail asking them to help the girls with their experiment.

The point is that e-mail is an important, new, dynamic way to communicate with people. Used correctly, it represents an important new technique for reporters. Used incorrectly, e-mail can produce unforeseen and unfortunate results.

4

Working the World Wide Web

In April, 1996, the leaders of the seven major industrialized nations of the world—known as the G-7—met in Moscow with Russia, Ukraine and Belarus to review the progress in nuclear power safety and the security of nuclear weapons in the former Soviet Union. Traditionally, two types of reporters would cover an event like this—correspondents who cover the top leaders of their countries and those who specialized in nuclear issues.

Those reporters would have access to the briefing documents prepared for the summit. They would have access to the experts whose views could make a difference to analyze and assess what took place. And it would be those reporters who shaped the public's perception of the success and significance of the meeting.

Traditionally, reporting on major international summits has been the domain of a select group of correspondents. But no longer. Prior to the summit, the Center for War, Peace and the News Media posted extensive briefing documents about the meeting on the World Wide Web. The briefing paper was written by Mark Hibbs, the European Editor of *Nucleonics Week*. Hibbs also posted a listing of ten sites on the World Wide Web with information on nuclear weapons issues. He included the names and contact information including e-mail addresses of fourteen experts on the subjects. He pointed interested people to two Usenet news groups that discussed nuclear issues.

In short, Hibbs provided reporters virtually anywhere in the world the opportunity to conduct original reporting on the summit. The only tool they would need to access all the information Hibbs provided was a well-configured Web browser.

But was Mark Hibbs himself a trustworthy source? In addition to the brief background bio provided on the summit briefing, a quick search of the Web revealed that he had received an M.A. in international affairs from Columbia University and had reported on nuclear security issues concerning Iraq, South Africa and Central Europe. The Web search showed that Hibbs was an authority in this area.

The World Wide Web has emerged as the most important new medium to distribute information since television. It allows reporters to access information from around the world virtually instantly. It also allows reporters to find information from sources that they previously would never have found. It allows journalists to be more thorough, more accurate, and more complete. And it allows people to publish information for an international audience in a cost-effective, efficient way. The World Wide Web is profoundly changing the practice of journalism.

Moreover, Web browsers such as Netscape and Microsoft Internet Explorer have become the preferred interface for many Internet applications. Properly configured, a Web browser can not only surf the Web, it can access Gopher sites (Chapter 5), operate Telnet and FTP (Chapter 6), be used for e-mail (Chapter 3) and Usenet news groups (Chapter 7), and interface with Internet Relay Chat channels (Chapter 8).

In this chapter you will:

- learn the basic structure of the Web, including its history and development.
- be introduced to the software you need to use the Web.
- develop search strategies to effectively apply the Web to your work.
- explore the possibilities of the Web as a publishing medium.
- receive tips about how to avoid common pitfalls and resolve basic problems that occur when people use the Web.

History, Development, and Structure of the Web

The World Wide Web was launched when Tim Berners-Lee, then a researcher with CERN, the European Particle Physics Laboratory in Geneva, Switzerland, developed what he called a hypermedia initiative for global information sharing. Since the mid-1970s, CERN had been a leader in developing and using computer networks. In 1988, CERN researchers had collaborated with scientists from the Amsterdam Mathematics Center to establish the European Internet—that is, a network of European computer networks all running the TCP/IP protocol described in Chapter 2.

As a result of their activity in developing networks over the course of nearly twenty years, researchers at CERN had developed a culture based on distributed computing. In a distributed computing environment, tasks are divided among many computers and researchers, who then swap and share needed information.

There were many problems inherent in a distributed computing environment. As Berners-Lee saw it, because different computers and software tools were not compatible with one another, it was difficult, time consuming and frustrating to share information among scientists.

Moreover, it was virtually impossible to easily move through related information stored on different types of computers. For example, Berners-Lee wrote in the original proposal for the World Wide Web that, if a researcher found an incomplete piece of software online with the name of Joe Bloggs on it, it would be difficult to find Bloggs' e-mail address. "Usually," he wrote, "you will have to use a different look-up method on a different computer with a different user interface."

The World Wide Web was Berners-Lee's solution to that problem. The objective was to provide a single user interface to large classes of information stored on different computers on the Internet. To achieve that objective, several elements had to be developed, including a simple protocol for requesting information that could be read by people (as opposed to information that can be read only by computers) using various computers; a protocol to convert the information into a format that both the sending computer and the receiving computer could understand; and a method for reading the information on-screen.

To achieve those goals, Berners-Lee proposed a system based on the concept of hypertext. With hypertext, information can be organized and accessed in a non-linear fashion. In other words, you can easily skip around to different sections of a document. For example, imagine you have a book and there is a footnote, labeled number three on page five. With hypertext, you can move from the footnote number on the page to the footnote itself, with the click of a mouse.

In Berners-Lee's vision, page three could be stored on one computer and the footnote on another. The development of hypertext links connecting information located on different computers became known as hypermedia.

Finally, the Web, as Berners-Lee outlined it, would use client/server architecture. As you know from previous chapters, within a client/server setup, client software running on one computer sends a request to a server computer, which then fulfills the request. Because, in most cases, any computer on a network can serve as either a client or a server, depending on the software that is being run, the number of Web servers could proliferate dramatically. Indeed, any computer with an IP (Internet Protocol) number potentially can be a Web server. And it is for this reason that the Web is so powerful for accessing and distributing information.

Linking all kinds of stored information on all kinds of computers in all kinds of different places, Berners-Lee suggested, would create a web of information. No single document would have links to all other related documents, but users could follow linked documents to find the information wanted.

Moreover, users could assemble their own collections of information stored locally and link to other computers on the Internet running Web server software. That information could then be accessed with Web client software. Those collections of locally stored information, which can include text, images, audio, video, and other types of data, have come to be called home pages, Web pages, or Web sites. A Web page is a collection of information available from a specific Web server, including links to other home pages running on other Web servers. The specific relationship of a home page to a server will be more fully explained in the section in this chapter about publishing on the Web.

Although Berners-Lee clearly laid out the structure of the Web and the strategy, the piece of the puzzle that turned it into a worldwide phenomenon was the development of Web browser software with a graphical interface. The browser is the client software the user employs to navigate the Web and display information.

Still an undergraduate at the University of Illinois Urbana Champaign, Marc Andreesen developed a browser, named Mosaic, that allowed users to navigate the Web simply by clicking the mouse button on text, icons, and buttons. Because Mosaic was developed under the auspices of the National Center For Supercomputing Applications at the University of Illinois, Mosaic was initially distributed for free via FTP, about which you will learn in Chapter 6.

Andreesen went on to help start the company Netscape Communications, which publishes a popular Web browser. Realizing the exploding popularity of the Web, software giant Microsoft responded by offering its own browser, Internet Explorer. Netscape and Internet Explorer have emerged as the most frequently used browsers.

The Popularity of the Web

After the emergence of Mosaic, the Web literally exploded. In the summer of 1993, there were approximately 4,000 registered names for Web home pages. In September, 1995, there were 118,000 registered names for home pages. By 1996, web servers were being measured in terms of servers per thousands of people in a given site. In Santa Clara, California, the heart of Silicon Valley, in January 1996 there were 554,967 Web servers, according to Matrix Information and Directory Services.

The popularity of the Web can be attributed to four factors. First, as noted earlier, it provides the first seamless interface to the entire Internet. The Web provides an umbrella for most other Internet tools, including Telnet, Gopher, Usenet, and other Internet applications you will learn about in subsequent chapters. To date, those tools generally do not have graphical user interfaces. Consequently, they tend to be more difficult to use.

The second reason the Web has become so popular is the vast amount of information available. All sorts of companies, agencies, and institutions, from the White House to local Pizza Hut stores, from Time Warner, the publishers of *Time* and *Entertainment Weekly* magazines, to elementary

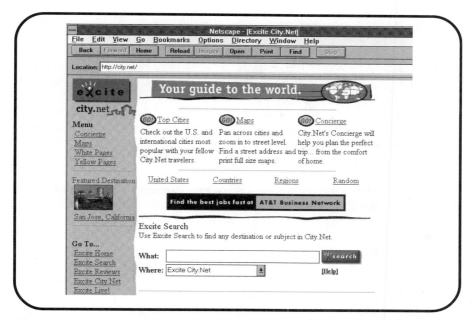

Fig. 4-1: One of the most extensive city directories on the World Wide Web is City.Net, accessed at http://city.net/.

school students, are distributing information via the Web. Major companies, such as Apple Computer Corp., have hundreds of Web pages.

Third, many companies, both large and small, believe that the Web and the Internet will become important mechanisms for conducting their businesses. Consequently, they are making huge and well-publicized investments to realize that objective.

Finally, the Web is both fun and efficient to use. You can find all sorts of interesting information, from academic research to city guides to directories and descriptions of microbreweries. Not only do many major libraries have a presence on the Web, so do most of the major movie studios. Not only can you find advanced scientific studies, law journals, state-of-the-art literary criticism and reams of census data, you can buy CDs, play advanced computer games, tour foreign countries, and download public domain software from the Web. For many people, the Web is useful both at work and play.

For example, Stefani Manowski was writing an analysis of the war in Bosnia. She normally would have done the background research by reading newspaper articles. Using the Web, she was able to download a daily English language news service from Croatia, one of the front-line states in the conflict. Later, she was able to track the activities of some of her favorite music bands, also using the Web.

The Structure of the Web

To successfully navigate the Web, it helps to understand the Web's basic structure. The Web is built on a three-part foundation: a scheme to identify and locate documents; protocols for retrieving documents; and a method for supporting hypermedia links for information stored in different files on different computers. The scheme for identifying and locating documents on the Web is called the Uniform (or Universal) Resource Locator—URL. The primary Web protocol is named the Hypertext Transfer Protocol (HTTP). The method for supporting hypermedia links is known as the Hypertext Markup Language (HTML). For moving among pages on the Web, understanding the URL is critical. For preparing information for distribution through the Web, knowing the basics of HTML is key. But, to understand the reach of the Web, having a grasp of the notion of transport protocols is essential.

Web Transfer Protocols

The main distinction between the Web and other ways to move information around the Internet, such as Gopher, is the model of data they use. For example, Gopher data is either a menu, a document, an index, or a Telnet connection (you will learn about Telnet in Chapter 6). On the Web, all data is treated as potentially part of a hypermedia document linked to other parts of the document residing on other computers. Consequently, in the Web, all data is potentially searchable.

Because of the model of data it uses, the Web is able to provide access to servers with information intended to be used with other transport protocols such as Telnet, FTP, Gopher, and Usenet. Nevertheless, a specific transport protocol—HTTP—has also been developed for the Web itself.

The HTTP protocol has several significant attributes. First, it is what is called stateless and generic—that means it can communicate with different computers running different operating systems. Second, it is object-oriented. Object-oriented software allows complex information to be treated as a single unit or object. Third, it can recognize and represent different types of data. That means the mechanisms to transport data can be built independently from the data itself. Finally, it communicates with other Internet protocols and gateways.

You can think of it this way: HTTP treats all data like containers in shipping. A container can be transported on a ship, truck, train or airplane. It doesn't matter what is inside the container; that will be revealed when the container is opened at its final destination. In addition to sending the containers, HTTP also handles all the paperwork needed to travel from port to port.

You really don't have to understand the mechanics of HTTP. But you must keep in mind that HTTP is designed to move data such as text, graphics, audio and video around the Web. Other tools are needed to actually see or hear the information when it arrive at its destination. Those tools will be more fully explained on the section about browsers later in this chapter.

Second, although HTTP was developed for the Web, it also can communicate with other transport protocols. Unlike other Internet protocols, which can only work with the cyberspace equals of, let's say ocean freight, HTTP can manage all the Internet methods of transportation. In many ways, the Web is the umbrella application for the entire Internet.

The Anatomy of an URL

To move information to and from a location, you must know that location's address. A Uniform (or Universal) Resource Locator is an addressing system for locating resources on the Web. In its most basic formulation, an URL (usually pronounced like the man's name, Earl) has two parts: the scheme or protocol used to access the information and an identifier of the information. The specific format by which the information is identified depends on the protocol used to access the information. In general terms, an URL is presented this way:

```
<protocol>:<information-identifier>
```

Because most of the information you will access via the Web uses HTTP as its scheme or method of access, most of the URLs you will see will be for HTTP. The general format for an URL for HTTP is:

```
<http://[host.]domain[:port number]/filepath/filename.html>
```

Information in brackets is optional. The host computer is the server from which your browser is requesting information. (The port number is the communications port the computer is using and is generally included only if the computer is using a non-standard port.) As you recall, every computer on the Internet has a unique identification or IP number. Those are long strings of numbers very difficult to remember. Fortunately, there is a way to assign a name—called an alias—for the those numbers. So, instead of remembering the numbers for a computer, you can remember a name. For example, *Scientific Computing & Automation* magazine has a Web site running on a computer at Cahners Publishing Company in New Jersey. The computer's IP number is 199.100.12.25. That computer has been assigned the name (or alias) of www.scamag.com. The URL for *Scientific Computing & Automation* is http://www.scamag.com/. The computer running the home page of the television network CBS has been assigned the name www.cbs.com. The URL for CBS is http://www.cbs.com/. Cable News Network is http://cnn.com/.

Once you reach the computer on which the information you want is stored, you then have to access the specific information in which you are interested. Information is stored on Web servers in the standard path/file format used by personal computers. The different directories, subdirectories and file names are separated in the URL by the / mark.

To fully understand the anatomy of an URL, consider this example. Every year, the Investigative Reporters and Editors organization sponsors a contest honoring the best investigative journalism. The 1995 winners are posted on the IRE Web page at http://www.ire.org/contest/winners.html. That means the information uses the HTTP protocol and is on a computer called www.ire.com in a directory or folder called "contest." The file that will be accessed is called "winners.html." That files contains text and graphics, plus links to information stored on computers elsewhere on the Internet.

As noted earlier, the Web supports access to a wide range of Internet protocols in addition to HTTP—including FTP, Gopher, Telnet, news and nntp (which are Usenet news groups protocols), mailto (electronic mail addressing), WAIS and other less-used protocols. Consequently, when you see an URL that begins ftp:// you recognize that you will be accessing information from an ftp server. Once you have jumped to that location, you may have to be able to use FTP commands to access the information.

In most cases, however, while you are using the Web, you will be using the HTTP protocol. You will move from link to link in hypermedia documents, in the process jumping to new URLs. It is the hyperlinks that make the Web such a dynamic service. The hyperlinks are based on HTML, the Hypertext Markup Language.

The Essentials of HTML

HTML is based on something called the Standard Generalized Markup Language or SGML. SGML is basically an international language to describe documents. It is an outgrowth of the methods proof readers used to mark documents before they were sent to be typeset then printed.

In essence, HTML codes are like word processing codes. When you are working with a word processor, tags are embedded in a document determining the way a document looks when it is printed. For example, working with a standard word processor, when you change a typeface in a document, a tag is placed in the document. Those codes are generally concealed from the user. In the same way, if you want to center, boldface or underline text, the word processor surrounds the words with hidden tags.

HTML has a series of tags which determine the way a document looks when it is viewed by a Web browser. It also has tags which link text or images in one document or file to text or images in another document or file. When you click your mouse on a link while using your Web browser, you will automatically access the linked information. That information could be text, images, video, audio, or computer programs that perform designated tasks such as searching a database.

Your Browser

Understanding the basic elements of the Web will help you maximize your benefits. But to use the Web, all you need is a Web browser, which is the term used for the client software for the Web. Unlike e-mail, for which you need your own mailbox, with the Web, you can basically use any computer running Web client software. The browser is the client software that makes the requests to Web servers for information then displays on your computer the information that is accessed.

Any computer linked to the Internet and running the TCP/IP protocol can run a Web browser. Generally, whoever provides your Internet access will provide Web browser software as well. The most widely used Web browsers are named Netscape and Internet Explorer. Like other software applications, browsers allow you to perform many tasks. The most important, of course, is that the browser allows you to request information from Web servers then displays the information. In addition, Netscape and Internet Explorer allow you to copy, cut, and paste information from the screen into word processing documents. There are also tools (bookmarks or hot lists) for saving the URLs of sites that you visit often and the sites passed through during a single session. Properly set up, current browsers allow you to send e-mail directly from them without exiting to a separate e-mail client program.

If you find yourself in the position of having to evaluate browsers, the most important consideration may be the speed at which the browser displays information. While the speed depends to a large degree on the Internet connection itself, the amount of Web traffic at the site you are visiting, and other factors, the way a browser handles data is a factor as well. Faster browsers will first display text then fill in the graphics. Some allow you to jump from Web site to Web site while the graphics are still filling in. Many functions of browser operation may be configured by the user.

Another important feature is called cache memory. With cache memory, information from one file can be temporarily stored in your computer's memory after you move to another page of information on the Web. Then, if you want to see the information from the first file again, it can be re-called from the computer memory, rather than from the original source of the information the Web. Loading information from memory is a lot faster than loading information from a Web server.

Browsers Are Moving Targets

The Web is changing rapidly. HTML is developing quickly and new data types are being made available. Consequently, not all browsers, particularly the older browsers, can display all the information available on the Web. While all can display text, some older browsers cannot display images stored in what is called the JPEG format. Few can play back audio and many cannot play back full motion video.

The inability to load all data types is not just a function of the software. It is a result of the Web connecting many different types of computers. For example, many browsers running under the UNIX operating system cannot play back QuickTime files, which are full motion video files.

If the browser you use does not display all the different data types available, you should consult your computer support staff to load the necessary additional viewers. The viewers are available via FTP, which you will learn about in Chapter 6. If you are setting up a browser to run on your own machine, it is fairly easy to locate JPEG and MPEG viewers and audio playback software. The names of some JPEG and GIF graphics viewers are Lview (Windows) and Jpeg View (Mac). Wham is a sound player for Windows; Sound Machine is for the Mac; MPEG Player 3.2 is a full-motion video viewer for Windows; Sparkle is for the Mac; Shockwave creates multimedia material for the Web for which you need a "plug-in" viewer.

Real Audio is a "plug-in" piece of software that allows audio to be broadcast over the Internet in real time (instead of waiting for the entire audio file to be downloaded first then played). If you wish to hear National Public Radio broadcasts via the Internet, you will have to download Real Audio.

Currently, almost all the browser "plug-ins" are free. The Netscape Web site (http://home.netscape.com/) has a large repository of free plug-ins with easy instructions how to download them.

A second factor to keep in mind, if you are configuring a browser on your own computer, is that the computer must be running TCP/IP. All Macintoshes with System 7.5 and above already have TCP/IP, as does Windows 95. With earlier versions of Windows, however, you will have to install TCP/IP yourself. If you are using a third-party Internet provider (i.e. not your university or employer) they should step you through the process.

Both Netscape and Microsoft are introducing new versions of their browsers at a heated pace. Generally, you can download test versions (called beta versions) of these browsers for free. Unfortunately, these test versions still have bugs in them and often crash unexpectedly. It is safer to use software that has been released commercially. The cost of a browser is usually low (some commercial versions may even be offered free via the Internet).

Fig. 4-2: Web browsers such as Netscape and Internet Explorer can be configured so that the program's default home page is a site designed for journalists, such as FACSNET, accessed at http:/www.facsnet.org/.

Working the Web

When you start a Web browser, the first thing that happens is that it calls out to a Web server. By default, Netscape opens the home page of Netscape Communications, its publisher. Because it is a very busy home page, people often change the initial home page—also called the default home page—to a chosen favorite. In some browsers, the default home page can be changed by pulling down on the options menu across the top of the browser and choosing "preferences." Many universities and employers use their own home page as the default. Others use the home pages of specific sources of information, such as academic departments. Journalists may want to use one of the "Journalists Hotlists" described in Appendix A as their default home page. For example, The FACSNET service for journalists at http://www.facsnet.org/ provides a wealth of links and information for working journalists (see Figure 4-2).

Once the browser is operating, you can then jump to virtually any location on the Web. If you know the URL of the information you want, you can pull down the file menu and choose "open location." You then enter the URL of the location from which you are requesting information.

When your browser requests information from a Web server, a three-part process occurs. First, if the Web server has an alias, your browser sends a request to what is termed a Domain Name Server (DNS), to determine the IP number for the computer. Once the IP number has been determined, the appropriate server is contacted and the information is requested. Finally, the data is transmitted to the browser on your computer for viewing.

For example, assume you are an environmental reporter and you want to access information from the Earth and Environmental Science Center at the Pacific Northwest Laboratory, the site of some of the most complicated environmental remediation work currently underway. You heard the Web site there has descriptions of the research being conducted. Under the file menu, you would select "open location," then enter the URL, which, in this case, is http://terrassa.pnl.gov:2080/.

The request from your browser is sent to the DNS to determine the IP number of the computer called terrassa.pnl.gov. The request is then sent to that computer and the information—in this case the Web site's opening page—will be transported to your browser for display.

But suppose you are not interested in all the environmental work being done at the lab. All you want is to periodically survey the technical reports and selected projects which they have published online. In that case, you can go directly to http://terrassa.pnl.gov:2080/ETDpub/projects/index.html. In reply, you will receive the file which contains a sample of their projects with links to information found elsewhere on the Internet.

There are two important lessons to be learned from this example. First, every file available via the Web has its own unique URL. You do not have to first access the home page of the Web site then travel down layers to find what you want. Virtually every file of information on the Web is accessible from every other place on the Internet.

Second, you don't actually log onto the remote computer. You simply make a request for information, which is then accessed and sent to your computer for display.

Opening a specific URL is only one way to travel the Web. Many people begin at specific starting places then just follow the links. For example, assume you are tracking the polls of the latest presidential campaign. In 1996, you could start at CNN's All Politics site (http://allpolitics.com/polls/) which offered the results of the latest tracking polls. From there you could jump to the home page of the Gallup Organization at http://www.gallup.com/, one of the premier polling groups, and review the back issues of their newsletters at http://www.gallup.com/newsletter/index.html. By moving from site to site, you could get a comprehensive picture of the polling developments during the race.

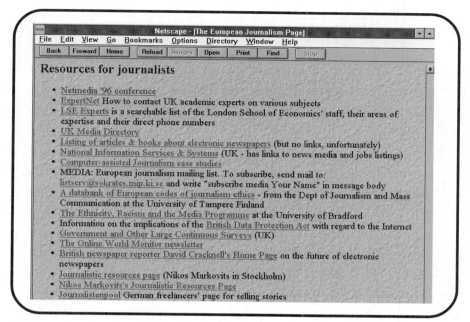

Fig. 4-3: Stovin Hayter's Eurojournalism Page, with links to many media sites and to network-based information of use to journalists, is a viable candidate for a default home page.

Here and Back Again

As you move from site to site on the Web by clicking on linked information, it is useful to know the URL of the Web servers you access. If you find useful information, you may want to return to the same site later.

The first step in staying oriented in cyberspace is knowing where you are. Under the options menu on the tool bar in Netscape and Internet Explorer, you can select "show location." Then, as you move from Web site to Web site, the exact URL for each file you access will be displayed.

As you move through the Web, you may find that you want to move back and forth among several pages. The most efficient way is to select the "go" command from the pull-down menu bar of the browser. You will see a history of the sites you have visited during that session. Highlight the site to which you want to return, and you automatically return there. Keep in mind, though, that if you visit a lot of sites during a single session, the history list may be truncated at some point.

If while moving through the Web, you find a site that you are sure that you will want to return to regularly, you can "bookmark" the site. When you are at the page of information to which you wish to return—perhaps

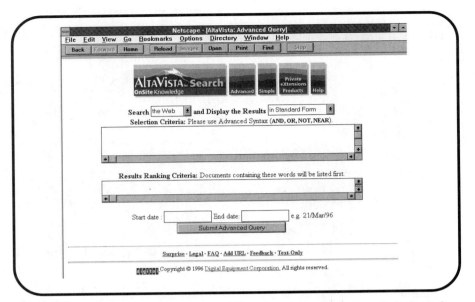

Fig. 4-4: The Advanced Search Page of Altavista (http://altavista.digital.com/) gives several options for narrowing search results.

the opening page of the site of a competitor such as Time Inc. (http:// pathfinder.com/)—select the "bookmark" command from the pull-down menu and select "add." The URL will automatically be added to a list of URLs bookmarked earlier. To access an URL on your bookmark list, simply select it and off you go.

Remember, however, that if you are working at a computer to which other users have access, such as a computer in a computer lab or a single computer in a newsroom, the other users could delete your bookmarked URLs if they choose. To be safe, you may wish to compile a list of the URLs of your favorite sites on paper or on a floppy disk. If your list is on a disk, you can cut from the list and paste the URLs into the Open Location line when you wish to revisit sites.

Finding What and Who You Need

New Web users frequently enjoy simply browsing Web sites, happily discovering interesting information. But few reporters have time for that. The Web is also a dynamic source for finding information that you need for an article or project, or to simply give you a better insight into the subjects you cover.

There are many different methods of locating information on the Web—
some systematic and some based on understanding the way the Web works.
For example, shortly after the new Republican majority assumed control
of the U.S. Congress in the Spring of 1995, Tanya Zicko was assigned to
write about proposed budget cuts in public broadcasting. She knew that
many companies and organizations use a standard format for their URLs.
The URL is www.company-name-or-initials.domain. As you learned in Chapter 3, the domain indicates the type of organization operating the computer
network on the Internet. There are six network top level domains in the U.S.

So Zicko sat down with her Web browser and entered http://
www.pbs.org at the "open location" line. She reasoned that the Public Broadcasting System would go by the initials PBS and that, because it is a non-
profit organization, it would be in the .org domain. She was right. She
accessed the opening page of the Public Broadcasting System's Web server.
There she found many press releases and transcripts of Congressional
testimony relating to her topic. She also visited www.cpb.org, the home
page of the Corporation for Public Broadcasting, PBS' parent organization, where she found additional information. Zicko's analysis was filled
with the most timely facts, figures and perspectives.

While many Web URLs follow the general format www.company-or-
organization-name.domain, many more do not. Moreover, many times you
will not know where the information in which you are interested is located. In those cases, there are two primary vehicles for finding information about the topics you want on the Web: Web search engines and Web
subject directories or catalogs.

As the Web began to grow in popularity, several teams of researchers
began to explore ways to automatically index all the information available
online. These researchers created software "robots" that travel through the
Web to identify new Web pages. They then index the pages according to key
words and other mechanisms. The researchers then created methods to access the index according to key words. Taken together, the indexing and accessing of Web information serves as what is called a search engine.

Currently, there are several active search engines available to users of
the Web. Among the more popular are AltaVista (http://altavista
.digital.com/, Figure 4-4), Infoseek (http://www.infoseekseek.com/), Lycos
(http://www.lycos.com/), and Webcrawler (http://webcrawler.com/).

Now many "meta-engines" that search and combine the results from
different individual search engines have emerged. Among the best known
are Inktomi (http://inktomi.berkeley.edu/) and the W3 Search Engines
(http://cuiwww.unige.ch/meta-index.html), which provides access to nine-
teen different search engines, including some for other Internet protocols,
such as Gopher and WAIS. The Web page at http://www.search.com/ provides access to several search engines and subject guides, which will be
explained in more detail shortly. Access to more than 400 search engines
is available at http://pacific.discover.net/~dansyr/engines.html.

In general, the search engines work like this. Once you access the search engine, you may enter key words describing the information you want. For example, assume you are writing an obituary about Spiro Agnew, a former vice president of the United States who died in 1996. You enter the words "Spiro Agnew" as key words into a search engine. The results will be a list of documents from the Web, Gopher, news groups, and other sources, in which the title of the document or some of the key information matches the key words you have entered. Every entry on the list is linked to the site, so you can then jump from site to site, looking for the precise information you want.

As you could tell from the URLs, some of the search engines are being operated by commercial companies, while others are offered by academic institutions. As a result, each search engine has somewhat different parameters.

While search engines are very powerful tools, they have very notable limitations. First, a search engine often will return only a small percentage of the Internet sites that actually match your search. For example, the key word search for Spiro Agnew on Webcrawler found 425 matches but only returned twenty-five for examination. Second, because searches

Fig. 4-5: The Scout Report is a Web publication dedicated to monitoring new sites on the Web.

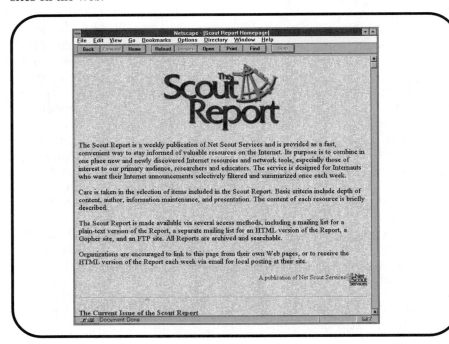

are driven by key words, the results may not always match your intentions. For example, the search for Spiro Agnew on AltaVista turned up everything from an issue of the ezine Dirty Phrack to a discography of the folk singer Tom Paxson.

To conduct a thorough search, you should run several searches, varying your key words from search to search. Furthermore, you should use several different search engines when you are actively seeking information.

Initially, searching for information via search engines is a lot like searching for needles in hay stacks. You may find yourself looking at many irrelevant pages before you find something appropriate. Once you find a good source, you will probably want to follow links on that page to other appropriate pages. To return to the results of your search, you can use the history list in the "go" menu as described earlier.

Using Subject Directories

Subject directories represent an alternative to search engines for finding information on the Web. In this approach, human beings actually select information for linking and assign the information to subject categories. You can click on the subject Art History, for example, and get links to forty or fifty sites on the Web that have information about Art History. The Poynter Institute's Nora Paul gives a good explanation of the different search engines and catalogs in her online book, *Computer Assisted Research: A guide to tapping online information.* The explanation is accessible at http://www.facsnet.org/report_tools/CAR/carfind.htm.

Four of the major subject directories are Yahoo (http://www.yahoo .com/), the Clearinghouse for Subject Oriented Internet Resource Guides at the University of Michigan (http://www.ba.cnr.it/docs/chhtml.html), and the World Wide Web Virtual Library (http://www.w3.org/vl/).

Search Engines vs. Subject Directories

If you know exactly the type of information you want, subject guides are often a productive way to start a search on the Web. Using subject guides is comparable to using the subject guides in libraries. You can easily scroll through many listings looking for the most promising.

On the other hand, search engines often turn up resources you would never find via subject guides. For example, many college students are creating their own home pages with links to a lot of other interesting Web sites. Search engines treat the home pages of college students the same as

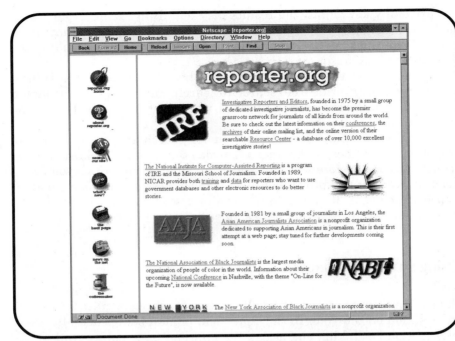

Fig. 4-6: A site maintained by Investigative Reporters and Editors (http://reporter.org/) specializes in linking sites maintained by reporters' professional organizations.

all other home pages and often will link you to an obscure but useful page of information you would not have otherwise found.

As you search for information, keep in mind that new Web servers with information are coming online every day. Several sites track new pages through a "What's New" section. The Webcrawler New Sites page is available at http://webcrawler.com/select/nunu.new.html. Netscape Communications has What's New and What's Cool directories at http://home.netscape.com/home/whats-new.html and http://home.netscape.com/home/whats-cool.html respectively.

If you are using Netscape or Internet Explorer, using search engines and net directories is extremely easy. Simply click the appropriate button on the menu bar and you are automatically connected to the right page to begin the search. Otherwise, simply enter the URL for the engine or directory you wish to use with the "open location" command. Also, many people bookmark their favorite search engines, making it easy to return.

Searching the Web for information can be time consuming. Consequently, if you know that you are going to be working on a project over time, it is worthwhile to subscribe to one of the appropriate online discussion groups described in Chapter 7. The URLs of Web sites of interest are usually posted in discussion groups. After you are familiar with the flow of information among group members, you can post a message asking for good sites with information about your project.

Nevertheless, the payoff of sustained searching can be dramatic. Tom Johnson, a professor at San Francisco State University, reported this result from a computer-assisted reporting conference he conducted in Lima, Peru. One person at the conference, who worked for a major Lima newspaper, wanted to know about the military expenditures of Chile. Using AltaVista, he entered the Spanish terms for Chile and arms and nothing much came up. Then he entered the words "Chile weapons" in English. Near the top of the list of sources was a site which maintained a database of arms imports and exports by country. The data base was maintained by a peace group in Sweden.

Other Kinds of Searches

Search engines and subject directories lead to information on the Web. But, some Web sites serve as an entry point to other types of information as well. For example, you can use InReference at http://www.reference.com/ to search the archives of more than 16,000 Usenet news groups and approximately 1,000 publicly accessible electronic mailing lists (Chapter 7). The Switchboard Web page at http://www.switchboard.com/ provides the telephone numbers of more than ninety million people. Infospace at http://www.infospace.com/ also provides directories of people, businesses and e-mail addresses. A section of the Reporter's Internet Guide at http://www.cfci.com/rig/ allows you to search the online archives of newspapers and speciality publications from around the world as well as lists of links of interest to reporters working different beats.

Moreover, several specialized Web sites have been created to specifically help journalists find the information for which they are looking. Although there is a more complete listing of Web resources for journalists in Appendix A, some of the top general purpose sites include FACSNET at http://www.facsnet.org/, the National Press Club at http://www.npc.org/, and the Poynter Institute for Media Studies at http://www.nando.net/prof/poynter/. The home pages of several organizations for journalists are linked at http://www.reporter.org/ (Figure 4-6).

When You Find What You Want

Usually, the primary purpose of surfing the Web is to locate information you can use for assignments. In most cases, that means you will want to save the information you find.

In many cases, the best approach is to print the information you wish to save for future use. Most browsers allow you several options to save and print information When you select the print command, the file at which you are looking is printed at the printer associated with the computer you are using. Remember, that printer may not be the one closest to you. So, if you are going to simply print the file directly from the browser, be sure to know where that file will be printed.

Printing from the browser has some drawbacks. The file at which you are looking may be quite long. Don't be fooled because a file appears to be presented in fairly small chunks and there are hyperlinks from section to section in the text. For example, it is easy to find *A Beginners Guide to HTML* on the Net online. The first screen you see is a table of contents. Click on any entry and you move down to that section of the document. But the whole guide is only one file, fourteen pages long. If you simply press the print command, the whole file will be printed—even if you only wanted to save one section on troubleshooting.

Most often, you will be interested only in a small part of the information you view. For example, you may not need the graphics on the page. If you only want to save parts of a document, you should open your word processor and cut and paste the wanted portions of the file on the Web into a document on your word processor. The cut and paste commands are under the Edit menu item on the browser. After you have cut and pasted all the information you need, you can treat the file as a regular word processing document.

The cut-and-paste approach is very effective if you wish to save bits of information from different pages. It is also a good approach if you wish to use the information on a personal computer off the network. If you use the cut-and-paste approach, be sure to carefully document where you found the information. The easiest way to accurately document the site from which you accessed information is cut and paste the URL from the "Show Location" line.

If you do want to save a long file, you may want to store it electronically on your personal computer. You can do this using the Save As command under the file menu on the browser. Alternatively, you can mail the file to your e-mail address. To use the e-mail feature of the Netscape browser, however, you must know how to configure the mailer. You will need to know the IP number or alias of your mail server and other information. Moreover, if you are using a public access computer, anybody can change the configuration.

Sourcing Cyberspace Material

A cardinal principle of journalism is to indicate to the reader or viewer the source of your information. Traditionally, that process has meant quoting people whom you have interviewed or referring to a report or document. On the other hand, if the information has come from a press release or is generally known, most journalists don't cite the source.

Sourcing material you find on the Web presents three problems. First, no standard citation format for Internet material has evolved. Second, the Internet is always changing. There is no assurance that the information you found today at one address will still be at the same location, should somebody what to check the sources later. In fact, most of the basic background information about the Web itself has been transferred from the server at CERN in Switzerland (info.cern.ch), to one at MIT (www.w3.org). While, in this case, users are forwarded to the new location, that will not always be the case. Third, URLs are often long and cumbersome to include in the body of an article. It is also easy to make a mistake in transcribing an exact URL and they can be time-consuming to verify.

The precise method of indicating the source of material you have obtained via the Web should be determined by your publication. If you have found a report or a document on the Web, you can refer to it as you would any report or document; that you found it via the Web makes no difference. But, if the material you are using was created specifically for the Web, you may want to indicate when and where you found it. The precise URL is probably not needed. After all, when reporters quote people, they rarely indicate whether the interview took place over the telephone, in person, or at lunch. On the one hand, Internet information does not have to be held to a higher standard than other information. On the other hand, the Web and the Internet do not free reporters from the obligation to indicate the sources of their information.

It is important, however, to develop a consistent method of citing material obtained via the Web. The minimum information should probably include, if it can be determined, the name of the person who created the material, the affiliation of that person, and the base URL showing where you found the material. In that case, if someone wants to follow up, they can communicate directly with the creator of the material you used.

A New Medium

In 1996, Brock Meeks won the Computer Press Association's top prize for an investigative news story. Meeks was the Washington correspondent of *Wired* and *Hot Wired* magazines, but he won the prize for a story that appeared in the *Cyberwire Dispatch,* of which he is publisher, editor and correspondent. *Cyberwire Dispatch* is available via e-mail and is archived at http://cyberwerks.com:70/0h/cyberwire/cwd/. Meeks is using new technology to assume the honored journalistic role of the angry lone voice that can make a difference.

And Meeks is not alone. Thousands of people have created their own Web pages and Web-based publications. Although some of the more ambitious efforts using the Web as a new publishing media will be examined in Chapter 11, many individual reporters and students may find it advantageous to create their own Web pages.

One of the reasons so many Web pages have been created is that simple Web pages are very easy to make. The only requirement for creating a Web page is to be able to post HTML documents on a Web server. Many schools and third party Internet providers routinely offer Web server space to students and subscribers.

There are many excellent books about HTML and Web publishing. Briefly, HTML is a plain ASCII text format and can be created using any word processor or text editor, though many find it easier using specialized programs such as Microsoft's Front Page (http://www.microsoft.com/) and Adobe's Page Mill (http://www.adobe.com/). Some of the latest generation of word processors include an automatic conversion to HTML option. After the document is completed, it is saved as an HTML file (or HTM if you are working in the DOS/Windows environment) in ASCII format.

As you will recall, HTML allows you to format a document and link sections and documents by embedding tags within text. Together, the tags and text are called the source code. Tags are embedded using angle brackets < >. Some common tags are <TITLE> for the title of the document, <H1> for a headline and <P> to separate paragraphs. A title is generally displayed separately from the text and is used to identify the contents. There are six levels of headlines (H1 to H6), with H1 being the most prominent. Unlike word processors, HTML text needs the <P> to separate paragraphs. Browsers ignore indentations and blank lines in the source code.

The main feature of HTML is linking documents and sections of documents—either text or images. Browsers highlight hypermedia links so users will know to click on them to be connected to another file. All links use the anchor tag <A>. The link includes the name of the document to which the link connects plus the text or image which is to be highlighted. The name of the document begins with the letters HREF and is enclosed by quotation marks. The full form for an anchor tag is <A HREF="name-of-document">highlighted text</A>. This form can be used to link documents running locally on the same Web server and documents that are running on different servers.

Most Web browsers can also display what are called in-line images; that is, images next to text. In most cases, the images should be in a GIF or JPEG format. To include an in-line image on your Web page, use the tag <IMG SRC=image_URL> The URL is the file name of the image and must end in either .GIF for GIF files or either .JPEG or .JPG for JPEG files.

The tags outlined above are enough to create very simple Web pages. For an example of a simple page using just the tags above you can visit http://144.126.5.84/ols/oljexample.html.

More sophisticated pages use short computer routines termed CGI's (an acronym for Common Gateway Interface) to enable data base searching, creating links to sections of an image and other advanced features. Moreover, HTML is still being developed and there are many other tags that can be embedded.

A good method of learning HTML programming is to study other pages on the Web. To see the source code for pages you are viewing, simply select "source" under the View menu item on your Web browser.

Individual students and reporters may wish to create their own Web pages for several reasons. It can be an excellent method to showcase your work. And, it can be a way to express yourself in an unfettered fashion. An example of journalism students' Web pages can be found at http://www.scs.unr.edu/unr/journalism/index.html. A basic understanding of HTML and Web publishing is an excellent skill for journalists to acquire. In many ways, the Web is like the early days of television. It represents a nearly unlimited opportunity for journalists.

When the Web Goes Wrong

Many people believe that the Web is the nascent Information Superhighway. Nonetheless, it does not work flawlessly.

Perhaps the main problem with the Web is that few people realized how popular it would become in such a short period of time. So, much like the streets in a rapidly developing city, there is a lot of traffic and an occasional traffic jam.

For a user, a traffic jam makes itself felt in several ways. First, if you are requesting large amounts of information, it may take a long time for the information to arrive and to be viewed by your browser. In general, text is the fastest to load. Images represent a lot more data than simple text and take a longer time to be displayed. Audio and video are extremely data intensive. Depending on the exact link to the Internet, it is not uncommon for it to take several minutes to retrieve twenty seconds of audio.

The speed at which information is transferred and viewed depends on the traffic on the Internet itself, the speed at which information is transferred from the Internet to the network on which the computer you are using is located—the computer which manages that transfer is called your gateway computer—and the traffic on your local network. The busier the Web and your local network, the slower the information will be transferred.

Sometimes the traffic jam is not on the Web or your gateway or local network, but at the server from which you request information. Servers can only manage requests for information from a set number of browsers at any one time. If that limit has been exceeded, you may receive a message indicating that your connection has been refused and you should try again later. This is a fairly common occurrence with very busy Web sites.

Another common problem is that the connection between your browser and the Web server may be unexpectedly disconnected. You may not realize that you are off line for some time, particularly if you are mainly viewing pages that your browser has cached. One indication that you have been disconnected comes when you request information from an URL you know is correct and you receive a message saying that the Domain Name Server cannot find the computer. Or, it may respond "host not found." If you receive that message consistently as you try different servers, you can be almost certain your connection has gone down and you should restart your browser or redial your provider.

As you know, URLs are generally composed of long strings of characters. It is very easy to make mistakes when you enter an URL into the open location line. If you have incorrectly entered the name of the Web server on which the information you want resides, you will receive a message "host not found." When that happens, you should check the first part of the URL.

If you incorrectly entered the directory path and file name for the information you want, you will probably receive a message which says "404 File Not Found." That means you have sent your request to a legitimate Web server but the specific file you asked for could not be located. If you spend long periods of time on the Web, you will have to manage your own computer memory as well. Remember, Web information is often stored in the computer's cache memory for easy recall. If the cache is full, you may not be able to open additional programs, such as a word processor should you need to. Therefore, it is prudent to have all the application programs you need open before you begin your searches.

Finally, as you move through the Web, from time to time you will come to sites that will ask you to register. Some will allow you to buy things online. While it is up to you to decide if you wish to register at a site, for the most part, transactions on the Internet are not yet secure. That means people can intercept and monitor information as it travels through the networks. The security risk may be about the same as giving your credit card number over the telephone. You should consider the Web a public place and act accordingly.

Some sites ask you to register and select a password even though they are not secure sites. In those cases, don't use the same password you use for your ATM card, computer access or any other meaningful, secure account. One technique is to use your name as your password for sites which are not secure. One advantage is that your name is easy to remember when you return. And, be sure to record the name and password you have entered for each site at which you have registered.

Conclusion

With the World Wide Web, you can search the world for the information you need. Literally millions of people are making information available on Web servers to be accessed by people with Web browsers. Browsers with graphical user interfaces such as Internet Explorer and Netscape are easy to acquire and easy to use.

On the other hand, with the World Wide Web, it is as if the Library of Congress just opened, but people are still relatively unfamiliar with books. It is thrilling to be able to access all sorts of information. But inevitably, at some point you will want to locate information for specific purposes.

Finding specific, high quality information is still a challenge. To integrate the Web into your work, you will have to invest time to gain experience. You will want to develop your own hot list and bookmarks. You should leave enough time in each project to follow links to see where they lead. You should explore.

As you obtain access to more information, you will face new demands.

For example, Kara Kiefer decided to write an article about assisted euthanasia. As she pursued the story, she read an article in *The New York Times* that referred to a New York State Legislative Report on law and dying. She knew she needed that report so she went to the Web. Working through subject guides, within an hour, she found a copy of the original report on the Web site of the Indiana University Law School.

Kiefer's success meant that she then had to read a long, complicated report. Finding the report on the Web meant she had to do more work. But her finished product was also much better.

Chapter **5**

Gopher Jewels

Science writers gathered for a June 1996 conference in Santa Fe, New Mexico, asked a basic question, "Is there a difference between the World Wide Web and the Internet?" The same question arose at a conference of journalists in London, England, the next month.

Print, broadcast, and film media have lavished so much attention— and imagination—upon the wonders of the World Wide Web that many have the impression the Web *is* the Internet. At least, others feel, the entire Internet is encompassed by the Web. Publishers of Web browsing software encourage the confusion because browsers like Netscape and the Internet Explorer have the power to read and to display most major Internet documents and to fetch others.

Long before there was a World Wide Web, the Internet connected universities, scientists, scholars, libraries, government agencies, research institutions, and almost anyone else who might benefit from sharing information. And, before there were any point-and-click Web browsers, there was another text-based browser that helped tame the internet—Gopher. To this day, much information of value to journalists is stored on Gopher servers, and other strengths of Gopher indicate that journalists should master its workings.

In this chapter, you will learn the relative strengths of the Internet Gopher and how to:

- Use Gopher to navigate quickly among network sites worldwide and bring information to your desktop.
- Use Veronica and Jughead search programs to locate information stored on Gopher servers.
- Use Gopher servers to access FTP, Hytelnet, Usenet and other network resources.
- Gain access to Gopher clients if one is not freely available on your host.

This chapter assumes that you are familiar with your computer and its operating system and that you have access to the Internet. Like World Wide Web browsers, Gopher clients can provide access to nearly all of the other Internet tools. Most of the examples described in this chapter refer to text-based Gopher clients of the type available on college campuses, through Free-nets, and through "shell" accounts provided by many Internet service providers. The section labeled "Some Other Gopher Clients" near the end of the chapter discusses some of the clients available for personal workstations. Regardless of the client you use, you will be able to perform the same actions, subject to the restraints mentioned in the text.

The Strengths of Gopher

Although Gopher documents are accessible through World Wide Web browsers, a solid understanding of Gopher will serve the online journalist well. Three Gopher characteristics in particular recommend its use: 1) the mechanics behind delivery of Gopher information, 2) the way Gopher information is organized, and 3) the relative stability of the Gopher protocol standard.

One of the great strengths of Gopher is its text-based delivery. That makes delivery of Gopher documents faster (all other conditions being equal) than a graphics-laden Web document. If what you need is words, you can access Gopher with the simplest of computers using the slowest of modems, and you won't have to wait forever. Text files are small, compared to graphics files, and they move relatively quickly over the Internet. Some Gopher clients can display graphics files, but that is not Gopher's strength. Most Gopher clients can retrieve binary files through FTP, and some can even display HTTP (Web) documents.

Documents and folders on Gopher servers are organized into hierarchical menus. There is a direct, linear path from a top (or root) Gopher menu, through logical choices "down" to a document at the bottom of the menu tree. For people accustomed to working with the way libraries organize information by related topics, Gopher menuing seems natural.

Finally, the Gopher protocol has been around since 1991 and has been well-established since 1992. The Gopher standard for storing and delivering documents is not changing rapidly, in the way that HTML is. The net results are that all Gopher sites "are equal" and one has fewer problems with systems crashing or network hangups under the Gopher standard. In claiming that all Gopher sites are equal, we mean that one does not encounter Gopher sites "optimized" for one browser or another as one does on the World Wide Web. Even though some "Gopher Plus" sites offer added utility, lesser browsers do not omit much.

Reliability and Credibility

One other "fact of life" about the Internet recommends Gopher to journalists. This has to do with the credibility and reliability of documents found on the Internet. In theory, anybody can place any type of document on an Internet server and make that document available to the world. In practice, this happens with increasing frequency on the World Wide Web, but not on Gopher servers. Internet Service Providers (ISPs) frequently offer "free" Web page storage to people using their services. A new industry has arisen selling others a presence on the World Wide Web.

The result is that a lot of material is served up in "Web Space" by persons having no particular credentials, no experience, no special authority, or understanding of their topic. Aside from credentials, there is no requirement for truth on the Internet. Anyone can claim to represent "Engineers for Alternative Energy" and place credible-looking documents on the Internet.

Because of the popularity and the ease of World Wide Web access, many spurious documents turn up in searches.

Theoretically, the same thing could happen in Gopherspace. In practice, it rarely does. As an older technology, a less flashy one, and less widely documented, Gopher servers tend to exist exclusively at universities, government agencies, and serious research facilities. Thus, the relative number of entirely spurious documents in Gopherspace is much smaller, and persons deliberately trying to execute a Net charade face a more complicated task with Gopher.

Menu Hierarchies

If your campus host computer has a Gopher client, you can connect to the University of Minnesota main Gopher server by typing:

gopher gopher.micro.umn.edu <CR>

or by signaling your Gopher client to "open the location" gopher.micro .umn.edu. In either case, you are greeted by a simple menu offering you twelve choices, the last of which promises information about the University of Minnesota campus (Figure 5-1).

To select the campus information you may do one of three things. First, you might type the number of the entry you want to select (12). Second, after using your down cursor arrow to point at menu choice 12, you may press the "Enter" key on your keyboard. Third, you may press the Right Arrow key after pointing at the menu choice. Gopher brings a new menu to your screen that displays 18 choices and informs you that you are looking at the first of two screens (lower right hand corner indicates "Page

```
             Internet Gopher Information Client v2.1.3

                        gopher.micro.umn.edu

         1.  Information About Gopher/
         2.  Computer Information/
         3.  Discussion Groups/
         4.  Fun & Games/
         5.  Internet file server (ftp) sites/
         6.  Libraries/
         7.  News/
         8.  Other Gopher and Information Servers/
         9.  Phone Books/
         10. Search Gopher Titles at the University of Minnesota <?>
         11. Search lots of places at the University of Minnesota  <?>
    -->  12. University of Minnesota Campus Information/




    Press ? for Help, q to Quit, u to go up a menu          Page: 1/1
```

Fig. 5-1: Gopher organizes Internet information into menus. Cursor keys move a selector arrow (here on choice 12) up and down. Pressing the Enter key or Right Arrow key selects the item on which the pointer rests.

1/2." See Figure 5-2). You selected one menu choice that took you to another menu rather than to a text file (or graphic or sound file). In turn, the new menu might take you to yet another menu.

This structure of layering (or nesting) menus one beneath another is known as a hierarchical menuing system. It is characteristic of Gopher and used at many Telnet sites (Chapter 6). Under such a system, you select one menu choice after another, burrowing deeper into the information system, until you open a terminal document, usually text. It could be a graphic or other file, or you might select a menu choice that tells Gopher to hand you off to a Telnet session or to some other network client (such as a Lynx World Wide Web browser).

Navigating Gopherspace

Gopherspace—as that part of the Internet accessed by Gopher clients is termed— is by nature organized into menus, which in turn are organized in hierarchical fashion, generally with menu items on related topics. You call up (bring to your screen) Gopher documents by moving a cursor device to the item of interest and selecting it by pressing the Enter key or the

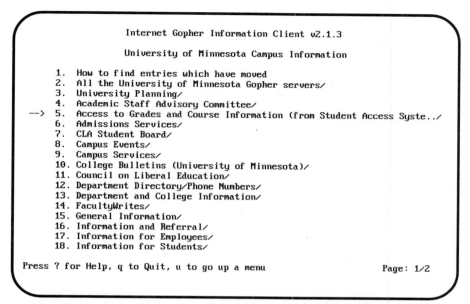

```
           Internet Gopher Information Client v2.1.3

           University of Minnesota Campus Information

      1.  How to find entries which have moved
      2.  All the University of Minnesota Gopher servers/
      3.  University Planning/
      4.  Academic Staff Advisory Committee/
 -->  5.  Access to Grades and Course Information (from Student Access Syste../
      6.  Admissions Services/
      7.  CLA Student Board/
      8.  Campus Events/
      9.  Campus Services/
     10.  College Bulletins (University of Minnesota)/
     11.  Council on Liberal Education/
     12.  Department Directory/Phone Numbers/
     13.  Department and College Information/
     14.  FacultyWrites/
     15.  General Information/
     16.  Information and Referral/
     17.  Information for Employees/
     18.  Information for Students/

 Press ? for Help, q to Quit, u to go up a menu            Page: 1/2
```

Fig. 5-2: Having selected "University of Minnesota Campus Information" from Minnesota's top Gopher menu, you are greeted with a new menu that is two screens full. The lower right hand part of the screen tells you that you are on Page (screen) 1 of 2.

Right Arrow key, by typing the number of the menu item, or, in some graphical clients, by double-clicking your mouse pointer on the item.

Once you have selected a document and brought it to your screen, you may have options to print the document, e-mail it to yourself, save it to disk, or close it. Gopher allows the option of doing many other things as well. From within Gopher you may visit other sites by "pointing" your Gopher at them. You may set, retrieve, edit, and view bookmarks. You may launch sessions with other Internet tools, such as WAIS, Hytelnet, Telnet, and FTP. You may call up searching mechanisms, such as Archie, Veronica, and Jughead. You may scroll backward and forward through documents and move up and down the menu hierarchy. You may call up information about a document without actually retrieving the item in question. All of these actions are available through a small set of keyboard commands. Graphical Gopher browsers permit you to do these things through the use of drop-down or pull-down menus activated by a mouse.

Some Gopher Commands and Conventions

The way Gopher lists menu items provides the user information about the menu listing. In Figure 5-3, menu lines 4, 5, 7, and 8 end with a slash

```
                Internet Gopher Information Client v2.1.3

                     Judiciary from Marvel (LOC)

        1.  About the Judicial Branch (US Govt. Manual, Via U.Mich.)
  -->   2.  Supreme Court Justices (Via CQ)
        3.  Search - US Court Clerkship Requirements (Via Columbia) <?>
        4.  Supreme Court Decisions (via UMD)/
        5.  The Judicial Branch (Supreme Court... via UMD)/
        6.  U.S. Code (Search GPO Access through Texas State Library Link) <?>
        7.  U.S. Code (via GPO Access Depository Library Sites)/
        8.  U.S. Code Gopher (U.S. House of Representatives)/




  Press ? for Help, q to Quit, u to go up a menu              Page: 1/1
```

Fig. 5-3: This Gopher menu lists three different types of choices, indicated by the character at the end of each line. A slash mark (/) denotes another menu; a bracketed question mark (<?>) suggests a search dialog; and no mark or a period marks a text document.

mark (/), indicating that each line marks a directory that will have further choices if it is selected. The item selector arrow in Figure 5-3 points to menu choice 2, which has no punctuation at the end of the line. Lines with no punctuation, or with periods at the end, indicate text files. If you select one of them, the text displays on your screen.

The bracketed question marks <?> at the end of choices 3 and 6 denote menu choices for which the user will be asked to provide key words. You could search for U.S. Court clerkship requirements (item 3) or for matters covered by U.S. codes of law (item 6). Sometimes one finds a Gopher menu item labeled "Under construction." This indicates choices that may not be fully functional. In Gopher, as with other network programs and utilities, patience is required. It is not unusual to find Gopher menu choices for which no files, directories, or information is available. When such an item is selected, Gopher returns a message stating that nothing is available. You might want to try that choice again at a later date. There are other kinds of temporary frustrations encountered on the network.

When you press your Return key (Enter key) or Right Arrow key, Gopher goes to work retrieving the item in question. If it is a directory (items 4, 5, 7, and 8 in Figure 5-3), that directory will appear on the screen when it has been retrieved from its point of origin. The menu item in question may be on the currently logged computer or on another computer halfway around the world. While Gopher is working, a message in the lower right-hand corner of the computer screen reports "Retrieving xxxxxxxx /" where the xxxxxxxx may be a file or a directory, and the slash mark spins to show work in progress. When Gopher has retrieved the item in question, messages across the bottom of the screen report status and user options. Across the bottom of the Gopher menu screen runs a list of three basic commands:

- Entering "?" for help produces a list of Gopher commands and their results (See Figure 5-4).
- Typing "u" moves the user up one level on the Gopher menu hierarchy.
- A "q" starts a dialog asking whether you really want to quit Gopher. (A capital "Q" quits without question.)

If you select a file from the menu, that file displays on your terminal one screen at a time. Across the top of the screen (bottom on some clients), a message reports what percentage of the file has been viewed. For some clients, you receive a message when all the file has been viewed that pressing "D" starts a dialog allowing the selected file to be downloaded to your personal computer. On some clients the message does not appear, but the command is still available, as are commands to save the file or to have it mailed to you.

A list of common Gopher commands is given in Figure 5-4. Gopher is case sensitive. If you are looking at a menu comprised of your bookmarks and you want to download a file at which you are pointing, enter an upper case "D." However, if you enter a lower case "d" while you are pointing at a bookmark, the bookmark is deleted. Also worth noting about Gopher is that commands for moving around often have synonyms. To move down a screen, you could press the Page Down key. However, if you are logged onto a host system using a communications program that is command compatible with ProComm, Page Down starts the download process. In that case, you should use one of the other keys, such as the spacebar or the "+" key.

"U" for Up or "B" for Back?

Two actions that at first seem identical are not. These are the "u" key and the "b" key. Figure 5-2 shows the first page of a Gopher menu that is two pages long. Some Gopher menus ("All the Gophers in the World," for example) may be more than 100 pages. The bottom right-hand corner of a Gopher menu screen tells you where you are in the current menu. In Figure 5-2 the whole menu is two pages (two screens) long. You could get to the second page (or subsequent pages) by pressing your Down Arrow key repeatedly. When the arrow moves below the last item on the current page, the next screen displays. A quicker way, however, is to use the space bar, which will take you to

the next page. So will the "+" key, the ">" key, or the Page Down key (if you
have that key, and it is not intercepted by your communications program).
This is where the "b" key becomes handy. If you are several pages into a
Gopher menu, pressing the "b" key moves you back one page of the menu.
Pressing "u" (up), however, takes you entirely out of your current menu and
moves you up one level in the menu hierarchy.

Fig. 5-4: Common keyboard commands for Gopher are summarized in a chart
like this when you ask Gopher for help.

Gopher Keyboard Commands

To move around
Use the arrow keys or vi/emacs equivalent
Right, Return .... "Enter"/Display current item.
Left, u .... "Exit" current item/Go up a level.
Down .... Move to next line.
Up .... Move to previous line.
>, +, Pgdwn, Space .... View next page.
<, -, Pgup, b .... View previous page.
0-9 .... Go to a specific line.
m .... Go back to the main menu.

Bookmarks
a .... Add current item to the bookmark list.
A .... Add current directory to bookmark list.
v .... View bookmark list.
d .... Delete a bookmark/directory entry.

Other commands
q .... Quit with prompt.
Q .... Quit unconditionally.
s .... Save current item to a file.
S .... Save current menu listing to a file.
D .... Download a file.
r .... goto root menu of current item.
R .... goto root menu of current menu.
= .... Display information on current item.
^ .... Display information on current directory.
o .... Open a new gopher server.
O .... Change options.
f .... Connect to anonymous FTP server.
w .... Connect to http, gopher, FTP, or telnet URL.
/ .... Search for an item in the menu.
n .... Find next search item.
g .... "Gripe" via email to administrator of item.
Ctrl-L, Ctrl-R, Ctrl-W .. Redraw (Wipe) the screen.
Ctrl-T .... Show host's local date and time.

```
Link Info (0k)                                                          100%
+------------------------------------------------------------------------+
#
Type=1
Name=Campus Wide Information Systems
Path=1/internet/cwis
Host=marvel.loc.gov.
Port=70
<URL:gopher://marvel.loc.gov.:70/11/internet/cwis>
```

Fig. 5-5: The Gopher link information screen describes the menu item to which your cursor is pointing. Invoked by typing the "=" key, it indicates the host computer, the type of document, path to the document, and the URL.

Pressing the "=" key in Gopher brings to the screen a report that tells the networker where (what machine, in which directory) the selected item is physically located (Figure 5-5). Here is another distinction between Gopher and Telnet. When you use the Telnet protocol to access a distant computer, you are a captive of that site. With few exceptions (in particular, some large government sites offer gateways to other government sites), your menu choices do not connect you to computer networks other than the one you first connected to.

In Gopher, however, you might start with a Root menu that resides on a machine in your home town. If you select a menu choice that calls up a new menu/directory, that menu, and any number of items on it, may actually be called up from a machine in another state—or even another country. It is possible that the ten to fifteen menu items on a typical Gopher directory could be located in ten to fifteen different places. Point the selector arrow at the item you desire. Gopher "knows" where the requested file or directory resides and goes out and fetches it for display on your screen. Whether the requested file or directory comes from France or rests on a machine next door, you see the same dialog, the same types of displays. Again, pressing the "=" key will report where your menu choice really resides.

Using Gopher Bookmarks

Because Gopher facilitates movement so easily from one menu to another and another and another, and so on, it is very easy to lose track of where you are. Two Gopher features help keep track of where you are. The "=" sign already mentioned is available to anyone, even with only Telnet connections to Gopher.

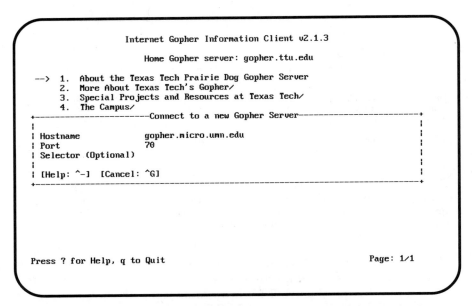

```
           Internet Gopher Information Client v2.1.3

               Home Gopher server: gopher.ttu.edu

   -->  1.  About the Texas Tech Prairie Dog Gopher Server
        2.  More About Texas Tech's Gopher/
        3.  Special Projects and Resources at Texas Tech/
        4.  The Campus/
  +--------------------------Connect to a new Gopher Server---------------------+
  :                                                                             :
  : Hostname                gopher.micro.umn.edu                                :
  : Port                    70                                                  :
  : Selector (Optional)                                                         :
  :                                                                             :
  : [Help: ^-] [Cancel: ^G]                                                     :
  +-----------------------------------------------------------------------------+




   Press ? for Help, q to Quit                            Page: 1/1
```

Fig. 5-6: The "Other Gopher" dialog is launched by typing "o" at any Gopher menu. You then type in the host address, and, if necessary, the port number.

Assume for a minute that you connected to Gopher by Telnet to consultant.micro.umn.edu or some other Telnet host. Browsing, you moved down through a series of menus until you happened onto a menu full of the very crime statistics you need. You suspect from signatures on some of the files that they are updated regularly, and you would like to return where you are later, but you have not kept thorough notes. You could point at a file or a menu, press the "=" sign, and write down the host address and the path information provided. (See Chapter 6 for path shorthand.) The next time you want to access your precious crime statistics, start by connecting to your usual Gopher. Once connected, press "o" and type in the host address you recorded from the earlier dialog. That should connect you to the right host, and, with luck (or good path notes), you will again find the files you seek.

There is a more graceful way of keeping track of where you are in Gopherspace. If the machine you use as your connection to the Internet houses a Gopher client, you may employ Gopher bookmarks. Placing bookmarks in Gopherspace is very easy. If you want to mark an item on a Gopher menu, just move the arrow selector to the item and press the letter "a" (lower case). A dialog box pops onto your screen highlighting a suggested name for the bookmark. This is the name that will appear on your bookmark menu when you recall your bookmarks later. If you want to return to the menu now on your screen, press "A" (upper case) and you will see the same type of dialog box. If you accept the suggested name, press the Enter key, and the bookmark is recorded. Otherwise, you may type in a name to suit your taste. The display given when you press "=" (Figure 5-5) is actually the information stored in your bookmark.

To recall your bookmarks, press the "v" (for view) key. Gopher displays your list of bookmarks in menu format, replacing whatever menu was on the screen with your bookmark list. Again, just point your selector at the menu item (or type in its number), and press the Enter key (or Right Arrow key) to call the item to your screen.

Searching with Veronica and Jughead

Many Gopher sites offer as a menu choice something like "Search Gopherspace using Veronica." The menu listing may be followed by a bracketed question mark <?> because the user must provide search parameters. Such a choice is offered on the Library of Congress Gopher, marvel.loc.gov. From the root menu choose "Internet Resources" (choice 11 at this writing) then choose "Veronica and Jughead" (choice 13 at this writing). You will then be asked to input the term(s) or key words for which you want to search. One of the strengths of Veronica is that it allows you to narrow your search using Boolean (AND, OR, NOT) logic.

Figure 5-7 displays a typical search dialog in which we have asked Veronica to find all the Gopher files and directories (wherever in the world

---

Fig. 5-7: Veronica searches accept Boolean logic. In this search we are asking for a list of Gopher items that have two words, "campus" and "crime," in them.

```
              Internet Gopher Information Client v2.1.3

                   Search Gopherspace using Veronica


        3.  Find GOPHER DIRECTORIES by Title word(s) (via NYSERNet    ) <?>
        4.  Find GOPHER DIRECTORIES by Title word(s) (via PSINet) <?>
    +---------------Search GopherSpace by Title word(s) (via PSINet)---------------+
    |                                                                              |
    | Words to search for                                                          |
    |                                                                              |
    | campus AND crime                                                             |
    |                                                                              |
    | [Help: ^-] [Cancel: ^G]                                                      |
    +------------------------------------------------------------------------------+
    -->  13. Search GopherSpace by Title word(s) (via PSINet) <?>
         14. Search GopherSpace by Title word(s) (via SUNET) <?>
         15. Search GopherSpace by Title word(s) (via U. Nac. Autonoma de MX.. <?>
         16. Search GopherSpace by Title word(s) (via UNINETT/U. of Bergen) <?>
         17. Search GopherSpace by Title word(s) (via University of Koeln) <?>
             Simplified veronica chooses server - pick a search type:

    Press ? for Help, q to Quit, u to go up a menu                    Page: 1/2
```

they might be) that use both "campus" (the search is not case sensitive) AND "crime" in their names. When Veronica is done searching, she reports results of the search in Gopher menu format. That is, you are given a customized Gopher menu that looks like any other Gopher menu. It also works like any other Gopher menu. You select an item in any of the normal ways, and Gopher reaches out and connects you to that site.

Sometimes Veronica search results report what seem to be multiple occurrences of the same item. They could, however, represent Gopher directory choices with the same names but in different locations. To tell the difference, you have only to point at each item and press the "=" key to get Gopher's report on the item location. You sometimes get duplicate listings because Gopher administrators (the people who set up the server offerings) in different locations may elect to establish menu choices leading to the same document. Because the same menu item occurs in multiple locations, Veronica reports once for each occurrence.

Jughead operates much the same way as Veronica. In fact, you could conduct precisely the same search with Jughead that we made previously in Veronica and get similar results. There are, however, some subtle differences in search capabilities. At each Jughead and each Veronica site there are files describing search parameters of the respective programs. If you wish to become a Gopher guru, you will want to study each document. Most sites have short documents explaining how to perform searches. Veronica has been available a little longer than Jughead and is more widely distributed.

Some Great Gophers

Your own campus information is probably not the only network resource you will find listed on your campus Gopher server if your campus has one. Many colleges and universities have special topic areas in which they excel. The Massachusetts Institute of Technology and Cal Tech in Pasadena, California, are noted for outstanding science programs. Harvard is known for its business school. Schools have done much the same thing on the Internet. Cornell and Washburn universities have developed outstanding online resources in the field of law. Sam Houston State University has an especially rich collection of pointers to online economics resources.

Several schools have set up Gopher servers that are distinguished in one way or another as gateways to a wide variety of resources. A few outstanding Gophers include:

1. University of Minnesota, where Gopher was created
2. University of Michigan Library
3. "Live Gopher Jewels" at the University of Southern California
4. Rice University's Riceinfo Gopher
5. University of California Irvine's PEG
6. University of California–Santa Cruz's InfoSlug
7. Library of Congress

Each of these Gopher sites is described briefly on the following pages. If you have a Gopher client, you should use the addresses described for each site. If you have only a World Wide Web browser, you may still access Gopher sites through the File/Open Location dialog. Begin by typing "gopher://" followed by the Gopher address. Thus, the Gopher at riceinfo.rice.edu would be addressed by a Web browser as "gopher://riceinfo.rice.edu" and you would have access to all the same information.

University of Minnesota

Minnesota's Gopher may be accessed at gopher.micro.umd.edu. As the "mother of all Gophers," the Minnesota Gopher provides access to many other Gopher servers. In fact, one of the menu choices at the Minnesota Gopher promises "All the Gophers in the World." If you select this choice, you will be asked to select a continent or subcontinent first, then you can choose from a menu of nations. Within nations you might be asked to select regions or states, and gradually you are taken to a list of local Gopher sites.

This process may be useful to you if you know (or suspect) ahead of time that the information you desire is located at a certain site. Because many Gopher sites provide phone books or directories, this resource can be very useful. If you know someone is affiliated with Washington and Lee University, for example, you could start at the Minnesota Gopher, select "All the Gophers in the World," "North America," then "United States," "Virginia," and so forth until you get to Washington and Lee. Choose the phone book entry, if it's available, and search for the person you choose.

This ability to reach "All the Gophers in the World" is useful to enough people that many Gopher sites offer it as a choice. In some of those cases, that menu choice actually points at the menu choice of that name at the University of Minnesota. Thus, even though you started at your own home Gopher, when you make this choice you actually are connecting to the Minnesota server.

University of Michigan Subject-Oriented Guides

Instead of organizing information geographically, sometimes it is more useful to group documents according to subject or topic. Libraries assign catalog numbers to books based upon subject area classifications. Hence, different textbooks for introductory biology will be placed on the shelves in the same area in the library. They all will be grouped together. Similarly, many Gopher servers follow subject-area organization.

Just as the Minnesota Gopher points to Gophers worldwide, listed by geography, a Gopher server at the University of Michigan library points to Gophers worldwide, organized by subject areas. "The Argus Clearinghouse" at the University of Michigan may be accessed at una.hh.lib.umich.edu by selecting choice 11, "inetdirs."

"Live Gopher Jewels" at Southern California

Rich Wiggins is a Gopher scholar who has maintained a list of outstanding Gopher sites. To qualify for inclusion in the "Gopher Jewels" list, a site must exhibit a truly outstanding collection of information resources on one topic. Wiggins has also maintained a discussion list inhabited by others who are interested in outstanding collections of information made available by Gopher servers. Contributors to the list often suggest or discuss inclusion of new Gopher sites on the list. The subject-oriented list is available from many sites. But at the University of Southern California, the list is "live," meaning you can actually call up a site by selecting it from the list.

The Live Gopher Jewels site is especially useful to journalists for two reasons. First, to be included on the list a site must have already been screened for quality of information. It is not likely that bogus sites or spurious work gets listed here. Second, the subject tree organization of resources is generally easy to follow; hence, it is fairly easy to find material on any given topic, especially broad topics.

The Live Gopher Jewels may be reached at cwis.usc.edu choosing first "Other Gophers" then "Gopher-Jewels." While the USC Gopher is home to the Live Gopher Jewels, other sites have pointers to USC, and still others around the world "mirror" (provide a working copy of the resource) the site at Southern California. What distinguishes the Gopher Jewels site from other subject-oriented sites is that all sites included on the list have been examined and "certified" as excellent resources.

Rice University's Riceinfo Gopher

A number of universities have set up Gopher servers with the stated purpose of providing excellent general information resources. Rice University is one such site. The Riceinfo Gopher is basically the campus-wide information server. But two of its main menu items provide pointers (or links) to a wealth of other resources. One menu choice is "Information by Subject Area." This choice provides links to the University of Michigan site, "The Argus Clearinghouse" (mentioned earlier in this section), to Jughead and Veronica searching programs, and to a menu of subject-oriented directories. Another choice from the Root menu at Riceinfo promises "Other

Gopher and Information Servers." In turn, this last choice contains links to two different "All the Gopher Sites in the World" lists. You can access the Riceinfo Gopher at riceinfo.rice.edu.

UC Santa Cruz "InfoSlug"

Another Gopher site billed as a superior all-around resource is located at University of California at Santa Cruz's InfoSlug. The machine gets its name from the university mascot—the large, bright yellow Banana Slug that inhabits redwood forests in California coastal areas. InfoSlug provides pointers to many outstanding Gopher resources. If you select "The Government" from InfoSlug's root menu, you will have access to an outstanding list of California state and United States federal government information sources.

If you select "The Community," you are presented with a long list of Santa Cruz area resources of particular interest to students. Similarly, selection of "The World" from the root menu calls up a directory containing a handful of menu choices that lead to other worldwide network resources. InfoSlug may be accessed by pointing your Gopher at gopher.ucsc.edu.

UC Irvine's "PEG"

If you ask Gopher to open cwis.uci.edu, you access the campus-wide information server for the University of California at Irvine. One of its menu choices is "Accessing the Internet." On the menu retrieved by selecting "Accessing the Internet," one menu choice is "PEG." "PEG" is an acronym for "Peripatetic Eclectic Gopher." As the name implies, PEG has wide-ranging (eclectic) interests, providing links to an expansive range of topic material.

PEG's directory links to mathematics, medicine, politics and government, and physics and the women's resources are especially rich. And, PEG's "Virtual Reference Desk" provides access to scores of reference documents and to other Gopher sites offering reference materials on a wide range of subjects.

Library of Congress

For many reasons, it is understandable that, if the United States Library of Congress wanted to provide information by Gopher, it would have a far-reaching Gopher server. That in fact is the case. Accessed at marvel.loc.gov, the Library of Congress Gopher provides pointers to the same types of worldwide resources mentioned for other Gophers as well as pointers to United States government information servers and to the extensive holdings of the Library of Congress itself.

Some Other Interesting Gophers

By following links on any of the Gophers just described, you could ultimately find your way, as one frequent menu choice suggests, to "All the Gopher Servers in the World." Or, following subject leads on the Gophers just described, you could find information on almost any topic you might find of interest. A few other Gophers you might find interesting are:

- Texas A&M Gopher, gopher.tamu.edu, a good general, all-around Gopher.
- University of Melbourne (Australia), gopher.austin.unimelb.edu.au, has, among other things, great sources on medicine and health, as well as telephone and e-mail directories from throughout the world.
- Environmental Protection Agency, gopher.epa.gov.
- United States Department of Education, gopher.ed.gov.
- United States Congress, gopher.senate.gov and gopher.house.gov.
- United Nations, nywork1.undp.org.
- Cornell University Law school, fatty.law.cornell.edu, provides access to a wealth of legal material, including searchable indices of United States Supreme Court decisions.

File Capturing Options

One of the more common reasons for accessing files in Gopherspace is to retrieve documents needed as source material for research papers. When you find a document of use to you in Gopherspace, you may wish to print it or to save it to a file on your computer. Gopher permits these and other options. To do this, you need to be aware of two things: where the Gopher client software you are using is located, and how that software is configured with regard to printing.

If you have gained access to Gopher through a Telnet link (described later in this chapter), you will not be able to print files directly because the Gopher client in question sits on a computer somewhere far away from you. If you gain access to Gopher through a central host on your campus, then you need to find out from your computer service contact where files are printed.

On some campuses where you access Gopher on a central host, your files will not print on paper at all. Instead, if you tell Gopher to print a document, that document is "printed" to a computer file in your disk space on the host computer. It might be given a name such as "Gopherprint$123456." Whatever name it is given, you now have the job of printing the file. That may be as simple as issuing a command such as print queue Gopherprint$123456 <CR>. Instead, you may have to download the file to your personal computer or workstation then print from there. You need to ask your instructor and/or campus computer system contact the proper course to take.

If, on the other hand, your Gopher client software resides on your personal computer or workstation, your document may well print out on whatever printer is connected to your computer or its network. Ask the person in charge of the lab you are using.

Even if you gain access to Gopher by way of a Telnet connection (see section on "Alternative Access"), you can e-mail the document to your mailbox. When you are viewing a Gopher text document, typing the letter "m" will initiate the mail option dialog. This option is also open to you if you access Gopher through a local client or a central host client on campus; you just would use a different command sequence.

The third option for capturing documents in Gopher is through the "save" command. Again, when you scroll through a Gopher text document, you have the option of typing "s" to save the document. If you choose this option, the document will be saved on your disk space if you are using a client on a central host on campus. You then must download the file to your computer or print from the central host. If your Gopher client is on the computer you are using, then you may save to the computer's hard disk or to a floppy. Having done that, you then have the option of importing the file (or portions of it) into your word processor and doing with it anything you normally do with a word processor document.

Finally, there is the "Download" option for those who access Gopher through telephone lines. When you are viewing a Gopher document, all you need to do is type "D" to initiate the Download dialog. You will be asked what communications protocol (such as Xmodem, Zmodem, Kermit) to use for the file transfer. And you may be asked to assign a name to the file.

Dealing with Network Gridlock

Because the volume of Internet traffic has exploded since 1992, more popular network sites may be more in demand than the existing network structure can manage. If you try to connect to a site where there is already too much traffic, you are likely to get one of three kinds of messages. The friendlier, more enlightening messages (less common) tell you something such as "there are already too many people connected to 123.456.78." The second kind of message simply says something such as "unable to connect to 123.456.78." Another common occurrence is that your computer screen holds for several minutes with a message such as "trying to connect," or "retrieving directory," and finally returns a message about being unable to connect because the connection process "timed out."

A student confronted with any of these situations might adopt the following strategy:

1. Try going to an alternative site for the same information. If you can choose an alternative from the same menu, do so. If you have to go to another Gopher or perhaps a Telnet site, do so.
2. If you received the message when you selected a menu item from Gopher, you might try asking Gopher for the address of the site (pressing the "=" key) then, if possible, connecting there directly from your system prompt.
3. If the site is accessible by another method (Telnet, HTTP), try that method.
4. Try again in a few minutes.

When Gopher Hands You Off to Another Client

Gopher is easy to use and can put you in touch with a lot of information. The Gopher menu and command structure are uniform worldwide. Whole libraries of information are made easily available. Gopher administrators have grouped gateways to like information together in many instances, making it easier to find what you need. Veronica and Jughead searching tools expand the finding capabilities for a student on the prowl for some particular kind of data.

One of the limitations of Gopher, however, is that there is a lot of information available on the network which may not be indexed for Gopher searching devices. There is even more information that is not stored at Gopher sites or under the Gopher umbrella. You might find pointers to some of that information if a Gopher menu happens to point to a Telnet or HTTP site. But, to get to the Telnet site, you must leave Gopher. And Veronica and Jughead won't tell you what is at the Telnet site other than what is shown on the Gopher menu pointing to that site.

However, many Gopher servers offer a menu choice such as "Internet Resources" or "Other Internet Resources." The Library of Congress Gopher server (marvel.loc.gov) has such a choice on its root menu. Typically, selecting this menu choice brings up a new menu populated with several selections offering use of network tools that reach beyond the limits of Gopher. The Internet Resources menu from the Library of Congress Gopher offers access to Archie and FTP (Chapter 6), to university campus-wide information systems, to Free-Net systems, Hytelnet (Chapter 6), WAIS servers (Chapter 9), and to Veronica and Jughead servers. One can also find guides to Mail Lists (Chapter 3), Usenet news groups (Chapter 7), and to the World Wide Web.

Alternative Gopher Access

For the user, a Gopher session at first glance looks and behaves very much like a Telnet session (see Chapter 6). Once connected, the network user faces a menu of less than twenty choices. Figure 5-3 shows the Judiciary menu from the Library of Congress (LOC) Gopher. If the local host has a Gopher client (each student will have to ask the network access provider), one has considerably more freedom in moving around Gopherspace. Usually all that is necessary to start a Gopher session (if your host has a Gopher client) is to type the word "gopher" at the system prompt then to press Enter. Typing the word "gopher" followed by a Gopher server's address takes the student to the Gopher site she chooses. For example, one might access the Library of Congress Gopher by typing

gopher marvel.loc.gov <CR>

Another path to the Library of Congress Gopher from a local Gopher site would be first to launch the local Gopher, then to "point" the Gopher at a chosen destination site. Typing "o" (lower case) brings up a window (Figure 5-6) in which you are asked to enter the address of the destination Gopher (the one to which you want to connect). In this case, you would type simply

marvel.loc.gov <CR>

Finally, one may access some public Gopher clients by using the Internet Telnet program (Chapter 6). Thus, typing the command

telnet consultant.micro.umn.edu<CR>

launches a remote log-in to the "Great Mother Gopher" at the University of Minnesota. Some other public Telnet addresses that allow access to Gopher clients include

- gopher.who.ch, log in as "gopher."
- gopher.uiuc.edu, log in as "gopher."
- info.anu.edu.au, log in as "info" (Australia).
- gopher.chalmers.se, log in as "gopher" (Sweden).
- ecnet.ec, log in as "gopher" (Ecuador).
- gan.ncc.go.jp, log in as "gopher" (Japan).
- panda.uiowa.edu, log in as "panda."
- gopher.ora.com, a commercial site, log in as "gopher," specify VT100 terminal.

Not all Gopher servers may be accessed via Telnet. Some may be reached only through another Gopher client or other network front end. If you have to Telnet to access Gopher, you will not be able to take advantage of Gopher's Bookmarks feature nor the Save (file) feature. But one great feature about Gopher that sets it apart from Telnet is that Gopher presents the same face and responds to the same commands wherever the Gopher server is. On the other hand, with Telnet, each site has its own "face" and responds to its own commands.

Some Other Gopher Clients

The discussion in this chapter so far has described Gopher as it is seen and used from a local or remote host computer. If you have direct network access from your workstation, then you may be able to use one of the other Gopher clients such as:

- TurboGopher for Macintosh.
- PC Gopher for DOS.
- WS Gopher or BC Gopher for Windows.

Each of these clients is mouse-sensitive, permitting you to make Gopher menu selections by pointing and double-clicking. In each case, these clients strip away the Gopher menu item numbers, so you lose the option of making Gopher choices by entering menu item numbers. What you see instead are bracketed letters (PC Gopher) or graphics denoting whether an item is a folder (directory), a file, a search, or a handoff to another client (Telnet or Lynx). And in each case, bookmark information is stored on the local computer.

This last characteristic, storing bookmarks on your personal workstation, means that, if you are using a machine that other students use, your bookmarks are likely to be mixed with other people's bookmarks. There are ways to deal with this. Under "Configuration," PC Gopher allows you to specify the location of your bookmark file. You could specify a floppy disk (which will mean slow access) or some private directory on your machine's hard drive. With the other clients, there are solutions commonly referred to as "workarounds."

What is involved here is that you identify the file in which the bookmark information is stored. To begin your workaround, make a copy of the file ("duplicate" on the Mac), and give it some other name, such as "bookmark.bak." During your Gopher sessions, you can store all your bookmarks as you wish. At the end of your Gopher session, rename your bookmark file to something like "mybkmark.lst" and save it to your floppy disk

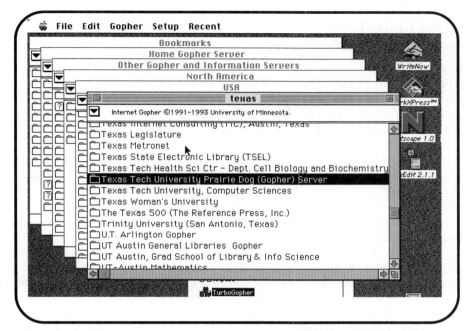

Fig. 5-8: Graphical interface Gophers, such as TurboGopher, shown here, may open several windows at once, giving you a stair-step track of the menu choices you have made.

for safekeeping. Before you end your session, you must remember to rename the "bookmark.bak" file to its original name so that people using the computer after you will have bookmarks. In BC Gopher, bookmarks are stored in a file called "bcgbkmrk.ini" stored in the \windows directory. For WS Gopher, the bookmarks are stored in the "wsgopher.ini" file in the directory where WS Gopher program files reside. You must be especially careful with your handling of this file, because it governs a lot more than just bookmarks for WS Gopher. For TurboGopher, you have the option under the "File" menu to save a bookmark file wherever you choose. Then under the "Gopher" menu you may import a bookmark file.

Each of these clients opens a new window on your screen when you select a Gopher menu item. It is common to have several windows cascading across your screen as you choose one item after another. Beware, however, that you can tax your system resources with too many windows. Each window you have open requires a piece of memory. At some point—maybe five windows, maybe a dozen—you will find that the client does not want to open any more windows.

Conclusion

Regardless of the client you use, Gopher software organizes network information into hierarchical menus. Browsing software allows you to read documents on-screen, moving forward and backward through the document and through Gopher menus. When you find a document of particular use to you, your client may permit you to print the document, save it to disk, or send it to yourself as e-mail.

Each client allows you to get information (location, name, and type of document) about documents toward which your software is pointing. Each client allows you to store this information in bookmarks so that you can easily retrieve the document again. Some Gopher clients will retrieve and display (or play) graphics and sound files, but Gopher primarily caters best to text files.

Veronica and Jughead programs allow you to search Gopherspace for key words. Several Gopher sites offer subject-oriented menu trees to a vast expanse of information stored worldwide. Whichever Gopher client you use, the client software puts the same "face" on Gopher sites wherever they are. In the final analysis, Gopher is a powerful, rich, and useful tool for navigating the Internet.

Chapter **6**

Telnet & FTP: Internet Core

At 4:31 a.m. Monday, January 17, 1994, ground in California's San Fernando Valley shook with a violence that produced the most costly natural disaster in U.S. history. A magnitude 6.8 earthquake jolted densely populated suburbs northwest of Los Angeles. Apartment buildings collapsed. Water mains and gas lines broke. Fires erupted throughout the valley, and sections of freeway buckled. Electrical power and telephone communications were interrupted. In all, 57 people died and 20,000 lost their homes in the Northridge earthquake.

The Northridge quake of 1994 was a news story of major significance. But, in the predawn hours that Monday, there was no way of knowing how serious the quake was. News people at the scene had difficulty sizing up the damage. Normal lines of communication performed erratically. Public safety officials who weren't at the strike points of the quake were hard to find for quotes and information at 5 a.m. It was a holiday (Martin Luther King Day) for many, the climax of a three-day weekend. For the thousands of reporters nationwide who were not in Southern California and the millions of Americans in their audiences, it was even more difficult to get information. The broadcast networks and wire services were painfully slow in sending out news.

There was no way of knowing how serious the quake was as the nation awakened that day—unless you had access to Telnet. "Tel-net" allows us to log onto (become a part of) computer networks at remote distances just as "tele-vision" allows us to "see" things happening a long way away.

In this chapter, you will learn how to:

- log onto remote computer systems.
- read files on a remote computer system.
- navigate menus during a Telnet session.
- capture remote text files on your personal computer.
- use Hytelnet to find computer sites of interest.

- move comfortably through FTP server directories.
- fetch ASCII and binary files using FTP.

This chapter assumes that the reader understands the concept of usernames and passwords used during log on to control access to computer systems. Additionally, this chapter expects the reader has an Internet connection and that the reader has some understanding of Internet addresses (e-mail, Chapter 3).

Telnet and FTP are basic, or core, Internet applications. They were among the first tools available to facilitate the swapping of files and information among computers, the primary function of the Internet. All computers running TCP/IP can perform Telnet and FTP. That means, no matter how you access the Internet, you can use Telnet and FTP. If you use a third-party Internet provider to access the World Wide Web, you also have access to Telnet and FTP. If you have to log onto a central computer for Internet access, you also can use Telnet and FTP.

The fundamental character of Telnet and FTP has two implications. First, as you search through the Net with your Web browser, you will be pointed occasionally to Telnet or FTP sites. To use the information, you will have to know how Telnet and FTP work. Second, as you become more sophisticated in using the Internet, you will be able to use these tools to perform tasks that are not efficiently performed via the World Wide Web or e-mail.

Basics of Telnet

The good news and beauty of Telnet is that it is the simplest of all Internet tools. When you are logged onto a system that provides Internet access, you need only to type the word "telnet" (or some local equivalent) followed by the Internet address (numerical or verbal) of the site you want to log onto. For example, by typing

telnet fedworld.gov

you can connect to the National Technical Information Service bulletin board system that provides a gateway to online services of many federal agencies. The process is much like connecting to your local BBS. Telnet is especially suited to delivering text information.

Telnet has three drawbacks: 1) You have to know ahead of time the address and log-on procedure for the site you are visiting; 2) Most sites allow you only to browse text files; they rarely will allow you to mail or download files; and 3) There are only limited indices of Telnet sites on the network, and usual search routines don't regularly turn up Telnet sites. Additionally, there is a side effect to Telnet that can be disquieting to journalists using Macintosh or Windows operating systems—the distant computer you log onto cannot see your mouse. This means that you must type all your commands to the distant machine from the keyboard.

```
        State of California - Governor's Office of Emergency Services
                ENERGENCY DIGITAL INFORMATION SERVICE (EDIS)
                           Latest Messages

    Number  Headline                       Select   Date/Time      Source

    0380    NEWS RELEASE.................   c2bp-   Jan 13 16:29    bfd
    0381    TEST MESSAGE.................   d0-p-   Jan 14 05:47    fema
    0382    TEST MESSAGE.................   d6cp-   Jan 14 09:24    sdsd
    0383    TEST MESSAGE.................   d6cp-   Jan 14 09:31    sdsd
    0384    TEST MESSAGE.................   d6cp-   Jan 14 09:43    sdsd
    0385    EDIS SYSTEM TEST.............   d0-o-   Jan 14 10:00    OES
    0386    TEST MESSAGE.................   d2bp-   Jan 14 13:59    sfoes
    0387    EDIS SYSTEM TEST.............   d0-o-   Jan 15 10:00    OES
    0388    EDIS SYSTEM TEST.............   d0-o-   Jan 15 16:16    OES
    0389    TEST MESSAGE.................   d0-p-   Jan 15 16:19    edis
    0390    EARTHQUAKE INFORMATION.......   c0-q-   Jan 15 19:13    NWS
    0391    TEST MESSAGE.................   d2bp-   Jan 15 21:46    sonsar
    0392    EDIS SYSTEM TEST.............   d0-o-   Jan 16 10:00    OES
    0393    URGENT NEWS RELEASE..........   b0-p-   Jan 17 05:25    edis

    Enter Message Number (blank to exit): 0393
```

Fig. 6-1: The Emergency Digital Information Service (EDIS) is a Telnet offering of California's Office of Emergency Services. On the morning of the Northridge earthquake, the first OES release on the quake appeared as item 0393 (bottom of menu) at 5:25 a.m.

On the day of the Northridge temblor, networked journalists who issued the Telnet command

telnet oes1.oes.ca.gov:5501

about 5:30 a.m. were greeted by the menu in Figure 6-1.

The Emergency Digital Information Service (EDIS) operated by the California governor's Office of Emergency Services (OES) is a simple Telnet site. It offers a menu of fourteen "Latest Messages" from the EDIS. Each message is numbered, and one line of information about the message gives a headline, select code, the date and time the message was posted to the system, and the source. A line across the bottom of the screen instructs the visitor to "Enter Message Number (blank) to exit:" At 5:30 a.m. January 17, half the "Latest Messages" were three days old, and more than half the messages indicated system tests rather than newsworthy information.

The screen image in Figure 6-1 shows we have entered "0393," the number of the latest message on the screen. It is headlined "Urgent News Release" and is timed at 5:25 a.m. January 17, some 54 minutes after the quake hit. After typing in the number of the desired message, the journalist online presses the Enter key. The message displayed appears in Figure 6-2.

The first message posted to the EDIS site on January 17 gave quake statistics in tentative terms and ended with a plea and a promise from the

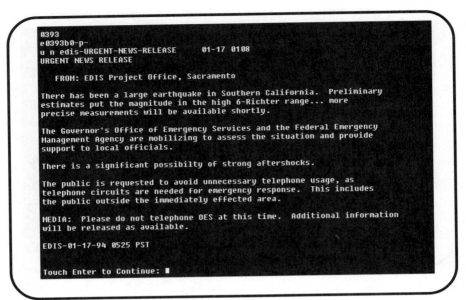

```
0393
e0393b0-p-
u n edis-URGENT-NEWS-RELEASE      01-17 0108
URGENT NEWS RELEASE

   FROM: EDIS Project Office, Sacramento

There has been a large earthquake in Southern California.  Preliminary
estimates put the magnitude in the high 6-Richter range... more
precise measurements will be available shortly.

The Governor's Office of Emergency Services and the Federal Emergency
Management Agency are mobilizing to assess the situation and provide
support to local officials.

There is a significant possibilty of strong aftershocks.

The public is requested to avoid unnecessary telephone usage, as
telephone circuits are needed for emergency response.  This includes
the public outside the immediately effected area.

MEDIA:  Please do not telephone OES at this time.  Additional information
will be released as available.

EDIS-01-17-94 0525 PST


Touch Enter to Continue: ▮
```

Fig. 6-2: First "official" word of the Northridge earthquake appeared on the OES/EDIS Telnet site in Sacramento 54 minutes after the quake. The first message was tentative and ended with a plea for media representatives NOT to telephone the OES.

OES: "MEDIA: Please do not telephone OES at this time. Additional information will be released as available." The plea to media folks not to telephone OES was understandable. OES kept the promise in such a way that made telephoning them unnecessary. Throughout the day, this on-line Telnet information was constantly updated. Morning postings included Caltrans (the state's highway maintenance agency) listings of highway closures and damages.

Also enumerated were utilities interruptions, aftershock times and magnitudes, Red Cross relief efforts, disaster declarations, press briefings, media advisories, FEMA (Federal Emergency Management Agency) involvement, structural damages, deaths, evacuations, and shelter locations. There were reports of oil spills, an hydrochloric acid spill in Saugus, a derailed train spilling 5,000 gallons of sulfuric acid in Northridge, and school closures. Postings to the list included law enforcement tactical alert notices, accounts of the U.S. Air Force flying U-2 surveillance missions, the California Conservation Corps assembling resources lists, neighboring counties sending in public safety officials, National Guard deployments, and more.

During the first days following the Northridge quake, the Office of Emergency Services EDIS Telnet site was a one-stop shop for all the hard statistics of a major breaking news story, and it provided many insights and leads for sidebars and color pieces. During the first two days after the quake, new intelligence was posted every few minutes. For weeks following the quake, OES continued to provide new information. As the relief efforts shifted to relocating the homeless and providing federal disaster relief assistance to victims, pertinent information continued to be posted several times a day.

This Telnet operation serves as an example of how online information services can aid journalists in the news business as well as the agency sources on whom news people rely. The OES/EDIS Telnet operation provided most of the benefits of a news conference, only better. News people had no need to physically arrive at a site. Those "arriving" online late could still pick up the "fact sheets" and news releases. Pertinent quotes did not have to be re-keyboarded, but could be moved directly into the journalist's copy. Using online technology, journalists in places as remote from Los Angeles as Sioux City, Iowa, or Boston, Massachusetts, or Temple, Texas, or Paderborn, Germany, could "attend" the conference and get all the pertinent data in the freshest form.

The system worked well for OES, too. Uninterrupted by calls and visits from media folks or by the need to orchestrate formal conferences, state information officers could gather necessary data from all their people at the scene, package the information once, and post the material to the Telnet bulletin board. The only thing missing from this virtual "conference" was that the press could ask no questions. No interview questions were raised at the OES/EDIS Telnet bulletin board. The online journalist has other tools for interviewing sources when personal visits are impossible and telephone communications are not reliable.

Telnet Lets You "Drive" Distant Computers

The basic function of Telnet is to allow you to log onto another computer on the Internet to view the information and use software available there. The computer may be far from your office or in a lab next door. For example, some Internet access providers do not support Internet applications such as Internet Relay Chat (IRC), which is like talking via computers and will be described in Chapter 8. Through Telnet, you can log onto a computer that does support IRC and join the conversations taking place in IRC channels.

On another level, Telnet allows you to search the library holdings at colleges throughout the world. The CARL public access library system described in Chapter 2 is based on the Telnet protocol. Furthermore, many government Bulletin Board Systems (BBSes) and campus-wide information systems (CWIS) are accessible via Telnet. For scientists, Telnet allows researchers in one location to use sophisticated software stored on computers elsewhere.

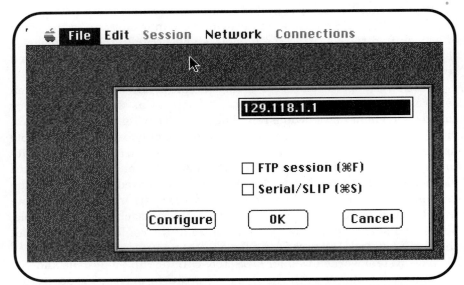

Fig. 6-3: In the NCSA/BYU Telnet program for the Macintosh, which also has FTP capabilities, the user types the address of the computer to which he wishes to connect in the "Connect" window.

Accessing distant computers is a useful feature of Telnet. Journalists on the road can take advantage of local network connections offered by providers such as America OnLine or CompuServe. Then, by using Telnet, the journalist can log onto host computers "at home" and manage e-mail there. Wherever you are in the world, if you have Telnet access to the Internet, you can, in turn, access machines anywhere else in the world with which you have an account.

Using Telnet Clients

On one level, Telnet is the easiest Internet tool to use. On another level, it is difficult. Telnet does only one thing—it establishes a connection from one computer to another. In essence it is a way for your computer to "call" another computer and open a line through which you can communicate.

In many implementations, Telnet is not a point-and-click operation in which you use your mouse. Instead, you type a command telling your computer you wish to call another computer. You use this command-line entry to launch the Telnet program and to enter the Internet Protocol (IP) number of the computer with which you wish to establish communications. On many computers, to launch the Telnet client, the word Telnet is typed followed by the appropriate IP number (or character address).

On clients running through graphical operating systems, the Telnet client works much like other software designed for the specific environment. For example, on NCSA/BYU Telnet (Figure 6-3), a popular Telnet client running on Macintosh computers, a click on the program icon launches the Telnet client. Then, under the File command on the menu bar, select "Open Connection." Next, enter the IP number or computer name (IP numbers and computer names were explained in Chapter 4) in the appropriate box. A similar process occurs in Windows Telnet clients.

In addition to NCSA/BYU Telnet, there are several other Telnet clients that can run on personal computers. For the DOS platform, many universities make available a package from Clarkson University named Clarkson University TCP, or CUTCP for short. Like NCSA/BYU Telnet, CUTCP contains both Telnet and FTP clients. If you use CUTCP, what is seen on the screen is very much as shown in Figures 6-1 and 6-2 except that the bottom line of your screen carries certain messages. Typically, the left part of that line would display the first part of the address of any machine to which you are connected.

QVT Net is a multi-client package for the Windows environment that is popular on many campuses. It runs Telnet, FTP, and e-mail, in addition to serving as a Usenet News reader. When it is launched in Windows, the program places a small button bar on the screen. A single click launches a terminal (Telnet) session, FTP, or Usenet news reading session.

Regardless of the client you use, once you have launched the Telnet application, you will need to enter the computer to which you want to connect. Remember, as with the World Wide Web, the people responsible for computers on the Internet can associate a name with the IP number. In those cases, instead of entering the IP number itself, you can use the name of the computer. For example, let's say you want to Telnet to the library catalog at the University of California. You don't need to know the IP number of the computer on which the catalog resides. If you know the computer is named Melvyl.berkeley.edu, all you need to do in Telnet is type Melvyl.berkeley.edu. Or, if you are using a graphical Telnet client, type Melvyl.berkeley.edu in the Open Connection box.

Closing Telnet Connections

Although opening a connection via Telnet is easy, closing a connection can be a little more challenging. If using NCSA/BYU Telnet, select Close Connection, under the File button on the menu bar. If you are not using NCSA/BYU Telnet or another client with a graphical interface, the process can get a little tricky. When you first connect to a site, you don't know what type of computer is at the other end or what kind of software it is running, so you cannot be sure exactly what command will close the connection.

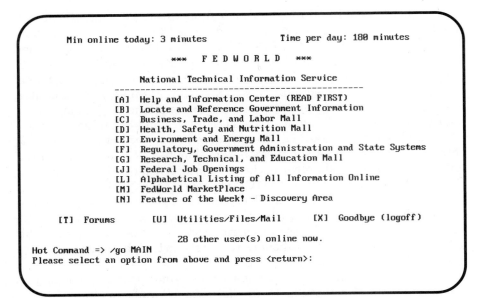

```
       Min online today: 3 minutes              Time per day: 180 minutes

                        ***   F E D W O R L D   ***

                    National Technical Information Service
       ----------------------------------------------------------------
       [A]  Help and Information Center (READ FIRST)
       [B]  Locate and Reference Government Information
       [C]  Business, Trade, and Labor Mall
       [D]  Health, Safety and Nutrition Mall
       [E]  Environment and Energy Mall
       [F]  Regulatory, Government Administration and State Systems
       [G]  Research, Technical, and Education Mall
       [J]  Federal Job Openings
       [L]  Alphabetical Listing of All Information Online
       [M]  FedWorld MarketPlace
       [N]  Feature of the Week! - Discovery Area


   [T]  Forums        [U] Utilities/Files/Mail        [X]  Goodbye (logoff)

                       28 other user(s) online now.
Hot Command => /go MAIN
Please select an option from above and press <return>:
```

Fig. 6-4: Top menu of the FedWorld BBS system offers several kinds of information through its menu choices. The FedWorld GateWay to other agencies will be accessed three menu levels down after selecting choice [F].

After you have opened a connection, for the most part, you must use the commands of the computer you called.

Sometimes information detailing how to disconnect is provided when you first connect. For example, a site might display, "Escape character is '^]'." What that means is that by typing Ctrl-] (holding the Control key down and pressing the right brace key), you can escape the program and disconnect.

The combination (Ctrl-]) is common on the Internet. Other common commands for leaving programs include:

- Typing "Q" or "QUIT."
- Typing "E," "X," "EXIT," or "Ctrl-X."
- Typing "Ctrl-Z."
- Typing "Bye," "Goodbye," or "G."

A Sample Telnet Session

Opening and closing the connection marks the beginning and end of a Telnet session. What happens in between is important. Accessing information stored on the computer you called is the hard part. First, while thousands of computers are accessible via Telnet, many are not open to the public. You have to know specific log on procedures. If you are logging onto a computer on your own campus or news operation, presumably you know the log on procedures. Except for libraries, most Telnet sites require that you have a user name and a password (i.e., an account on that machine or knowledge of a public access account). For example, if you Telnet to Arizona State University by typing the command

telnet asu.edu <CR>

you will be informed that the system is for authorized use only. If you do not have an appropriate user name and password, you will not be able to log on.

Other public Telnet sites may provide you with connect screens that offer advice for logging on to access special services. FedWorld is a BBS-type system available through Telnet. To access FedWorld by Telnet, type

telnet fedworld.gov

When you connect, you are prompted for your name. The first time you log on, enter "new," and FedWorld will ask you to fill out a form giving your organizational affiliation (your school or company), phone number, and address. You then choose a password, and you are encouraged to write it down so that future log-ons will proceed more quickly. FedWorld offerings include gateways to dozens of BBS systems run by various federal government agencies.

Fig. 6-5: The Government Administration Mall menu, three levels down into the FedWorld system, offers as Choice [1] the "GateWay" to dozens of U.S. federal government agencies.

```
Now searching for "admin"...

###:Name                          :Comment
---------------------------------------------------------------------
   5:IS-SIS (IRS)                 :IS Support Info System
   9:ADA-BBS (DOJ)                :Amer. With Disabilities Act Info
  13:EBB (DOC)                    :Economic data and information
  15:GSA/IRM BBS (GSA)            :Information Resources Management Issues
  16:EPUB (DOE)                   :Energy information and data
  17:FDA's BBS (FDA)              :FDA info and policies
  18:CDRH Elect Docket (FDA)      :Center for Devices Radiological Health
  20:FEBBS (FHWA)                 :FHWA information and data
  22:FEDERAL BBS (GPO)            :GPO and Govt Data (Fee Based)
  23:OSS-BBS (GSA)                :GSA On-line Schedules System
  25:JAG-NET (USN)                :Navy Judge Advocate General
  29:RIBBS (USPS)                 :US Postal Service Rapid Information
  33:1040 BBS (IRS)               :Electronic Tax Filing Information
  35:OIS (Bureau of Prisons)      :US Bureau of Prison employees
  39:SALEMDUG-BBS (FEMA)          :State and local FEMA user groups
  40:SBA On Line (SBA)            :SBA Information & Data (Full Service)
  41:GAO WATCHDOG (GAO)           :Identify Waste Fraud and Abuse
  42:SBAI-BBS (SBA)               :Small Bus. Admin internal BBS
  44:OPM Mainstreet (OPM)         :OPM - Job Info, Personnel Guidance
<Q> quit to prompt, <N> scroll, RETURN to continue
```

```
Now searching for "admin"...

###:Name                          :Comment
----------------------------------------------------------------
  5:IS-SIS (IRS)                  :IS Support Info System
  9:ADA-BBS (DOJ)                 :Amer. With Disabilities Act Info
 13:EBB (DOC)                     :Economic data and information
 15:GSA/IRM BBS (GSA)             :Information Resources Management Issues
 16:EPUB (DOE)                    :Energy information and data
 17:FDA's BBS (FDA)               :FDA info and policies
 18:CDRH Elect Docket (FDA)       :Center for Devices Radiological Health
 20:FEBBS (FHWA)                  :FHWA information and data
 22:FEDERAL BBS (GPO)             :GPO and Govt Data (Fee Based)
 23:OSS-BBS (GSA)                 :GSA On-line Schedules System
 25:JAG-NET (USN)                 :Navy Judge Advocate General
 29:RIBBS (USPS)                  :US Postal Service Rapid Information
 33:1040 BBS (IRS)                :Electronic Tax Filing Information
 35:OIS (Bureau of Prisons)       :US Bureau of Prison employees
 39:SALEMDUG-BBS (FEMA)           :State and local FEMA user groups
 40:SBA On Line (SBA)             :SBA Information & Data (Full Service)
 41:GAO WATCHDOG (GAO)            :Identify Waste Fraud and Abuse
 42:SBAI-BBS (SBA)                :Small Bus. Admin internal BBS
 44:OPM Mainstreet (OPM)          :OPM - Job Info, Personnel Guidance
<Q> quit to prompt, <N> scroll, RETURN to continue
```

Fig. 6-6: The FedWorld GateWay to U.S. federal government agencies offers access to dozens of agencies through numbered menu choices.

FedWorld and some other Telnet sites require you to specify a terminal type during the log on process. This is done so the host computer, the computer to which you have connected, knows how to read your keyboard and in turn how to speak back to your computer. Most communications software and Telnet client programs allow your computer to "emulate" one of several different "dumb" terminals, often connected to larger computers. Commonly accepted terminals on the Internet are the DEC VT100 or VT102. If the site to which you are connecting asks for VT100 or some other emulation, be sure you configure your software to that specification. A few sites require an IBM 3270 terminal emulation. If you do not know what is required or accepted, try VT100 or TTY first.

At the FedWorld site, the registration process on your first visit establishes for you a user profile that FedWorld "remembers" for all subsequent visits. When you get past the registration and introductory screens, you are taken to a top menu in which you must choose whether you want to enter the FedWorld system, an Internal Revenue Service system, or the Nuclear Regulatory Commission Online system. Choosing FedWorld brings up a new menu that offers several new choices (see Figure 6-4). Selecting item "[F] Regulatory, Government Administration and State Systems" takes us to a menu from which we can choose "[B] Government Administration Mall" (Figure 6-5).

Through this system of menu hierarchies we finally work our way down to the FedWorld Government Administration GateWay Systems (choice [1]) that provides access to dozens of U.S. government bulletin board systems (Figure 6-6). At the height of the system in 1994, more than 120 government agencies were represented. With the increasing popularity of the World Wide Web, many agencies have now elected to serve up their information in the Hypertext Transfer Protocol (HTTP) environment of the Web rather than the more limited Telnet BBS protocol.

Staying Found among Menu Hierarchies

At the FedWorld site, we had to navigate "down" through several levels of menus, each with several choices, in order to reach the FedWorld gateway to other government information servers. This hierarchical menu structure, found frequently at Telnet sites, is the same type of arrangement found at Gopher servers (Chapter 5).

Unlike Gopher and Web browsers, Telnet clients do not have handy bookmark utilities that allow you to mark a site that has information which you may want to use again, so you can automatically return to that place. You have to keep track of the access path to the information you wanted.

This makes working through Telnet sites an adventure somewhat like the one described in the Greek myth of Theseus and the Minotaur. In that tale Theseus, the hero, was able to slay the monstrous Minotaur and escape a maze by marking his movements with a ball of string. Entering a Telnet session is much like entering a maze in search of the monster called information. It is easy to move randomly about the computer site's menus, browsing information that is neither useful for your news story nor particularly interesting.

However, when you do find something that you expect may be useful now or in the future, you will want to be able to return to that information. If you want to return, unravel a ball of twine along the way by making path notes. Record the Telnet address. Then, as you move down through menus, keep notes of which choices you selected.

For example, assume you "happened" onto the FedWorld GateWay to government agencies and decided it would be a worthwhile resource to return to for future story research. If you were casually browsing—without unraveling your ball of string—you might have a hard time finding that resource again.

Here's an example of the path you might follow:

1. Connect to the system via Telnet to fedworld.gov.
2. At the system menu (after logging on), select Item 1, "FedWorld."
3. From the "FedWorld" top menu (Figure 6-4), choose Item "[F],

Regulatory, Government Administration and State Systems."

4. At the "Regulatory, Government Administration and State Systems" menu, select "Government Administration Mall" (choice [B]).

5. From the "Government Administration Mall" menu (Figure 6-5), select "[1] GOVADMIN GateWay Systems," which then takes you to the gateway menu (Figure 6-6).

A relatively standard shorthand for tracking network navigation would summarize the actions this way:

> "Path = 1/F Reg Gov Adm/ B Gov Adm Mall / 1 GateWay."

The shorthand means "start at the Top Menu (1), choose Item F, then Item B, then Item 1." The first word or two of each menu choice is kept with that choice's number as a security check. The path shorthand would be attached to the site address (fedworld.gov) in order to provide a full record of where you had been.

Capturing a Telnet Session with Log Utilities

When you bring files to your computer screen during a Telnet session, you are doing just so much reading unless you take advantage of a utility built in to nearly every communications program on the market—session logging. Session logging is like computerized photocopying. It copies all the text that passes your screen and writes it to a disk file that you name. You then have the full text on your computer so that you use it without having to re-enter it.

If you are using a PC with ProComm communications software, start a log file by typing "Alt-F1." If you are networked using DEC Pathworks, the command is "Ctrl-F1." In either case, you are prompted to name the file you wish the session log to be stored in. If you are using Clarkson University's Telnet package (CUTCP described earlier), launch what the software terms a "capture session" by typing "Alt-C." The resulting log file is saved under the name of "Capfile." In the NCSA/BYU Telnet package, the session capture option is under the Session menu. Whatever your software, check your manual (or ask your systems administrator) for the procedure to start a log file or to log a session.

Most programs also allow you to suspend the log temporarily during a session. In ProComm, once a log file is opened, it may be toggled on and off with the command Alt-F2. In Pathworks, the Ctrl-F1 combination is a toggle. In the Clarkson University package, Alt-C acts as a toggle to turn the capture procedure on and off.

In Macintosh or Windows-based computers, you have a second option for saving information you find in a Telnet session. You can highlight text and copy it to the clipboard then paste the text into a document in your word processor. In Windows or in Macintosh System 7 (or later), you can actually have the word processor running in the background and switch between the word processor and your Telnet client.

Getting Help

As you explore your possibilities with Telnet, at times you may become confused about what to do. You can usually get online help in one of three ways:

- Type "?"
- Type "H" or "HELP."
- Enter the number, letter, or name of a menu choice.

Help screens generally summarize available commands. If you are accessing the network by telephone, be alert to the commands of your software program. For example, Ctrl-] is a common Telnet escape command we have noted. However, if you are using ProComm communications software, that key combination merely toggles on and off a status bar across the bottom of the screen; the command is not passed on to the Telnet host.

Finding Directions with Hytelnet

While FTP, Gopher, and the World Wide Web have extensive search tools to help you locate information you may want, the tools for Telnet are less developed. From time to time, a World Wide Web search will lead to a Telnet server. Sometimes you will read about a good Telnet site. The tool developed (by Peter Scott at the University of Saskatchewan) for helping you use Telnet to find information is called Hytelnet.

Hytelnet is a client program that puts a menu interface on publicly accessible Telnet sites and gives you online help logging onto remote sites. Library systems, CWISes, and community free-nets (public Internet systems maintained in a specific location) are among the more interesting sites indexed by Hytelnet.

On the Hytelnet menu, menus and submenus are organized by subject. Terms in bracket < and > are selector items, and the cursor highlights them one at a time. When you choose a highlighted item by pressing the Enter key, you either get a new menu, a text document, or a Telnet connect dialogue box telling you about the site you have chosen. The dialogue box usually provides the Telnet address, log-in instructions, and a brief description of what you will find at the remote computer.

The simple command structure for Hytelnet can be confusing at first. It can take a little time to get used to the difference between using the Left Arrow which takes you to the previous document and the "b" or "-" commands which take you back one screen in the same document. To quit Hytelnet, enter "q."

```
Password:
<
<                               Welcome to
<                        THE OAK SOFTWARE REPOSITORY
<                A service of Oakland University, Rochester Michigan
<
< If you have trouble using OAK with your ftp client, please try using
< a dash (-) as the first character of your password -- this will turn
< off the continuation messages that may be confusing your ftp client.
< OAK is a Unix machine, and filenames are case sensitive.
<
< Access is allowed at any time.  If you have any unusual problems,
< please report them via electronic mail to archives@Oakland.Edu
<
< You are user #229 out of 400 maximum users on Thu Jul 13 08:53:22 1995.
<
< Oak is also on the World Wide Web, URL: http://www.acs.oakland.edu/oak.html
<
< File searching is now available!  Example command:  site exec index 4dos
<
<Please read the file README
<   it was last modified on Fri Mar 24 18:59:19 1995 - 111 days ago
<Guest login ok, access restrictions apply.
OAK.OAKLAND.EDU>
```

Fig. 6-7: Oakland University's Oak Software Depository's FTP greeting message lets you know of a shorter log on process peculiar to the Oak site.

While Hytelnet facilitates the use of Telnet sites, it does not have key-word searching capability. You cannot enter a key word and locate Telnet sites which have that information. Moreover, Hytelnet is not widely distributed. If your host does not have a Hytelnet client, you can access by telnetting to

- hytelnet.cwis.uci.edu (login: "hytelnet").
- pubinfopath.ucsd.edu (login: infopath, use selection 9).
- or laguna.epcc.edu (username: library).

Additionally, some Gopher sites provide links to public Hytelnet clients. On the World Wide Web, at least one search site, the Tradewave Galaxy, gives as a search option the ability to probe the Hytelnet data base. The Galaxy is located at http://galaxy.einet.net/.

A Few Other Telnet Sites

A few other Telnet sites that might be of interest to journalists, depending upon beat assignments, follow. They might also be accessed just for practice sessions. Try these sites:

- **neis.cr.usgs.gov**, Username: "QED," access to USGS earthquake information.
- **fdabbs.fda.gov**, log on as "bbs," password "bbs," access to U.S. FDA files.

```
<Opening ASCII mode data connection for /bin/ls.
total 1386
-rw-r--r--   1 w8sdz     OAK           0 Nov 13  1994 .notar
drwxr-x---   2 root      operator   8192 Dec 31  1994 .quotas
drwx------   2 root      system     8192 Dec 30  1994 .tags
-rw-r--r--   1 jeff      OAK     1172471 Jul 13 03:20 Index-byname
-r--r--r--   1 w8sdz     OAK        1237 Mar 24 18:59 README
drwxr-xr-x   4 w8sdz     OAK        8192 Jun 21 19:42 SimTel
d--x--x--x   3 root      system     8192 Jan 19 20:26 bin
d--x--x--x   2 root      system     8192 Jun 12 02:23 core
drwxr-x---   3 cpm       OAK        8192 Jun  9 20:18 cpm-incoming
d--x--x--x   5 root      system     8192 Dec 30  1994 etc
drwxrwx---   2 incoming  OAK        8192 Jun 21 11:36 incoming
drwxrwx---   2 nt        OAK        8192 Jul 13 08:47 nt-incoming
drwxr-xr-x   3 w8sdz     OAK        8192 Apr 13 19:46 pub
drwxr-xr-x  15 w8sdz     OAK        8192 May 30 23:03 pub2
drwxr-xr-x   8 w8sdz     OAK        8192 Jul 11 23:42 pub3
drwxr-xr-x   4 w8sdz     OAK        8192 Jun 21 19:42 simtel
drwxr-xr-x   2 jeff      OAK        8192 Apr 17  1994 siteinfo
drwx------  44 w8sdz     OAK        8192 Jul  2 19:27 w8sdz
<Transfer complete.
1133 bytes transferred at 18727 bps.
Run time = 0. ms, Elapsed time = 484. ms.
OAK.OAKLAND.EDU>
```

Fig. 6-8: The FTP "dir" command produces a detailed directory. At the far left of each line are descriptors that tell you whether the object is a file or a director. At the far right of each line is the object's name.

- **info.umd.edu**, no log on required, access to the University of Maryland campus system, using a Lynx client.
- **debra.dgbt.doc.ca:3000**, no log on required, access to AIDS and epilepsy information files.

If you are accessing the Internet through a World Wide Web browser, you can access all the Telnet sites described here, if your browser is properly configured and has the necessary supporting software. The manner of opening a Telnet site from your browser is first to select the "Open Location dialog from the File menu, then type "telnet://" followed by the Telnet address. Thus, to open the FedWorld Telnet site, type in the address "telnet://fedworld.gov."

Moving Files with FTP (File Transfer Protocol)

Although reading and logging information found via Telnet serves many purposes, often you will find information on the Internet that you will want to grab and transfer to your own computer. It may be a large file located somewhere else or it may be a great piece of software available on the Net. FTP is also an excellent method for getting Frequently Asked Question (FAQ) files that abound on the Internet and address many topics.

Like Telnet, FTP is one of the basic Internet applications. It is the method used to transfer files among computers on the Internet. File Transfer Protocol is a name given by computer programmers to a series of conventions that enable one type of computer operating under its own set of rules to send/receive files to/from another type of computer operating under another set of rules. Thus a UNIX machine connected over a network passing through a machine running VMS can exchange files with an IBM mainframe operating under still another set of rules then pass the file on to your Macintosh or PC.

From the user point of view, there are some similarities between Telnet and FTP. Both are found on any computer connected to the Internet running TCP/IP. In their basic format, both are command-line driven. In both cases you can connect by naming the protocol (FTP or Telnet) then adding the Internet address of the host or server to which you wish to connect. In both cases, you frequently go through a log on procedure once you are connected.

FTP is perhaps the least friendly of all the Internet protocols. It is "strictly business" and assumes you know the rules. Fortunately, there are only a few simple rules to learn. Those rules govern: 1) connecting to and disconnecting from FTP sites, 2) getting and reading directories, 3) moving between directories, and 4) retrieving files with the proper protocol.

Making the FTP Connection

FTP connections are made exactly the same way Telnet connections are. Using an FTP client, establish your FTP connection by typing ftp and the name or IP number of the computer with which you want to connect.

For example, there is a large repository of software available at Oakland University in Rochester, MI. To begin the process of transferring files from there to your computer you would type

ftp oak.oakland.edu <CR>

As an alternative, you can launch the FTP client first then from its prompt (typically "ftp>"), type

open oak.oakland.edu

to get the same results.

In either case you are greeted by the dialog shown in Figure 6-7. At the logon prompt type "anonymous" (without the quotes). When you are asked for the password, enter your complete e-mail address. This process of logging on with the username "anonymous" and your e-mail address as your password is known as "Anonymous FTP."

In addition to being the prime method for serving up software on the Internet, Anonymous FTP is the way to obtain many text files. For example, one can get the text of Federal Communications Commission rules and proposed rules, the text of Supreme Court decisions, National Institutes of Health data files, Securities and Exchange Commission filings, and Commerce Department data. Also available by Anonymous FTP are U.S. Navy policy and strategy documents, immigration information, NASA

Fig. 6-9: The more commonly used FTP commands help you move through the remote server directory structure, get directory reports and retrieve files. Commands that turn features on, such as hash, bell, and interactive, can be turned off by issuing the same command with "no" added to the front of the word. For example, "nobell" turns off the bell which sounds at completion of file transfer.

Basic FTP Commands

abort	Terminate current operation
ascii	Set file transfer mode to ascii
bget	Retrieve a file in binary mode
bput	Send a file in binary mode
bell	Ring bell when file transfer completes
binary	Set file transfer mode to binary
bye	Close the connection and exit
case	Toggle mapping of local filenames to lower case
cd	Change current working directory on remote host
cdup	Change working directory on remote host to parent directory; synonym = cd ..
dir	Display contents of a directory in long form
dis	Close the connection
get	Retrieve a file from remote host
hash	Print # for each packet sent or received
help	Display help messages for all ftp commands
interactive	Prompt with each filename for mget, mput and mdelete commands
ls	Display contents of a directory in short form
mget	Retrieve a group of files from the remote host
open	Open a connection to a remote host
put	Transfer a file from client machine to remote host
pwd	Print remote host's current working directory
quiet	Do not display transfer statistics
remotehelp	Display list of FTP commands implemented by the server
stat	Display contents of a directory in short form
show	Show current status
verbose	Display server replies & transfer stats

```
-rw-rw-r--   1 ftp      other     294693 Mar  2 13:53 pany.bones.tar.Z
-rw-rw-r--   1 ftp      other      84420 Oct 13  1993 pcucp.tar.gz
-rw-rw-r--   1 ftp      other      62832 Oct 15  1993 references.Z
-rw-rw-r--   1 ftp      other     232364 Oct 15  1993 review.txt.Z
-rw-r--r--   1 root     other      81565 Sep 23  1993 rzsz9103.tar.Z
-rw-rw-r--   1 ftp      other      30720 Apr 19 18:46 system.zip
-rw-rw-r--   1 ftp      other      13113 Oct 13  1993 wdial101.zip
drwxrwxrwx   2 2016     2001        1024 Feb 28 12:23 wynn
Transferred 1595 bytes in 4 seconds (0.389 Kbytes/sec)
226 Transfer complete.
ftp>
ftp> hash
Hash mark printing on (1024 bytes/hash mark).
ftp> bget htmlwrit.zip
200 Type set to I.
200 PORT command successful.
##150 Opening BINARY mode data connection for htmlwrit.zip (315243 bytes).
###############################################################################
###############################################################################
###############################################################################
##############################################################Transferred 315
243 bytes in 599 seconds (0.513 Kbytes/sec)
226 Transfer complete.
200 Type set to A.
ftp>
```

Fig. 6-10: The entire process of downloading a binary file using FTP marked by hash marks (#) is shown.

documents and graphic images from space missions, and gigabytes of software for all types of different computers.

Because anyone can log on using Anonymous FTP, host sites grant limited or "restricted" access to people doing so. The FTP greeting screen at Oakland University Software Repository (Figure 6-7) concludes with the line "Guest login ok, access restrictions apply." If you have an account with the host site, enter your assigned username and chosen password. You then presumably have more liberal access than people logging in anonymously. In either case, each site is limited in the number of persons who can log in at one time. The Oakland University site greeting screen says that its limit is 400 users. Other sites may handle fewer.

Navigating FTP Server Directories

One reason that using FTP is complicated is that, once you have connected to the host computer, you often are using UNIX-like commands. The commands and results will look very cryptic to people accustomed to Macintosh and Windows interfaces.

For example, after you have logged onto the FTP server at Oakland University, you will be staring at a command line prompt (here an asterisk) with no menu. If you type the command "dir" you will see a detailed directory. Figure 6-8 (page 121) shows the result of asking for a directory immediately after logging onto the Oakland University FTP site anonymously. FTP reports back that the "PORT" command was successful, that an ASCII (text) "file" is being opened (the file is actually the directory), and that the transfer of information from the distant server to your local client is complete. Before displaying the list of files and directories, FTP reported that there were ten files and directories.

The fifth item listed in Figure 6-8 is a README file that you are encouraged to read. (To read the README file, you will have to "get" it using the procedure outlined below then open it using a word processor.) Most of the remaining objects listed are all directories. You know this because the first character in the 10-character string at the left of the lines describing those items is a "d" followed by an "r." The left-most characters on the line describing the README file are "-r."

Near the end of the directory in Figure 6-8 are three directories labeled "pub," "pub1," and "pub2." These are standard designations for publicly accessible directories. You change to the pub directory by using the "cd" (for change directory) command:

cd pub <CR>

Be very careful to observe differences in upper- and lower-case letters because many FTP sites are case sensitive. FTP will report back to you that the PORT command was successful if you typed it properly.

Below the "pub" directory are several other directories containing still other directories in a hierarchical fashion. A close relative of the "dir" command is "ls" for "list." The "ls" command displays a short directory, listing only the file names and no other information about them. The "ls" command tends to give you results more quickly than the "dir" command, but less information is reported. Consequently, you don't know if an item in the list is a directory leading to files or if it is a file. Still, if all you need to know is the exact name of a file so that you can "get" or "bget" it, then "ls" does the trick.

Getting or Bgetting a File

Usually the reason for using FTP is to retrieve a file you already know something about. FTP is not an especially friendly or efficient browsing tool. You may know, for example that the most recent set of Supreme Court rulings are at ftp.cwru.edu or that data from the National Archives are at nih.gov. If you've done an Archie search (which will be discussed later in this chapter), you have full path information. In other words, you will know which directories you have to move through to arrive at the directory in which the file you want is located. In most cases when using FTP, you know where you are going and what you want to do ahead of time.

Let's assume you want to create your own pages on the World Wide Web. By monitoring a mailing list, you learn that the program "HTML Write" has been placed on an FTP server at Brigham Young University. It has the file name htmlwrit.zip and is located in the /tmp directory. Figure 6-10 shows the dialogue with the FTP server which occurs during the process of retrieving the file.

You connect to the BYU server by typing

FTP ftp.byu.edu <CR>

and use the "cd" change directory command to move to the "/tmp" directory. From there, the "dir" directory command is used to:

1. confirm that the file was where it had been reported;
2. get the exact name of the file, noting case of letters; and
3. ascertain the approximate size of the file.

Table 6-1: File name extensions provide clues to the nature of a file's contents and storage format. This table summarizes some of the more common file name extensions encountered on the Internet.

File Ext.	Archive?	PC?	Mac?	Extraction program to use
ARC	yes	x		PKUNPAK, ARCE
ARJ	yes	x		ARJ
COM	maybe	x		If archived, is self-extracting
CPT	yes		x	Compactor
DOC	no	x	x	Usually text-only file; may be MS Word (PC) file
EXE	maybe	x		If archived, is self-extracting
HQX	yes		x	BinHex
LZH	yes	x		LHARC
MAC	no		x	is a runnable application
PIT	yes		x	PackIt
PS	no	x	x	PostScript coded file; send directly to PS printer
SEA	yes		x	Self-extracting
SIT	yes		x	Stuff-It
TAR	yes			Should be decompressed on host/server
TXT	no	x	x	ASCII (text) file readable on any computer
WK*	no	x	x	Lotus 1-2-3 files usable by spreadsheet programs
WP	no	x		Word Perfect file
Z	yes			Should be decompressed on host/server
ZIP	yes	x		PKUNZIP, UNZIP

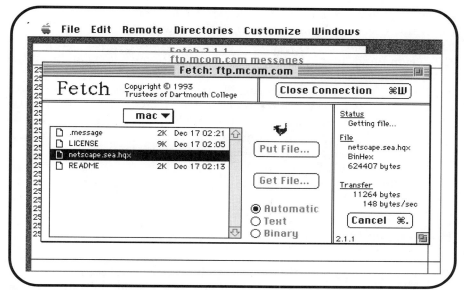

Fig. 6-11: FTP clients such as Fetch (here) and WS-FTP put a point-and-drag interface on the FTP process. Web browsers such as Microsoft Internet Explorer and Netscape also perform FTP functions.

The "ls" list command would have answered the first two questions but would provide no insight on the file size. Because the file was more than just a few bytes, it would have been prudent to have entered the FTP "hash" command, which tells the FTP server to report the progress of the file transfer. It does so by sending "#" marks to the screen for each "packet" of file data it delivers. After entering the hash command, the actual transfer can begin.

HTML Write is a binary file to be read by a computer and not a text file (for reading by human beings). There are two common command sequences for retrieving binary files. Using the command "bget" followed by the file name (in this case htmlwrit.zip) instructs the server to "get" a file with the specific file name in binary mode. In a two-step process you would enter the commands:

binary <CR>

get htmlwrit.zip <CR>

If the file you want is a text-only (ASCII) file with no special formatting commands or any other programming code, you can use FTP in the ASCII mode, which is usually its default. In that case, you can use the "get" command rather than "bget." Sometimes several files are stored together. To transfer them as a group, you can use the command "mget."

Most types of files require binary transfer. You can usually determine the type of file it is by its file extension, the part of the file name that follows the period. Some common file extensions requiring binary are "sea" (Macintosh self-extracting archive), "ps" (PostScript), "exe" (an IBM executable file), and graphics files with extensions such as "tif," "pnt," "pcx," "gif," "cgm," and "mac." The most common file name extension for ASCII (text) files is "txt."

Interestingly, you may successfully transfer text files in binary mode, but you may not move binary files in ASCII mode. Users of popular Macintosh client programs such as NCSA/BYU Telnet must first turn on "MacBinary" (under the File menu) to transfer some files successfully. It is generally advisable to enable MacBinary at each FTP session.

When the server has finished moving the file, it reports the time required (599 seconds in the example) and the rate of transfer.

Handling and Using Files

Once you have mastered the steps in grabbing a file and transferring it to your computer, there are several other factors to consider. First, if you are transferring the file to your account on a central computer, you have to be sure that you have enough disk space to receive the file. If you don't, the transfer will be automatically terminated.

Second, if you transfer the file to a central computer, you will probably want to download it to a personal computer open and read it using a word processor if it is an ASCII file, or use it, if it is software. Many files that are transferred using FTP are compressed. Not only do compressed files take up less storage space on a hard drive, they are more quickly transferred across the Internet. However, once you receive a compressed file, you must first decompress it before you can use it.

By convention, the file extension—the part of the file name after the "."—indicates whether a file has been compressed and, if it has, by what compression method. The name of the file used in the example was htmlwrit.zip. The extension ".zip" indicated that the file had been compressed and archived using a program such as PKzip. In order to use the program, it would have to be "unzipped." PKunzip and PKzip are IBM-compatible shareware programs used to compress and decompress files and are widely available on college campuses, bulletin boards, and the Internet.

Other common compression schemes are Stuffit for the Macintosh, which produces the extension .sit, and must be decompressed with a program named Unstuffit, Compress/Uncompress (file extension .Z), and Pack/Unpack on UNIX (file extension .z). Finally, many people use a program called Binhex to convert Macintosh files into a binary format. They have to be read and reconverted using Binhex as well. All compressed and Binhex files must be moved through the Internet in a binary format.

Fortunately, most compression software and Binhex is available via FTP. Some FTP sites will tell you in their welcoming screens about other compression schemes that the host site can uncompress "on the fly" if you follow instructions. See Table 6-1 for a list of common file compression/ archive formats and the software needed to unpack the archive.

The Final Step

When you download a file via FTP, the file is moved from the remote server to the machine where the client software resides. If you are dialing in with a modem to access a host machine which has the FTP client you use, FTP brings the file to your disk space on the local host. You then will have to download the program to your computer using Kermit, Zmodem, or some other protocol your host recognizes. If, on the other hand, you are directly connected to the Internet with a network card and hard wire, or if your dial-in host provides SLIP access, then the file moves directly to your per-sonal computer—if your FTP client software is on your computer.

Making FTP Easier

If FTP sounds complicated, it can be. But it is also one of the most efficient ways to transfer large files, software, and data. FTP is also key to much of the collaborative work done by scientists on the Internet. For example, the Cooperative Human Linkage Center is a collaborative effort among researchers to map the human genome. In it, experimental data collected at the University of Iowa is automatically transferred via FTP for analy-sis at the Fox Chase Cancer Research Center in Philadelphia.

Fortunately, tools are developing to make FTP easier. As noted in Chap-ter 4, Web browsers have become all-purpose Internet tools. At times, if you are absolutely sure of the precise name and location on the network of a file stored on an FTP server, you can use your World Wide Web browser to retrieve the file. Your web browser may even provide some directory list-ings, and let you browse those directories on a remote site. The standard address for accessing an FTP site with a World Wide Web browser is

FTP://ftp.computername.domain/filedirectory/filename

In some cases, the Web browser will completely automate the FTP process for you. For example, if you wish to download an updated beta version of Netscape or Internet Explorer, you can go to the Netscape or Microsoft Web site and, through a point and click process, complete the FTP transfer (including the file decompression, which will be explained later in this chapter.)

The Telnet clients for Macintosh, DOS, and Windows described earlier in this chapter also permit you to use FTP. For Macintosh and Windows machines there are also some very nice stand-alone clients that partially overcome the command line interface limitations of FTP. In the Macintosh program, Fetch, and in such Windows programs as WS-FTP, you use a point-and-drag style of interface. In either program you simply point your mouse at the file on the remote server and drag it to a folder (directory) on your machine (Figure 6-11). They also allow you to display on your screen text files (such as README files) that reside on the distant server and they may also automate the sending and receiving of files.

FTP in Action

Although a little tricky to master, FTP can be very useful for journalists who need to access large files and graphics. For example, Aimee Kalnoskas, a science writer, was preparing a story on the work of the Cornell Theory Center (CTC), a major supercomputing center funded by the National Science Foundation and associated with Cornell University. Researchers at the CTC had created several striking visualizations of their research. Each visualization was more than a megabyte large.

Kalnoskas wanted to use the images to illustrate her story. Instead of having the researchers send more than a megabyte of information via e-mail or put the images on a disk and send them via regular mail, she had them put the images on an FTP server. She then fetched them within a matter of moments. You can FTP large files much faster than you can e-mail them and there are fewer limitations on what you can send. Often, authors who collaborate in writing books will transfer chapters via FTP.

Similarly, journalists and students who are publishing their work on World Wide Web sites will probably need to master FTP. The most efficient way to post material on a remote Web server is via FTP. Of course, Web servers are rarely "anonymous" FTP servers as well. Instead, you will need to have permission and a password to post material on a Web server. On the other hand, FTP means a journalist working for an online publication whose server is located in, let's say, Seattle, can post information via FTP from Washington D.C. as easily as a journalist sitting right next to the server itself.

Finding Files Using Archie

Archie and FTP go together. Like its comic book cousins Veronica and Jughead, which you learned about in Chapter 5, Archie is a network detective. Archie scours a constantly updated index of data bases and archives for any "hits" on key words you provide. What Archie returns to you is a list of directories and files whose names contain the word(s) you have given.

The listing of those files and directories is organized by host site. Below the name of each host site is a list of the directories and files whose names match your query. Archie indicates whether the matching object is a file or a directory then reports full path information for getting to the directory or retrieving the file by FTP.

Because it is used often by scientists and computer programmers to find software, Archie is often one of the first Internet clients system administrators put on a host. If your computer runs Archie (it will often be on the central computer on which you have your e-mail account), to launch an Archie search, type the word Archie followed by a key word describing what you want to find.

If your host does not have an Archie client and you do not have one on your machine, you have two options for accessing a public domain Archie client. You could access Archie clients by using Hytelnet or Gopher (Chapter 5) clients. At a general Gopher site or Hytelnet site, Archie access is generally found under an Internet Resources menu. The advantage of using Gopher is that you may not have to start a separate FTP session to fetch a file if you find one you would like. World Wide Web clients also permit this.

You also could use Telnet to connect to an Archie client. Some publicly accessible sites include:

- archie.ans.net (Advanced Network Services in Michigan).
- archie.unl.edu (University of Nebraska, Lincoln), log-in: archie (press Return at password).
- archie.doc.ic.ac.uk (United Kingdom).
- archie.sura.net (a consortium of Southern universities).
- quiche.cs.mcgill.ca (McGill University in Montreal, the home of Archie).

In all cases, the login word is "archie."

When you launch Archie, either from your host computer or from a remote site, you are given a brief message that tells you the default settings for searches at the site to which you are connected. You must take note of these settings; they determine whether Archie's search is case sensitive and whether Archie looks for whole words or reports a match when your search string shows up anywhere. These settings will impact heavily on the results of your search.

To use a specific setting, append it to the end of the Archie command. For example, to launch a search which ignores the case of the letters, type archie-s. This generally is the best kind of search. When you ask Archie to report the names and locations of files and directories containing a specific string of characters, you don't know ahead of time whether the name of a file is upper case or lower case; nor do you care, so long as there is useful information in the file.

Default search parameters at a remote site are often set at "sub," which means that the search is case insensitive and that anywhere Archie finds a match—whole word or partial—a match will be reported. Other Archie search settings include exact, regex, and subcase. Exact will report only exact matches (same case, whole word). Subcase looks for matches in terms of case, but does not require whole word matches. Regex sets the search to look for strings in UNIX terms. If Archie tells you that the search type is anything but "sub" you may want to change the setting. You do that by typing the command

set search sub <CR>

Starting an Archie Search

If you are at an Archie prompt (which is the case when you launch the program from a remote site), the way that you initiate an Archie search is by typing the word "prog" or the word "find" followed by a space and the string of characters (key words) you want to find. Pressing the Enter key starts the search. Otherwise, just enter the word Archie and the search string.

Let's assume you have an assignment to create a page for a World Wide Web site and you want to find an HTML editor to help you. You would conduct an Archie search using the key word HTML_editor. The underline was included because file names cannot have blank spaces in them and key word searches often find file names.

When Archie completed the search, you received a list of files and directories matching your search terms. A standard search did not return any results, but a case insensitive search found several matches.

The report contains several tiers of information. The first tier (far left of the screen) reports the anonymous FTP host site. The second tier reports the "Location," which actually is the directory path leading to the file that registered the hit.

The third and final tier describes the file or directory itself. In this search, one site reports a file named "HTML_Editor_1.0.sit.hqx." The name in this case tips you off that the file is a Binhex file compressed using Stuffit because it ends in ".sit" and ".hqx," which are standard designations for such files. Archie reports the size of the file (554564 bytes), as well as the time (23:16 or 11:16 p.m.) and date (Mar 30, 1995) it was last revised. The time and date information can be of help if you are looking for information about a particular event or a specific version of a piece of software. The size information will give you a sense of whether you're looking at a novel-length document, a huge software program, or a one-page document.

As the Archie report results scroll past your screen, you can stop the scrolling by typing Ctrl-S. Once stopped, you can begin the scroll again with Ctrl-Q. If your communications program permits, you can create a log file and capture the Archie report as it passes. You also have the option of mailing the results to yourself. At the end of the search, you remain in the Archie program and have the option of issuing a number of commands. To mail the results of your search, type

mail username@host.domain <CR>

and substitute your e-mail address for the string "username@host.domain."

When you are done with Archie, type "q" for quit. Generally, you will be released to your host server. The "qarchie" server at archie.sura.net (login: qarchie) accepts an abbreviated set of commands and does not drop you immediately back to your host. Help, in Archie, is accessed by typing "help" just as it is in many other Internet programs. When you ask for help, you are given a set of help topics upon which you may get further information. If you want to see a full set of Archie commands and what they do, give Archie the command

manpage <CR>

and you will see an Archie manual which is about twenty typewritten pages long.

While you can find text files on the Internet in this way, Archie and FTP are uniquely suited to finding and retrieving software archived at FTP sites around the world. But, it is not always easy to tell whether a file is a text file or a binary (program) file. The naming conventions—discussed under FTP—provide clues. The Archie "whatis" command can also provide information about files. If you type

whatis baseball <CR>

for example, "whatis" searches the Archie Software Description Data Base for the string "baseball," ignoring case. In the data base are names and short descriptions of many software packages, documents, and data files on the Internet. When Archie finds a match, it will report proper file names and their descriptions. A "prog" or "find" search on the file names will then tell you where to get the files. That is a job for FTP.

Words of Caution

However you bring text and software "down from the net," remember that much of it is copyrighted. With software, shareware programs put you on your honor to pay for them if you decide after a reasonable trial period that you like a program well enough to use it. Freeware is, as the name implies, free, but is still copyrighted. Other programs are in the public domain, which means that nobody holds the copyright.

Still other programs available in Internet archives are software in some state of testing. During testing periods, users are encouraged to report software bugs to the authors in exchange for free use of the program.

Whatever the situation, it's up to you, legally and ethically, to know the terms under which the software is distributed. Generally there is some type of notice provided with each program, often in the "README" file or the opening screen.

Chapter **7**

Groupspeak: Lists & News

A powerful explosion ripped through the Albert Murrah Federal Building in Oklahoma City on the morning of April 19, 1995. Armed with scant details, rumors, and a few solid leads, dozens of journalists "gathered" online in the hours immediately following the blast. They continued sharing notes and asking each other for help on aspects of the story that stretched out for weeks.

Lines of inquiry on e-mail discussion lists included leads on Muslim terrorists, Michigan Militia, other attacks on federal buildings, and the making of the bomb itself. The Internet abounded with answers, if only you knew what questions to ask and where to look. Journalists "gathering" in CARR-L (Computer Assisted Research and Reporting List), IRE-L (Investigative Reporters and Editors List), and SPJ-L (Society of Professional Journalists List) and other online discussion lists exchanged hundreds of messages on the topic in the weeks following the blast. Nearly two dozen such lists provide homes for journalists to discuss their craft.

When Karla Homolka pleaded guilty to the mutilation murders of two girls, a Canadian court banned publication of any details of her trial until the trial of her husband Paul Bernardo was completed. The court reasoned that defendant Bernardo's right to a fair trial outweighed freedom of the press in this case. The judge was particularly worried that the American press just across the border would violate the ban, so he excluded foreign media from the courtroom and forbade anyone to publish any circumstances of the deaths mentioned in Homolka's trial until the conclusion of the Bernardo case.

The judge's ban could not stop the flow of information about the trial to mass audiences in the United States and around the world. Soon after Bernardo was arrested, several electronic bulletin boards containing facts and rumors about the affair were launched. On July 14, Justin Wells and Ken Chasse set up a Usenet news group about the trial on Chasse's Sonic Interzone BBS, a public access bulletin board in Toronto. The Usenet news group, which was named alt.fan.karla-homolka, distributed information around the world about the trial, in defiance of the publication ban. Net-connected Canadians and other interested folks found information on the case in news groups and in e-mail discussion lists.

In this chapter we will discuss:

- e-mail discussion lists of interest to journalists.
- common listserv commands used to subscribe to and manage traffic in discussion lists.
- commands to search listserv archives.
- Usenet news groups, including what Usenet is, how news groups are organized, and how to access network news.
- the promises and pitfalls these services hold for reporters.

Discussion Lists and Listservs

E-mail discussion lists have emerged as potentially significant tools for journalists. If you have e-mail access to the Internet, you can participate in these groups.

Discussion lists can be thought of as electronic salons in which people holding similar interests gather to talk about issues of concern. It works in this way: Individuals send e-mail to a specific address for the particular discussion list; that mail is automatically distributed to everyone who sub-scribes to that list; and everyone who subscribes to the discussion or dis-tribution list receives every message sent to the list.

There are two addresses associated with e-mail discussion lists. The first is the address of the list distribution software, a specialized mailing program designed to manage the list functionality and located on a host server. This is generally called the Listserv, named after the Bitnet soft-ware created to manage e-mail distribution lists. We will use the term Listserv to refer to all such programs even though there is other software, notably Listproc and Majordomo, designed to perform the same operations.

The second address for the list is that of the discussion list itself. You send messages you want to share with the group to the discussion list address. Once your subscription is set up, this is the address you use most frequently as you participate in the discussions of the list. You send all commands governing your subscription including "SET" parameters (dis-cussed later), to the Listserv.

For example, if you wanted to subscribe to the CARR-L list mentioned above you would send a message to the Listserv:

Listserv@ulkyvm.louisville.edu

After you are subscribed to CARR-L list, you send messages you want to share with everyone to the discussion list:

```
   PINE 3.91    COMPOSE MESSAGE                    Folder: INBOX   3 Messages

   To        : listproc@lists.missouri.edu
   Cc        :
   Attchmnt:
   Subject :
   ----- Message Text -----
   sub IRE-L Elliot King
   set IRE-L mail digest




^G Get Help  ^X Send       ^R Read File ^Y Prev Pg   ^K Cut Text  ^O Postpone
^C Cancel    ^J Justify    ^_ Alt Edit  ^V Next Pg   ^U UnCut Text^T To Spell
```

Fig. 7-1: Subscribing to a discussion list and setting parameters for the list may be done with the same message.

CARR-L@ulkyvm.louisville.edu

The only difference in the two addresses is what is on the left side of the @ sign. In one case you are giving commands to the machine that handles your mail, the Listserv. In the other case, you are sharing correspondence with people, the list. Understanding the distinction between the list and the Listserv—and how you use each—will save you a lot of grief as you begin to use e-mail discussion lists in your work.

Subscribing to a List

The list service software at a particular location often manages many different discussion lists. The primary function of the list service software is to allow a person to subscribe or terminate a subscription to a particular list. To subscribe, you would send a message to the Listserv. In the body of the message, you would enter

> sub *listname your name*

where you insert the name of the list followed by a space, your first name, and your last name.

To terminate a subscription, address a message to the Listserv and in the body of the message type

> unsub *listname*

Instead of the command "unsub" you can also use the command "signoff."

For example, to subscribe to IRE-L you would address an e-mail message to listproc@lists.missouri.edu. In the body of your e-mail message you should type "sub IRE-L jane doe," substituting your name for jane doe. Figure 7-1 shows a sample message for subscribing to IRE-L and for setting the manner in which you get the list to digest (see the following section on setting parameters).

This exact procedure works for lists managed by Listserv or Listproc software, a large portion of the discussion list universe. Some mailing list software uses variations on this theme. Instead of sending the subscribe message to "listserv@(Location)" you would send it to "(name of list)-request@(location)." For example, to subscribe to the "Digital News" discussion list maintained by the Radio and Television News Directors Foundation (RTNDF) you would send an e-mail message to Digital_News-request@rtndf.org and on the subject line of your message put the word "subscribe."

Another popular list managing program is Majordomo, which uses a command structure of its own, but somewhat resembles Listserv and Listproc software.

Setting Your List Parameters

After sending a subscription request to a Listserv, you will receive a message welcoming you to the list, describing the list's purpose, and sometimes giving basic commands for controlling your receipt of mail from the list. Save these messages in a place where you can easily find them. Mail lists have frequent postings from people who are asking for help getting off a list or giving other commands described in the welcome message because they have failed to record the instructions.

After you receive the welcome message you will receive all e-mail messages that are being sent to the list. With some active lists, you may receive fifty or more messages a day. Consequently, you should check your mailbox regularly. If you subscribe to four or five lists, you could receive more than 100 e-mail messages a day. These messages will arrive one at a time and they will be interspersed with your personal mail. If you subscribe to more than one list, the messages will arrive in a random mix and you may have a hard time separating one set of messages from another, or from your personal mail.

To better manage the possible deluge of messages you receive from lists, you can set your mail to "digest" or to "index." When your list mail is set to "digest," you receive only one message a day from the Listserv. The message generally starts with a table of contents telling you how many messages there are for the day then listing the topics of the messages followed by the number of messages touching each topic. Following the table of contents, you get the complete text of each message sent that day.

When mail is set to "index," you also receive only one message a day. The index message, as the name implies, is only an index of the day's messages. Each message has a two-line entry that includes the message number, the name of the sender, and the subject. Usually, the index is followed by instructions about receiving the messages you want, and a sample script for sending to the Listserv to get the messages you seek.

In order to set your mail to digest, address an e-mail message to the Listserv. In the body of the message, type

```
set listname mail digest
```

where you provide the listname, such as IRE-L or SPJ-L. If you prefer the index format, just substitute the word "index" for the word "digest."

Other set commands that might prove useful include "nomail" and "ack." If you are going on vacation and you don't want your mailbox to fill up, you can send to the Listserv the message

```
set listname nomail
```

That will turn off your mail without unsubscribing you. When you return, just send to the Listserv the message

```
set listname mail
```

Ack and noack are also opposites. If, when you post messages to the list you want to see your own posting, you need to set your mail to "ack" (which means acknowledge. Some lists are set that way by default, others are set to "noack," meaning your own postings will not be sent to you.

For instructions on these and other commands, send a message to the Listserv. In the body of the message, type "info refcard" and you will get a short e-mail message identifying commands available to you.

Finding Relevant Lists

Thousands of e-mail discussion lists, treating all manner of topics, are scattered about the Internet. Two general kinds of lists will be of interest to Journalists: those catering to particular interests of journalists, and those specializing in topics relevant to the beats journalists cover. The challenge seems to be to identify relevant lists. Several tools exist to help find these.

First, there are about two dozen lists catering to the various crafts and interests of journalists. Some of these are listed in Table 7-1. We have used CARR-L, IRE-L, and SPJ-L as examples in this chapter. Messages on these lists routinely provide tips on how and where to find valuable information on the network. CARR-L is very strong here. Barbara Croll Fought at Syracuse University maintains a more extensive list of e-mail discussion lists focusing on public communications topics. Her list is available on the World Wide Web at http://web.syr.edu/~bcfought/nnl1.html.

Listserv	Listname	Topic of List
listserv@ulkyvm.louisville.edu	CARR-L	Computer assisted research and reporting
listserv@cornell.edu	COPYEDITING-L	Interests of copy editors, including grammar, punctuation, style concerns
Digital_News-request@rtndf.org	Digital_News	Implications of new news technology. "Subscribe" in Subject field.
listserv@listserv.syr.edu	FOI-L	Freedom of information issues
listserv@american.edu	INTCAR-L	Internationally oriented computer-assisted reporting
listproc@lists.missouri.edu	IRE-L	Interests of investigative reporters
listserv@acfcluster.nyu.edu	JHISTORY	Issues related to the history of journalism, job placements, and research
listserv@qucdn.queensu.ca	JOURNET	Journalism education and research
listproc@ripken.oit.unc.edu	NEWSLIB	Researching news stories
listproc@lists.missouri.edu	NICAR-L	Computer-assisted reporting
listserv@cmuvm.csv.cmich.edu	NPPA-L	Visual communicators, news photographers and graphics editors
listserv@vm1.spcs.umn.edu	RADIO-L	Digital audio broadcasting issues
listproc@listserv.umt.edu	RTVJ-L	Radio - TV journalism trade, ethics, classes, and equipment
listserv@psuvm.psu.edu	SPJ-L	Broad area, including SPJ chapter information

Table 7-1: Partial listing of e-mail discussion lists focusing on the interests of journalists and journalism educators.

In order to find discussion lists relevant to your beat, you may use one of several Web-based finding tools. The following sites are good starting points:

- http://tile.net/—The Tile.net site will help locate e-mail lists, news groups, and ftp servers.
- http://www.liszt.com//—Started at Indiana University, this server claims to have a data base of more than 65,000 discussion lists.
- http://www.neosoft.com/internet/paml/index-index.html— Stephanie da Silva's Publicly Accessible Mailing List index

- http://www.netspace.org/cgi-bin/lwgate—NetSpace Mailing List WWW Gateway has documents describing mail list commands as well as providing an index to discussion lists.
- http://www.nova.edu/Inter-Links/cgi-bin/lists—The Nova search engine returns lists and their descriptions based on key words you provide.

You can also request the very large "List of Lists" document by sending the message "send interest-groups" to mail-server@sri.com. The message "list global" sent to listserv@uga.cc.uga.edu will produce a similar list.

Posting Messages and Using Lists

Reading and participating in discussion lists can be extremely useful. It puts reporters in contact with people who generally know a lot about a specific topic. The reporter can then follow up with those people, ask where more information can be found, or ask who else would be a good source to interview. In other words, discussion lists can provide reporters with a wealth of leads to more information. We recommend that you "lurk" in a list for awhile before posting any messages to it. "Lurking" means that you "listen" or read without talking.

After you understand the tenor of the list and what kinds of discussion it encourages, you are ready to post. To post a message to a discussion group, you send e-mail to the list (not the Listserv) by following the normal procedures for sending e-mail. To respond to a posted message, with most lists you can simply use the reply function of your mail program while you are reading the message. Hundreds of different listserv-based discussion lists operate with people communicating about topics ranging from the use of computers in Eastern Europe to bird watching to jazz.

To Quote or Not to Quote

As you monitor discussion lists, from time to time participants will engage in an exchange that may relate directly to a story on which you are working. Should reporters directly quote from messages that have been posted on discussion lists?

This controversial question has been hotly debated and no clear rules have emerged. At one level, when people send messages to discussion lists, they know the message will be read by hundreds and perhaps thousands of people. Those people clearly have chosen to communicate publicly. On the other hand, they may not have realized that they are talking on the record to reporters, with the added factors that entails.

The copyrights associated with messages posted to discussion lists is an issue that has not been resolved. Should e-mail messages posted to discussion lists be considered the same as talk in a public forum or like published, written works in which authors have greater control over the dissemination of their words? If discussion list postings are copyrighted written works, what constitutes "fair use?" Legal issues will be further discussed in Chapter 10.

Ideally, you should use discussion lists as places to obtain leads to information. You should then follow up those leads through more interpersonal methods. The best journalism is frequently the result of one-on-one interaction between a source and a reporter. Learn from the material that is distributed; but, if you want to use that material in a story, try to establish one-on-one contact to clarify and develop the information.

Discussion List Archives

In general, when you subscribe to a discussion list, you will monitor or participate in an ongoing discussion. Often it is like walking into the middle of a conversation.

Commonly, the interaction taking place at any particular moment will not be of immediate interest or use. Months later, however, you may receive an assignment on a topic that was discussed earlier by a discussion group. Alternatively, after you receive a specific assignment, you may identify what you think is an appropriate discussion list and wish to know if the topic has, in fact, been discussed.

Fortunately, many discussion lists keep archives of their past postings. To receive an index of archived files you send a message to the listserv. The body of the message should state "index (list name)." You can retrieve messages that look like they may be of interest by sending the message "get (list name) (name or number of file)."

For some lists you may have to subscribe to review the archives of its messages. You can see which groups have archives at a specific location by sending the message "data base list" to listserv@location. In other words, to see what archives are available at the location at which the CARR-L discussion list is manager, you would send the message "data base list" to listserv@ulkyvm.louisville.edu.

Once you have the list of archives, it can be searched using key words by sending the message "search (key word) in (listname)." You can then retrieve the message using the procedure outlined above.

Listserv software supports several other data base features as well. For instructions about accessing advanced commands, send the message "info" to listserv@(location).

Listserv software permits some very powerful searching through a scripting language. If you wanted to get a listing of all messages sent to

CARR-L during 1995 that discuss the bombing of the federal building in Oklahoma City, you would send a message to the Listserv containing the following script in the body of the message:

```
//
Database search DD=rules
//Rules DD *
Search Oklahoma and (bomb or bombing) in CARR-L since
95 to 95
Index
/*
```

What is returned to you is a listing in index form of all the messages that meet your search criteria. Each message is assigned a number. Let's say your index came back with three documents you wanted to read, and they were numbered 3106, 3110, and 3112. You would then send the following script to the Listserv:

```
//        JOB
Database search DD=Orders
//Orders DD *
Select * in CARR-L.3106-3112
Print 3106 3110 3112
/*
//        EOJ
```

Using these scripts as models, you can search any Listserv archives for topics of your choosing simply by adjusting the name of the list, the topics, and the dates. You need to be sure your message is addressed to the appropriate Listserv.

To search Listproc archives you would follow the same process, except that the syntax for the search line follows this pattern:

```
Search IRE-L Oklahoma and (bomb or bombing) since 95 to 95
```

Usenet News Groups

In addition to e-mail discussion lists, news groups also serve as a network place for people to gather around predefined topics. Usenet news groups, which are sometimes referred to collectively as network news, make up a large distributed conference system in which people with shared interests interact with each other. In many ways, Usenet is like the forums on CompuServe, America Online, other commercial information services, and smaller electronic bulletin boards. People post and read messages on boards or in news groups organized around topics of common interest.

While Usenet news groups appear to be like e-mail discussion lists, they operate differently. Once you subscribe to a discussion list, every message posted to the list is sent to your account as electronic mail. When you read the messages posted to a news group, you are reading messages that are located on a server, not in your own account. In the same way, when you post a message, the message stays on a server. It is not automatically distributed to thousands of people.

Technically, Usenet news groups are not part of the Internet. Usenet is the name given to the network of servers whose system administrators have agreed to feed news to each other, adhering to a specific communication protocol. Consequently, it is a very informal network with no governing body and few specific usage rules. Each system administrator controls the traffic at his or her particular site. If you know of a news group (such as "alt.journalism") that your news site does not carry, you can ask to have it included. Some Usenet sites also have Internet connections, which is how some network news gets to the Internet. Similarly, many Internet host sites and gateways offer Usenet access.

The structure of network news has some advantages over listserv-oriented, mailing list-based discussion groups. Because the messages are not actually sent to an account but reside on a central server, people who are reading news group postings do not find their mailboxes filled with mail if a discussion gets lively. Nor do they have to suspend mail if they plan to go on vacation or cannot monitor their computer account for a couple of weeks.

On the other hand, not everyone with Internet access can conveniently access Usenet news groups. As noted later, people whose system administrators opt not to receive a news feed will have to access public systems. Also, most Usenet news groups do not archive their messages. That means you can only access current discussions.

Another concern for journalists is that the quality of the information communicated in these groups is very uneven. Some information is excellent. Some is just wrong. And, often, it is hard to tell which is which. Nonetheless, the amount of information circulated through network news is enormous, more than 12,000 network news groups involving more than 100,000 computer sites. An estimated twelve million people have accounts on computers carrying Usenet, and three million people read Usenet news at least occasionally. In 1994, one expert estimated that approximately 370,000 articles per week were copied worldwide through Usenet. This traffic represented roughly 20,000 printed pages per day of announcements, questions and answers, advice, bits of program code, and other information. A typical server subscribes to about 4,000 news groups and may receive more than twenty megabytes of information a day.

Network News Hierarchies

Network news groups are organized according to hierarchies ranging from the general to the specific. The name of each news group is divided from

Seven Major News Categories

comp .... Computer science and related topics
news .... Network news itself
rec .... Hobbies, recreational activities
sci .... Scientific research and applications
soc .... Social issues, either political or simply social
talk .... Forum for debate on controversial subjects
misc .... Anything that doesn't fit into the categories above.

Fig. 7-2: Traditional Top-level domains for naming of news groups. Others include "alt," "biz," and "bionet."

its parent and various subgroupings by a "dot" (period). For example, the news group alt.fan.karla-homolka was initially placed in the hierarchy of news groups reserved for discussion of alternative and controversial material. All news groups in this hierarchy begin with "alt."

The second element in the news group name "fan" designates fan clubs. Other fan clubs listed that begin with alt.fan. range from the Addams Family to Madonna to Dan Quayle. In fact, the Homolka murder case is not the only crime to have its own fan club. The highly publicized Amy Fisher-Joey Buttafucco attempted manslaughter case in which a teenage girl shot the wife of her purported lover was also the subject of a news group under the alt.fan hierarchy. So was the O.J. Simpson case.

Traditionally, Usenet news groups have fallen into seven categories, listed in Figure 7-2.

But news groups can also be created locally. And, because system administrators can arrange news feeds for any group that is of interest, many locally created groups gain as wide a distribution as standard network news groups and are generally considered part of the Usenet news group family.

Locally created news groups often use the "alt" prefix or create prefixes of their own. Some other common designations include "bionet" for topics of interest to biologists and "biz" for business-related subjects.

Although it seems as if much of the publicity given to Usenet news groups in the media has focused on groups discussing topics such as bestiality, bondage, or pornography, the range of discussion is extensive. For example, as many as 300 or more news groups discuss issues of interest to scientists in different disciplines.

There are news groups about major political events and leaders in both the alt and social hierarchies. The soc.politics designation includes politically oriented news groups. Soc.rights.human is a news group that discusses human rights issues. Finally, most major professional sports teams as well as many entertainment activities and industries are the topics for news groups in both the alt and rec hierarchies. For example, in the rec hierarchy there is rec.sport.baseball, rec.music.bluenote for discussions about jazz and the blues, and rec.mag for discussion about magazines.

Getting Access

The easiest and most efficient way to access Usenet news groups is for the system administrator to arrange for a news feed to your local system and to mount news reader software (i.e., a news client) for you to use. Two of the most common news readers in the UNIX environment are called nn and rn. To see if you already have access to network news enter "nn," "rn," or "trn" (an updated version of rn) at your system prompt. If not, you might also try "news" (which on some systems gives you news only for the system), "unews," "usenet," or "netnews." You can also consult your system administrator.

NN and rn are only two of the news readers available for reading network news. Other popular programs include Trumpet for MS DOS, WinVN for Windows, Nuntius for the Macintosh, and NNR and VMS News for VMS. The most popular World Wide Web browser software, Microsoft Internet Explorer and Netscape, have incorporated within them a very good news reading module. Like other client software described earlier, news readers organize the information on the servers on which the news groups are stored in ways that meet your needs. For example, messages on similar topics will be linked together in what are called threads, which can then be read in sequence. News readers also help you post messages to news groups.

Alternative Access to News Groups

Many system administrators do not want to support a network news feed. They fear the large volume of message traffic will strain their system resources, and they deem other tasks more important than reading network news. For you to configure a news reader to access a different network news server on your own is possible, but it can be a complicated and frustrating process. However, if the system you use is not running network news locally, you can access news groups via other publicly available avenues.

Many Gopher sites provide access to Usenet news. One such Gopher is at Washington and Lee University, gopher://liberty.uc.wlu.edu:70/11/internet/usenet/readers. You will be able to use the Usenet news readers at Washington and Lee University itself as well as those at selected other sites. The Internet is always changing, however, and some news readers may not be publicly available. Others may allow use only during restricted hours. On the other hand, the news reader at the Danish Academic Network, which is item 11 on the Washington and Lee Usenet news reader menu, provides search indexes as well as reading news.

The Solinet Gopher provides access to more than dozen publicly available news readers from gopher://gopher.solinet.net:70/11/SOLINETGopher/NewsGroups.

Another option for accessing Usenet news is a gateway between Usenet and Bitnet, which is the network on which most Listserv mailing lists operate. Those news groups that take advantage of the Usenet/Bitnet gateway can be accessed via e-mail using the same processes associated with a standard discussion list.

Most Usenet news groups, however, do not correspond to mailing lists, and they cannot be accessed by e-mail. For people who don't have easy access to Usenet, the "List of Active News Groups" can be retrieved from archives at MIT and UUNET using the procedures described under "Finding the Right News Group" later in this chapter. For a list of news groups that have a gateway to listserv discussion groups, see the "List of Active News Groups" posting in news.announce.newusers. To do that, you need to know how to navigate the Usenet.

Organizing Your News Groups

Before you begin to read messages, your first task when you access network news is to designate news groups with which you want to connect. Local servers may offer access to more than 7,000 news groups. When you first begin to read network news, the system assumes that you may want to read all the news from all the news groups. Consequently, the process of eliminating news groups can be time consuming.

Most news readers, however, have features that allow you to eliminate news groups according to major designations and categories. For example, you may not be interested in anything that has to do with computer science, so you will want to exclude all news groups that begin with the comp. prefix.

If you have a local news feed and local reader software, the specific commands you need should be available in the help files.

News readers keep a log of the news groups to which you subscribe and which articles within that group you have already read. Therefore, when you select that group again, you are brought directly to messages that have been posted since you last read the postings.

This information is stored in a file frequently called "NEWS.RC" on the machine where the news reading client resides. If the client resides on your Internet host, it is stored in the space you are allocated on the host. If you have a client on your personal computer, the file (or its equivalent) will be stored there. If you are using public access to Usenet through a

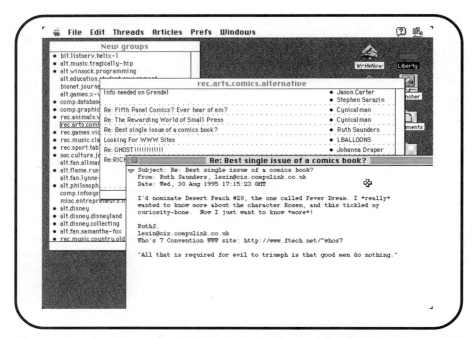

Fig. 7-2: Levels of Usenet news operations are graphically illustrated by these three windows from a Nuntius news-reading session. You select a news group from a list (left window), then an article from within the group, and finally you read the article (foreground, right).

Telnet or Gopher connection, you do not have the benefit of the NEWS.RC file tracking. If you are accessing Usenet from a BBS or commercial service, you must ask your service provider about this kind of tracking.

A word of caution regarding the NEWS.RC file and the way you exit from your Usenet reader. Both "quit" and "exit" commands may take you out of the news reader. However, when you "quit" from some programs, the reader does not update your NEWS.RC file. When you "exit," it does. Thus if you "quit" the reader keeps no record of what you have read or your subscription list.

Navigating Usenet Levels

When you read Usenet news, you enter a program that functions on three tiers: 1) a group listing/directory level, 2) an article listing/directory level, and 3) an article reading level. Additionally, you may be in screen mode or command mode at either directory level. This three-tiered structure and what it means to you as a user is the same no matter which news reading software you are using.

```
VMS NEWS v1.24 --- Newsgroups [TOTAL] 2818 (Posting OK)
==> 1992 info.sun-nets                                    -      2
    1993 info.sysadmin                                    -      1
    1994 info.theorynt                                    -    448
    1995 info.wisenet                                     -   3071
    1996 junk                                             - 659693
    1997 k12.chat.teacher                                 -    590
    1998 la.eats                                          -   2181
    1999 la.general                                       -   3744
    2000 la.news                                          -    221
    2001 la.seminars                                      -    247
    2002 la.slug                                          -     44
    2003 la.test                                          -     77
    2004 misc.activism.progressive                        -  13780 Mod
    2005 misc.answers                                     -    621 Mod
    2006 misc.auto                                        -      8
    2007 misc.books.technical                             -   2703
    2008 misc.comp.forsale                                -     65
    2009 misc.computers.forsale                           -    232
    2010 misc.consumers                                   -  32466
    2011 misc.consumers.house                             -  31720
NEWS:
%NEWS-I-GRPSEL, Newsgroup news.answers with 1319 articles selected
%CLI-W-IVVERB, unrecognized command verb - check validity and spelling
```

Fig. 7-3: A portion of the news group listings from a Usenet News server. To select a group, point to it with the cursor pointer (here on group 1992) and press the Enter key.

Although the Usenet navigating descriptions that follow describe commands you would give in a text-based news reader, the process is the same for graphical interface readers incorporated within Web browsers and in stand-alone programs. In the graphical environment basic navigation selections are made by clicking on text-icon listings rather than by typing commands, but the three-level structure of Usenet news and the selection process are the same.

When you first launch the news reading program, you enter at the group directory level. Figure 7-3 illustrates a directory of news groups. The message across the top of the screen indicates that this particular news server carries 2,818 news groups. The directory lists twenty groups to a screen. The top line also tells us the news reading program we are using (VMS News) and the version (1.24). Beside the number of the news group is the news group's name. The top domain categories for the groups shown here are "info," a broad information category; "junk," an active, nondescript category; "k12," a group for teachers and students in elementary and secondary schools; "la," a group for subjects about Los Angeles; and the ubiquitous "misc" category. Only this last category is one of the seven traditional top domains of Usenet news.

The Group Directory Level

In the news group directory, to the right of the news group's name, is a number that corresponds to the number of the last article posted to the group. The group "k12.chat.teacher" has had 512 postings and "la.general" has had 3,744. The first two groups in the "misc" domain have the word "Mod" to the right of the posting number. This indicates the groups are moderated. In such a group, a moderator screens all incoming messages before posting them for all readers to see. In unmoderated groups, people can post just about anything they please. The vast majority of Usenet news groups are unmoderated.

Using your cursor keys, you move the news group selector arrow through the list, in order to choose the group you want. Or you can also enter a number, and the news reader will take your cursor to that number. Because group numbers change, they are not reliable bookmarks for getting to the group you want. If you know the name of the group you want, you can enter the command Group followed by the group's name to send your cursor to that group. A shortcut for Group in the VMS News reader is simply "g." Thus, if we wanted to read messages in the group "misc.consumers," we could enter the command

g misc.consumers <CR>

Fig. 7-4: A listing of article postings to the news group "alt.california" on the day of the 1994 Northridge earthquake. News of the quake dominated the group.

```
  VMS NEWS v1.24 --- alt.california (#42) 4342 - 4383
==>  4361 Re: Quake Status.....??                                    4
     4362 Re: SO CAL EARTHQUAKES                                     19
     4363 Help passing 818 area-code messages?                      18
     4364 quake and Northridge                                      13
     4365 Re: SO CAL EARTHQUAKES                                     44
     4366 Re: Quake Status.....??                                    9
     4367 Quake Report 94 Jan 17                                    80
     4368 Re: SO CAL EARTHQUAKES                                     37
     4369 Re: quake and Northridge                                  30
     4370 Earthquake updates from Los Angelinos                     36
     4371 Re: Quake Status.....??                                    8
     4372 Re: Quake Status.....??                                   14
     4373 (213) 485-5191                                            10
     4374 Re: Quake Status.....??                                    7
     4375 Re: (oh s___!) Church and Child Molesters                 31
     4376 Re: Earthquake updates from Los Angelinos                 44
     4377 Re: quake and Northridge                                  20
     4378 Re: Help passing 818 area-code messages?                  40
     4379 Re: Quake Status.....??                                    3
     4380 Re: Quake Status.....??                                    9
  NEWS:
  %NEWS-I-NOARTSRV, Newsgroup la.news contains no articles [SERVER ERROR]
  %NEWS-I-GRPSEL, Newsgroup alt.california with 42 articles selected
                                                      Receive: On
```

Fig. 7-5: Some of the more commonly used Usenet news commands, here in their VMS News version. Other text-based readers will have similar commands. You can usually invoke "Help" to get instructions specific to your program.

Basic Usenet News Commands	
Bottom	Moves cursor to the bottom of the display. Goes to last entry in the group or article list
Directory	Displays a directory of news groups or news items within a group. Moves up one level in tier structure. Synonyms = "Dir" and "d"
Down	Moves down one screen. In directory levels, moves cursor down generally 20 items. In article reading level, scrolls to end of article or down one screen, whichever is first.
Exit	Leaves the news reader program, updating your NEWS.RC file.
Extract	Saves the current news article in an output file which you name on the same command as "extract." Thus "extract filename" Synonym = "Save"
Followup	Starts a dialog that posts to an entire news group your reply to news item.
Go	Selects (goes to) an article or news group specified by the number which follows the word "go."
Group	Selects (goes to) the news group named following the word "group." Accepts wild cards (*). Synonym = "g"
Help	Calls up the help facility, from which you may gain more detailed instructions.
Mail	Starts program to mail message to individual, not the group.
Mark	Marks specified articles as read/unread by user.
Next	Only in article reading level, this command takes you to the next article in the group. Synonym = "n"
Post	Initiates process of posting an article to the news system.
Reply	Posts a mail message directly to the sender of a news item without putting the message out to the whole net.
Scan	Command is followed by a pattern to search for. Works in Article reading level. Useful for finding a string in large articles. Example: Scan "*searchterm*" (quotes necessary).
Subscribe	Marks a group as one you want to monitor, so the news reader program keeps track of what you have read.
Top	Moves cursor to the top of the display.
Unsubscribe	Reverses Subscribe command.
Up	Opposite of Down; moves up one screen.

and our cursor arrow would point to that group. Having chosen the group we want, we receive a list of the articles available by pressing the Enter key while the cursor arrow is pointing at the chosen group.

While the examples here are taken from the news reader VMS News, other readers have similar—often identical—commands. In any case, you will understand how the news reading and posting process works and what commands to look for when you issue the "help" command to your reader.

You can scroll through the list of news groups one screen at a time by entering the command "down" to go down twenty groups or "up" to go up twenty groups. If you aren't sure of the exact name of a group, you may search for matches using the asterisk wildcard. Thus, if you want to find a group discussing consumer interests you could enter the command

> g *consumer* <CR>

and the news reader program will take your cursor to the next group that has "consumer" in its name. If what you get is not the group you wanted, you may repeat the command until you find the right group.

The Articles Listing Level

Figure 7-4 shows a listing at the article directory level of the group "alt.california" on the day of the Northridge earthquake. You select articles in a fashion similar to the way you select news groups. You move the cursor pointer to the article you want and press the Enter key. As an alternative, you can use the "Go" command, followed by the number of the article, to move your cursor to that article. When you are in the article directory, you must type the whole word; the "g" shortcut only works in groups.

In both directory levels, you are automatically placed in screen mode until you type something other than a number, a Return key, or a cursor arrow key. As soon as you type a letter (or press the space bar), you are taken into the command mode. In command mode, your Up and Down Arrows do not move the cursor. Neither does the Return (Enter) key select anything; instead, a Return signals to the news reader completion of a command. Most of the time this screen mode vs. command mode is fairly intuitive, and it goes on unnoticed. But, if you find peculiar things going on at one of the directory levels, you might wish to note whether you are in screen or command mode.

Once you select an article to read, you can scroll through the article one line at a time by using your Down Arrow, or you can scroll one screen at a time by typing the command "down." The "Dir" command and its shortcut "d" move you up a level in Usenet news. If you are reading an article, the "d" command takes you out of reading the article into the article directory. If you are in the article directory when you type the "d" command, you are taken to the group directory.

```
   VMS NEWS v1.24 --- alt.cd-rom, Art.#20583 (20557 - 20594)

   Generating ARTICLE header :-

   From: WURLR@ttacs3.ttu.edu (Reddick, Randolph L.)
   Newsgroups: alt.cd-rom
   Subject: CD-Machine
   Date: Wed, 29 Jun 1994 21:48:22 CDT
   Distribution:
   Organization: TEXAS TECH UNIVERSITY
   X-News-Reader: VMS NEWS 1.24




   Distribution ? world
   %NEWS-I-GRPSEL, Newsgroup alt.aldus.pagemaker with 5 articles selected
   %NEWS-I-GRPSEL, Newsgroup alt.cd-rom with 38 articles selected
```

Fig. 7-6: When you issue the "post" or "followup" command, the news reader asks you for header information, suggesting default values for you. For some fields you have no options. In this dialog, we are defining the scope of distribution as worldwide.

The Article/Messages Reading Level

When you select news group messages to read, what you see on-screen has all the appearance of an e-mail message or a message posting to a bulletin board. If you wish to respond, you have the option of writing a "followup" message, which then will be displayed to the network. Or, you can "reply," which will send a mail message privately to the originator of the message. See Figure 7-5 for a summary of commonly used news reader commands.

If you choose the "followup" or the "post" command, the header dialog will have a few more options than a mail header. Figure 7-6 shows a news group message posting header dialog. The "Distribution" field demands special attention. What you put in the distribution field governs how far your message will be disbursed. If you select "world," your posting or followup will go out worldwide. If you select "local," it will generally stay at the site to which you post. Other acceptable distribution categories are:

- CA, OH, NY, TX, etc. = specified state.
- can   = Canada only.
- eunet   = European sites only.
- na   = North American destinations.
- usa   = United States based servers.

An important restriction on distribution codes is that your site must be included within the zone you designate. If you post from Canada, you may not specify "eunet" distribution. If you post from Florida, you may not specify "PA," but you may specify "usa."

Most news readers track what you have read through a system of marking files. When you are in the article directory level, you are reading articles that are described by one-line subject tags. You may know that you don't want to read certain articles. By issuing the "mark" (or "skip" in some systems) command, you instruct the news reader to treat the article as if it had been read.

The mark (skip) command marks the article at which your cursor is pointing. You can also add qualifiers (or arguments) to the command. Thus "mark /all" will mark all of the current postings as if they have been read. More commonly, you would give the command, "mark num1-num2," substituting the actual numbers of the articles you want to skip.

Finding the Right News Groups

For journalists, network news can serve many functions. Reporters may want to monitor beat-related news groups to stay current on specific topics and to find potential story ideas. In that case, the reporter may have the time to select several news groups and monitor the messages on them for several days to see if the information is relevant.

In other cases, however, you will be on deadline and looking for precise information about well defined topics. You won't be able to leisurely survey twenty news groups to find what you need.

In those cases, you can start by reading the FAQ or "Frequently Asked Questions" posting, which generally describes the news group and its charter. The FAQ also often contains other valuable information and leads about the topic in question. Most news groups routinely repost their FAQs.

FAQs are also available via FTP (Chapter 6). Perhaps the most comprehensive listing of FAQs is at Massachusetts Institute of Technology. Connect to rtfm.mit.edu using FTP and do a standard anonymous FTP logon. Then, using the CD command, change directories to /pub/usenet/news.answers. At that point, type a directory command (DIR) and the list of news groups for which the site has an FAQ will scroll by. When you see the name of a news group in which you may be interested, write it down.

Most of the FAQs listed at the MIT FTP site consist of multiple files. Consequently, you will want to run the list command (ls) and the name of the news group in which you are interested. For example, if you are interested in the FAQ for the news group alt.baldspot, enter the command

ls alt.baldspot.

This will list all the FAQ files associated with that news group. Once you see the individual files, you can retrieve the one you want using standard FTP commands.

Because of the amount of information contained in the FAQ archives, some of the FAQs may be compressed. If they are, their names may end with a .Z. Some FTP servers will automatically decompress files if you omit the .Z when you ask for a local file name in the retrieval process. If the archive is busy, however, the decompress function may be disabled.

The site at MIT is often very busy, and you may not be able to get on the system. But there are several other good FAQ archives available. They include:

- N. America: ftp.uu.net   /usenet/news.answers
- Europe: ftp.uni-paderborn.de   /pub/FAQ
              ftp.Germany.EU.net   /pub/newsarchive/news.answers
              grasp1.univ-lyon1.fr   /pub/faq
              ftp.win.tue.nl   /pub/usenet/news.answers
- Asia: nctuccca.edu.tw   /USENET/FAQ
              hwarang.postech.ac.kr   /pub/usenet/news.answers

Another alternative for retrieving any of the mentioned FAQs is to request it from the e-mail server at MIT. To find out how to use the server to get what you want, send mail to "mail-server@rtfm.mit.edu." In the body of your message include the word "help." The server will return a mail message to you explaining how to get the documents you want.

Finally, some search sites on the World Wide Web will help you find news groups treating your topic. One of these, Tile.Net at http://tile.net/. Altavista (http://altavista.digital.com/), permits you to specify Usenet news groups as a target when you perform key word searches at the site.

Archived Usenet Information

Most news readers retain Usenet news group messages for a limited period of time. The quantity of messages being posted daily makes it impossible to save everything. Consequently, when you read news group posts, you will only be able to read the messages that have been posted within that specified period.

Old news group messages are rarely saved. There are often good reasons for this. First, to save all Usenet news group messages would be similar to saving a record of all telephone conversations. It represents a huge amount of data. Second, as the Usenet FAQ puts it, the signal-to-noise ratio, i.e. the amount of good, useful information compared to the amount of useless information on many news groups is very low. In other words, the information is not worth saving in many cases.

The information from some news groups is archived, however. The Sunsite server at the University of North Carolina, for example, archives the messages from many of the news groups carried by the Launchpad service discussed earlier. To make use of the archive, you can FTP to sunsite.unc.edu. The system administrators there, however, recommend you use WAIS. To find out more, you should FTP to sunsite.unc.edu and get and read the file /pub/wais/ftp-wais.readme.

If you don't have a WAIS or Gopher client, you can Telnet to Sunsite (sunsite.unc.edu) and log on as "swais" to test a sample WAIS client or log on as "gopher" to test a sample Gopher client. If you send e-mail to info@sunsite.unc.edu in the same manner as we describe for the MIT site (the body of your message reads "help"), you will be sent help information about how to use the different services the Sunsite server provides.

Key Word Searches and News Filtering

To locate the relevant Usenet news groups, you have two options. The most straightforward method is to simply scroll through the lists of news groups for which your Internet host has a news feed. Because the groups are arranged in a hierarchial manner, you may not have to scroll through all 4,000 to find the ones in which you may be interested. For example, if you are working on a topic related to history, it is unlikely that you will find any appropriate group in the .comp or the .sci categories.

This method of finding news groups is analogous to browsing the shelf in a library. Alternatively, you could use the World Wide Web search engines that will search news group archives. One of these, Tile.Net at http://tile.net gives you the options of browsing for topics or performing key-word searches. Other search engines, such as Altavista at http://altavista.digital.com, will perform keyword searches for news group postings on topics. Deja News at http://www.dejanews.com/ is a powerful search tool dedicated to searching news groups. It enables finding groups that treat specific topics, finding articles on topics across various groups, and even searching for people who have posted to news groups.

Once you have identified the news groups you wish to monitor, you must "subscribe," using the commands associated with the news reader you are using. In NN the "u" command is used to both subscribe and unsubscribe to news groups. In VMS News, use "sub" and "unsub" to subscribe and unsubscribe. In many Macintosh and Windows readers and the readers associated with Netscape and Internet Explorer, simply click on the appropriate icons.

A third approach for identifying useful news groups and discussion lists is to search through the e-mail archives to see who is discussing the topics in which you are interested. Stanford University's SIFT (Stanford

Information Filtering Tool) News Service digs through both e-mail discussion lists and Usenet news archives to find postings containing key words or combinations of key words that you specify. SIFT finds appropriate references and sends you an e-mail message describing in digest form what SIFT found. SIFT is accessed at http://sift.stanford.edu.

After you have identified appropriate news groups, your next step is to read the online discussions to see if the participants are discussing issues appropriate to your topic and if they seem generally knowledgeable about your subject. At this point you should just "lurk" in the background to ascertain the relevance and quality of the group information.

Your first selections may not be appropriate and you may have to subscribe and unsubscribe to several news groups and lists before finding the two or three best. Usually, you will want to participate in only two or three discussion lists or news groups. Reviewing the messages takes time, and interacting with online discussion groups will probably represent only a small fraction of your total research effort.

Proper Usenet Behavior

Like other groups of people interacting, people communicating with each other via news groups have developed their own rules of etiquette. If you begin to assert yourself in a group without understanding how to behave, at least some people in the group are bound to get mad at you. While you might think that might not make a difference, boorish behavior may mean that you will miss a good lead or contact.

People just starting to read network news should probably read several of the FAQs about Usenet itself prepared for new users. The news.answers news group carries most of the relevant FAQs for new users, including what to do if you have questions about network news. A primer by Chuq Von Rospach for new Usenet users is available in the news.answers news group. It summarizes the rules for working with the Usenet community.

As a journalist, you may not find yourself fully participating in the discussions in a particular news groups. More often, you will monitor the traffic—which is called "lurking" in online jargon—to identify people with whom you may either want to be in touch outside the context of the news group or contact to develop leads to other sources of information.

You can think of a news group as any other kind of public forum. As a reporter, if you attended a community meeting, you probably would not grab the microphone and begin interviewing a person you thought made an interesting comment. Instead, you would try to take the person aside, identify yourself as a journalist, and talk privately. You should follow the same process with a news group.

On the other hand, it certainly is not impolite to inform the group of the reason for your participation and invite people to get in touch with you via e-mail if they have information they wish to share.

Usenet, Listservs, and Journalism

Both network news and e-mail discussion lists represent methods of communicating with people around the world about predefined topics of interest. By talking to people, journalists can get interesting ideas for stories as well as interesting leads to information.

Understand, however, that just because someone is computer savvy enough to participate in a news group or discussion list, it does not mean he or she has any special expertise or knows anything factual about the issue. Many news groups are filled with rumors and mistakes, particularly about current affairs. Information gathered there has to be carefully checked out and verified.

And, while an argument can be made that people who are participating in a news group or discussion list are engaging in a public forum, they often do not know that a reporter is present and that their comments are "on the record." Consequently, online journalists repeatedly debate whether you can or should use information posted to a news group. You should carefully consider all the ramifications of your actions, including how much confidence you have in the accuracy of the information, how necessary the information is to your story, who will or could be hurt by the quote, and other issues before you make a decision.

On the other hand, Usenet news groups and e-mail discussion lists offer an intriguing possibility for journalists: the opportunity to include the views of informed non-experts in stories. Media critics have observed that, in many cases, the information reporters use comes from a narrow slice of elite and expert opinion.

Though there are many reasons for that, one is that it was hard for journalists to identify and interview non-experts whose opinions may be significant. With the emergence of Usenet news groups concerned with professional sports teams, sports reporters could include information from fans as well as the usual quotes from the players and management in their stories. The alt.fan discussion groups on Usenet give reporters easy access to loyal fans for all teams. Not surprisingly, the baseball strike in the summer of 1994 was a hot topic of discussion for some news groups.

Usenet news groups and e-mail discussion lists can provide journalists with access to people who may not be experts on a subject or part of the elite but yet are interested and have informed opinions. How that access is and should be managed and made to work for reporters has not yet been determined. Over time, however, it could change the flavor and sourcing of many different types of reporting. And even today, Usenet and discussion lists are viable for reporters gathering information and leads when more traditional means are cut off.

Chapter

8

Chat Zones, MUDs and BBSes

You may never have heard of Paso Robles, California. That doesn't matter. What matters is Vic's Cafe. Every city beat should have a place like Vic's Cafe in Paso Robles.

During World War II, many people visited Paso Robles while they were stationed at nearby Camp Roberts. The U.S.O. building on 10th Street later became home to the city's recreation department. The police department rose next door, the municipal court was up the street, and City Hall was catty-corner across the street. There was a park in the center of town— between 11th and 12th streets. On 13th Street, as Paso Robles entered the last quarter of the 20th century, not much different from the previous quarter century, stood Vic's Cafe. There Larry Eastwood ran a diner situated between the Continental Barber Shop and Redi's Western Wear.

The day started early at Vic's Cafe. Larry opened his doors around 6:00 a.m. City police, nearing the end of their early morning shift, were among the first customers. Their radio message, "10-7 Vic's" signaled the start of a new day. Jay Lyon, head of public works was there before 7:00. John Steaffens, a big, affable man who wore large plastic-framed glasses and had puffy cheeks, parked the pickup truck which identified him as fire chief right in front of Vic's Cafe. Proprietors of nearby businesses, sales clerks in downtown stores, and others dropped in. Politicians, police, public servants and just plain folks were there.

Before most other concerns opened, Vic's Cafe was awash with talk of the city's business. Talk ranged from whether or not the coach made the right decision at the Bearcats' last football game to what to do about water pressure at the old hospital, destined to become a Christian school.

Vic's Cafe was a reporter's heaven, a perfect place to measure the pulse of a community at the start of the day.

Late in the afternoon, about 5:00 p.m. or so, a slightly different crowd, generally with more commercial interests, began gathering at the Cattleman's Bar upstairs at the Paso Robles Inn. Other "watering holes," like Johnny Busi's Chianti Room (facing the park on Pine Street), attracted crowds of still another character. At midday, the post office served as gathering place for some folks. Orcutt's Market had its following as did Dauth-Leisy's. Some people preferred Bill Morgan's drug store, while others preferred the conversation at George Theraldsen's pharmacy. People involved in the community allied themselves with a couple of theater groups, the chamber of commerce crowd, Bearcat Boosters, Band Boosters, and a whole gaggle of service clubs.

There are a couple messages in all this.

First, people have ways of defining communities and of defining the "subcommunities" to which they belong. Second, members of any given "community" tend to congregate in well-defined places. The reporter assigned to City Hall soon learns the haunts of all those who make the decisions and call the shots. Beat reporters worth their keep find a Vic's Cafe where community pulse may be tapped. It's true in the real world as well as the online world.

This chapter is devoted to surveying that portion of the online world occupied by bulletin boards and the "real time" communities of MUDs and Internet Relay Chat.

In this chapter, you will learn:

- what you need to get online.
- how to find and log into local bulletin board systems (BBSes).
- a few things about "virtual communities" that exist online.
- how to capture the text of online sessions to disk files you can then edit in your word processor.
- how Internet Relay Chat (IRC) and MUDs work.
- what is offered for journalists on bulletin board systems, IRC, and MUDs.
- where to go for more help if you need it.

If you are already a veteran telecommunicator with hours of time logged in at commercial services and local BBS systems, you may want to merely scan the first part of this chapter.

Navigating the Neighborhood Bulletin Board

The Vic's Cafes of the world, the neighborhood grocery stores, barber shops, post offices, community centers, and churches all have counterparts in the online world. When personal computers first began to become a part of people's lives in the late 1970s and early 1980s, it was natural that people with computers would want to connect with one another. They created the virtual equivalent of the grocery store bulletin board. Some computer enthusiast would set up a machine in his or her bedroom or garage. The machine would run software that allowed other people with computers and modems to call in and post notices for all to see. Such a system was called a bulletin board system, or BBS. The person who owns the computer and sets up the BBS is called a sysop, short for system operator.

The BBS allowed callers to respond to the messages—publicly or privately—and, in some cases, allowed people to "chat" with each other in real time. In other words, if I called your BBS and wanted to chat with you, I could choose a menu item called "Chat" or "Page the Sysop." That might set off some type of alarm so that the sysop—who might well be doing other things at the time—could respond. The sysop also had the ability to initiate a "chat" session any time you called in. Often, the BBS ran on a machine the sysop also used for other purposes and used the only personal telephone line coming into the home. As a result, many of those bulletin boards were "open" only a few hours a day.

More sophisticated BBS software developed, personal computers became more powerful and less expensive, and local bulletin boards became popular "gathering places" for growing numbers of people with personal computers. Because people who "come together" online do not meet in any real space in the physical sense, the term "cyberspace" is often used to refer to the online world. Established hangouts or gathering places in the online world may be seen as virtual communities, and members of all such communities are sometimes called netizens.

Today, millions of persons daily "chat" with others online; do their banking, pay bills, and conduct business electronically; get news and weather reports by computer; make their own airline and hotel reservations; and even play games together. They "visit" libraries, read online magazines and newspapers, and save articles to their computers' clipboard or disk space. From their homes and offices they access encyclopedias and other reference materials, read movie reviews, carry on courtships, talk politics and sports, conduct meetings, and, in short, do everything people of the past did at the village square or general store. On a global scale, they do so with little regard to traditional geographical boundaries. The revolution in cyberspace presents myriads of opportunities for journalists.

Getting What You Need to Make Connection

For connection with the online world, you need: 1) a computer; 2) a telephone line and appropriate phone numbers; 3) a modem; 4) communications software; 5) healthy curiosity, a venturesome spirit, or gritty determination; and 6) (optional for some, but very useful) a friend who's been through all this before. If you don't have one, buy one. That is, stop by your local computer store, introduce yourself, and offer the person dinner

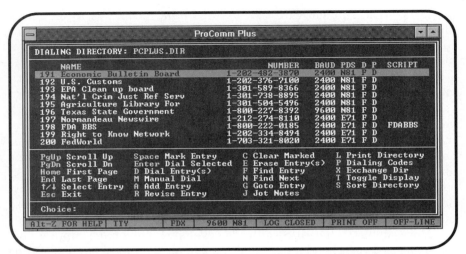

Fig. 8-1: Most communications programs have some kind of dialing directory or address book facility such as the one provided by ProComm Plus.

or something appropriate in exchange for helping you set up and get online. If you recently bought a computer, start with the person who sold it to you.

The computer: You don't need anything fancy here if you only want to get connected. A Mac Plus with 512K of memory will work. Original IBM PCs with the same amount of memory will do fine. It would be nice if the machine you plan to use has a hard drive, but even that is not necessary. In fact, these basic machines will make every connection and run almost every program this book describes except the graphical World Wide Web browsers or other Windows-based software. On the IBM compatible side, you need to assure that your computer either has a built-in modem or it has an available serial port to which you may connect an external modem.

The telephone line: Again, you don't need anything fancy. Standard residential service works fine. You should have a modular (RJ-11) phone jack to plug into, and you should have touch-tone service. But even these are not necessary, if you're willing to experiment and tinker. As for the phone numbers, you have several sources. For starters, go to the neighborhood newsstand and pick up the current issue of *Computer Shopper* magazine. Each month it carries an extensive listing of bulletin boards arranged by area code. The list describes each board's contents. Although it runs for dozens of large-format pages, the list is not comprehensive. Pick one or two near you. Log on, and you frequently find a comprehensive list of local bulletin boards.

Boardwatch Magazine was conceived with its reason for existence reporting on the bulletin board scene. Your local library may also have some useful books and directories. In fact, public libraries and their college counterparts are among the first service-oriented segments of society to go online. Many libraries provide access to their computerized card catalog and to other data bases via telephone hookup. If you know a library has a computerized catalog, ask for the dial-in number. Some will even be listed in the phone book, but you may have to have a library card to get access. Don't forget your local computer store friend. Usually the folks who sell computers and modems will have handy a phone number or two for local bulletin boards. As a last resort, you might try some of the BBS numbers listed under the national BBS section in this chapter. Most of those will be long distance, and you will have to pay the consequence. It is better to do your learning close to home.

The modem: For less than $100 you can buy a 14,400-bps (bits per second) external fax modem complete with communications and fax software. External simply means it is a separate, stand-alone unit that you can unplug from your machine and plug in somewhere else without taking anything apart. Internal modems usually are $20-$30 cheaper, but they are customized according to the specific computer types with which they are compatible and are not easily moved.

We recommend an external modem with visible display lights on it. These lights "report" the progress of your computer's communication with some other computer. This can be very helpful when you have asked some other computer to give you some information and nothing seems to be happening. If you can see those little modem lights flickering, you know that data is moving between the computers, even though you don't see any changes on screen. We also recommend you buy the fastest modem you can afford. Internal 2,400-bps modems for DOS/Windows machines will only work for text-only computing. If you buy an external modem you will also need a cable to connect the modem to your computer. The same external modem will work for either a Mac or a PC; only the cables are different.

Communications software: Generally, your modem will come with software and coupons for free time on CompuServe, America Online, Prodigy, or a similar service. The programs bundled with modems are usually adequate. Some are very good. If you must buy your own modem software you might try a shareware package such as Red Ryder (Macintosh) or ProComm (DOS). A commercial version of Red Ryder is sold under the name of White Knight. ProComm Plus is a commercial version of its shareware predecessor and comes in both DOS and Windows versions. Crosstalk is a commercial communications programs for both Macintosh and IBM compatibles. Qmodem (PC) and Zterm (Mac) are also popular shareware programs that are widely available. MacKermit is a shareware Kermit communications program that is widely available. Frequently packaged with modems intended for use on DOS machines are Bitcom,

QuickLink, and MTEZ. Bitcom is an older program which runs on machines that are only partly IBM compatible. MTEZ is a WordPerfect product that has fax capabilities and is ProComm command compatible. On the Macintosh side, Microphone joins White Knight among commercial products deserving consideration.

Whatever software you buy, be sure it will run on your computer. If you have a low-end computer, most of the newest, fanciest software may not run on it. Most communications software programs are pretty straightforward, simple, and will work on a large majority of the machines for which they were written.

Proper attitude: We can't do anything about your attitude. However, we can offer some tips. Regarding attitude, if you don't have healthy curiosity, you probably should not be a journalist. If you aren't tenacious and gritty, you aren't going to get what you need for a lot of stories. Getting online can only help you. Pat Stith of the Raleigh (N.C.) *News and Observer* told the Fourth Annual Conference on Computer Assisted Journalism at the National Institute for Advanced Reporting in Indianapolis in 1993, "It (computer assisted journalism) is not cheaper—it's better. Those individuals and organizations that get into it will get ahead, and the others will be left behind."

Right friends: A large amount of success in journalism depends upon nurturing good sources. The online world opens entirely new realms of sources once you are connected. As you tackle each new online area de-

---

Fig. 8-2: Communications programs allow "manual" dialing for access to bulletin board systems and other online services.

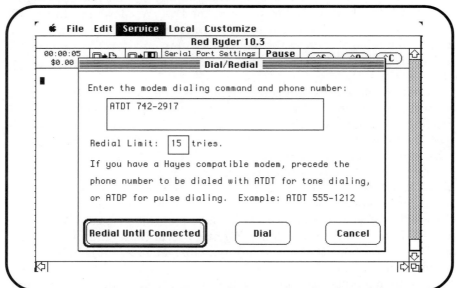

scribed in this book, you would do well to have a friend you can rely on to help you over the tough spots. Earlier we suggested the computer store people. Most towns of any consequence also have some kind of computer club or another. The members could be a great resource. Colleges tend to be computer intensive and they have myriads of students, graduate students, and professors with computing expertise. High schools sometimes have computer clubs, and their student leaders are often eager to share with others the joys of computing.

Making Your First Connections

Armed with local telephone numbers and all the hardware and software you need, you're ready to practice going online, moving around in cyberspace, and taking the pulse of virtual communities. Your first step is to launch your communications software program and to learn your way around it. You start a call to a bulletin board from within your communications program. Usually you have two ways to do this: automated or manual. Most programs permit you to build a directory of places you call frequently. In Red Ryder, you compile "Phone Books," and in ProComm you keep "Dialing Directories." The directory stores such information as bulletin board names, telephone numbers, terminal emulation required (if any), and communications protocol parameters (see Figure 8-1).

Fig. 8-3: Welcome screens at most bulletin boards will seek the identity of the caller by asking for your name. If the name matches an existing user list, the caller is asked for a password. If name and password don't match, the caller is usually asked to register.

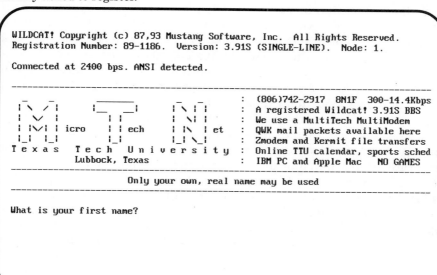

```
                        MicroTechNet BULLETINS

     1 - About MicroTechNet           9 - What's new in Wildcat! 3.90 (long)
     2 - Tips for using MicroTechNet  10 - To those with ACS VAX accounts
     3 -                              11 - How to use QWK mail packets
     4 - How do I download files?     12 - About the Discussion Conference
     5 - "What is a .ZIP/.SEA/... file?"  13 - What is "ShareWare"?
     6 - Not enough time to download? 14 -
     7 - "An Introduction to BBSs"    15 -
     8 - Repeat of "New User" Message 16 - Results of user poll (if any)

     17 - ATLC hours and phone numbers; TTU computer phone numbers
     18 - BBSs in the Lubbock area (from "Kaptain's Korner BBS", 762-5536)
     19 - TTU Campus Events Calendar (Thanks, D.S.!)

     TEXAS TECH UNIVERSITY ATHLETIC SCHEDULES
     20 - Football      22 - Men's Basketball      24 - Baseball
     21 - Volleyball    23 - Women's Basketball    25 - Others

     Bulletins updated: 1, 2, 3, 4, 5, 6, 7, 8, 9, 10, 11, 12, 13, 15, 16, 17, 18
     19, 20, 23
     Enter bulletin # [1..25], [R]elist menu, [N]ew, [ENTER] to quit? [  ]
```

Fig. 8-4: The Bulletin Menu of this BBS offers several explanatory options for new users. Calendar items for the board's community are also offered.

Your parameters should be set before you start the dialing process. A "safe" set of parameters for most bulletin boards includes a baud rate of 2,400 and either N-8-1 or E-7-1 for the data structure. What those labels mean is parity-data bits-stop bits. Thus N-8-1 means no parity, 8 data bits, and 1 stop bit. Many bulletin boards today can handle faster baud rates, but the faster modems can also talk to slower ones. As for the data structure parameters, the overwhelming majority of BBS systems run either N-8-1 or E-7-1. If you enter this information into your directory, you merely have to "point" at the bulletin board you want to call or select it with your cursor keys. You will launch a session with the selected BBS by double clicking on it or by pressing Enter when it is selected.

The second way to launch a dial-up connection is manually (see Figure 8-2). Your communications program assumes default parameters for baud rate, parity, data bits and stop bits. You can make changes as necessary. In Red Ryder, you adjust serial port settings (Apple-command U), and in ProComm, you adjust parameters (Alt-P). If all those things are set to the proper rate, you will have some procedure in your program to "open connection" or to "launch session." From this place in the program— sometimes called terminal mode—you will type modem commands. In Hayes-compatible language you would type:

ATDT 1-216-381-3320<CR>

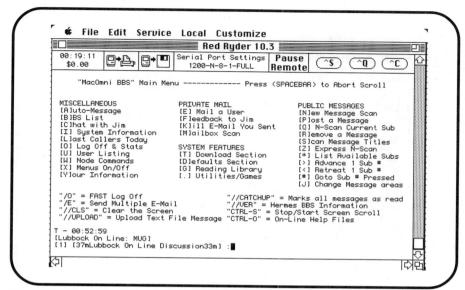

```
   🍎  File  Edit  Service  Local  Customize

========================= Red Ryder 10.3 =========================
00:19:11   🖥️▶🖨️  🖥️▶📀   Serial Port Settings  Pause    ⌒S   ⌒Q   ⌒C
$0.00                       1200-N-8-1-FULL       Remote

    "MacOmni BBS" Main Menu ------------- Press <SPACEBAR> to Abort Scroll


  MISCELLANEOUS             PRIVATE MAIL             PUBLIC MESSAGES
  [A]uto-Message            [E] Mail a User          [N]ew Message Scan
  [B]BS List                [F]eedback to Jim        [P]ost a Message
  [C]hat with Jim           [K]ill E-Mail You Sent   [Q] N-Scan Current Sub
  [I] System Information    [M]ailbox Scan           [R]emove a Message
  [L]ast Callers Today                               [S]can Message Titles
  [O] Log Off & Stats       SYSTEM FEATURES          [Z] Express N-Scan
  [U] User Listing          [T] Download Section     [*] List Available Subs
  [W] Node Commands         [D]efaults Section       [>] Advance 1 Sub #
  [X] Menus On/Off          [G] Reading Library      [<] Retreat 1 Sub #
  [Y]our Information        [.] Utilities/Games       [#] Goto Sub # Pressed
                                                      [J] Change Message areas

  "/O" = FAST Log Off                  "//CATCHUP" = Marks all messages as read
  "/E" = Send Multiple E-Mail          "//VER" = Hermes BBS Information
  "//CLS" = Clear the Screen           "CTRL-S" = Stop/Start Screen Scroll
  "//UPLOAD" = Upload Text File Message "CTRL-O" = On-Line Help Files

  T - 00:52:59
  [Lubbock On Line: MUG]
  [1] [37mLubbock On Line Discussion33m] :█
```

Fig. 8-5: Main Menu of the MacOmni BBS is typical of most solo bulletin boards. You are given choices that will take you to other parts of the system, such as the file download, message, and other sections.

"AT" tells the modem to wake up and stand at attention; "DT" means dial (D); using touch tone (T). A space follows, then the phone number followed by a carriage return (<CR> means you press the Return or Enter key on your keyboard). Some low-end communications programs may not like having all the hyphens in the telephone number. If you are manually launching communications sessions and having trouble, drop the hyphens. If you called the number we have just given, you would connect to the PC-OHIO bulletin board in Cleveland, listed frequently by *Boardwatch Magazine* as one of the top BBS systems in the nation.

If your screen fills with unintelligible garble instead of recognizable text, you should experiment with your communication parameters and perhaps your transmission speed. For example, if your parameters were set at N-8-1 and you got garble, hang up. Reset to E-7-1. If that doesn't work, set your transmission speed to 1,200 or 2,400 bps and try each set again.

It is generally easier to launch communication sessions from a dialing directory where you have prerecorded the names and phone numbers of those bulletin boards you like to visit. It's faster, it's less mistake-prone, and the directory (phone book) method also allows you to store scripts with your phone numbers so that your communications program will automatically log on for you.

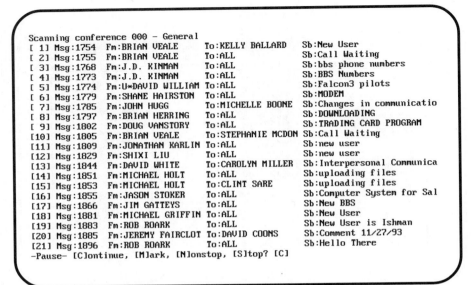

```
Scanning conference 000 - General
[ 1] Msg:1754  Fm:BRIAN VEALE        To:KELLY BALLARD     Sb:New User
[ 2] Msg:1755  Fm:BRIAN VEALE        To:ALL               Sb:Call Waiting
[ 3] Msg:1768  Fm:J.D. KINMAN        To:ALL               Sb:bbs phone numbers
[ 4] Msg:1773  Fm:J.D. KINMAN        To:ALL               Sb:BBS Numbers
[ 5] Msg:1774  Fm:U*DAVID WILLIAM    To:ALL               Sb:Falcon3 pilots
[ 6] Msg:1779  Fm:SHANE HAIRSTON     To:ALL               Sb:MODEM
[ 7] Msg:1785  Fm:JOHN HUGG          To:MICHELLE BOONE    Sb:Changes in communicatio
[ 8] Msg:1797  Fm:BRIAN HERRING      To:ALL               Sb:DOWNLOADING
[ 9] Msg:1802  Fm:DOUG VANSTORY      To:ALL               Sb:TRADING CARD PROGRAM
[10] Msg:1805  Fm:BRIAN VEALE        To:STEPHANIE MCDON   Sb:Call Waiting
[11] Msg:1809  Fm:JONATHAN KARLIN    To:ALL               Sb:new user
[12] Msg:1829  Fm:SHIXI LIU          To:ALL               Sb:new user
[13] Msg:1844  Fm:DAVID WHITE        To:CAROLYN MILLER    Sb:Interpersonal Communica
[14] Msg:1851  Fm:MICHAEL HOLT       To:ALL               Sb:uploading files
[15] Msg:1853  Fm:MICHAEL HOLT       To:CLINT SARE        Sb:uploading files
[16] Msg:1855  Fm:JASON STOKER       To:ALL               Sb:Computer System for Sal
[17] Msg:1866  Fm:JIM GATTEYS        To:ALL               Sb:New BBS
[18] Msg:1881  Fm:MICHAEL GRIFFIN    To:ALL               Sb:New User
[19] Msg:1883  Fm:ROB ROARK          To:ALL               Sb:New User is Ishman
[20] Msg:1885  Fm:JEREMY FAIRCLOT    To:DAVID COONS       Sb:Comment 11/27/93
[21] Msg:1896  Fm:ROB ROARK          To:ALL               Sb:Hello There
-Pause- [C]ontinue, [M]ark, [N]onstop, [S]top? [C]
```

Fig. 8-6: Scanning messages from the Message Menu produces a directory of messages on the bulletin board. By reading the subject entries, the dates, and the parties of the messages, you can choose which you want to read.

An Online Session

When you first connect to a local bulletin board, the computer you access usually opens with a short welcome screen spelling out some of the rules governing use of the BBS. Sometimes you get nothing on-screen until you press the Enter key a few times. After your host BBS welcomes you, it begins a login process by asking you for your name (Figure 8-3). After you type in your name, the BBS computer checks its data base for registered users. If the computer recognizes your name, it requests a password. If your name is not on the list of registered users, a public BBS will give you a brief welcome message and invite you to register. A private BBS may give you a second and even third chance to log in before disconnecting you. Figure 8-3 shows the greeting screen for visitors to MicroTechNet (aka MTN) in Lubbock, Texas. It specifies use of real names only and announces that the board carries no games. If you go through the process of registering, you are asked to answer several questions about your computer, your home address and phone, and, sometimes, your age and employment. Generally, only fully registered people have full access to the BBS.

When you have completed the name identification/registration stage, you are taken to a menu of choices, generally a message or bulletin menu or a main menu for the BBS. New users and visitors to bulletin boards often receive a series of bulletins designed to explain the board and how it works. Figure 8-4 shows the MicroTechNet Bulletins menu. Bulletins are numbered 1-25, and you bring a bulletin to your computer by typing the number of the bulletin followed by a carriage return (pressing the Enter or Return key). The bottom line asks you to enter the number of the bulletin you'd like to read. If you type "R," the menu will be redisplayed. The BBS computer keeps a log of your visits, so if you type "N" at the Bulletin screen, you will get a display of all new bulletins. Pressing the Enter key without giving any other direction tells the BBS to clear the screen and take you to the Main menu (Figure 8-5). The Main menu of most BBS systems offers options of reading and posting messages, joining conferences, and going to the file area where you can download (retrieve to your computer) or upload (send from your computer) files.

At the message menu, your choices typically include reading and posting messages, returning to the Main menu (or other menus), killing messages addressed to you, and scanning all messages not posted privately to others. A scan produces a list of messages posted, each with a one-line description of the message, who sent it, to whom it was addressed, the topic of the message, and the message's number on the bulletin board. Figure 8-6 shows a typical scan from MicroTechNet. By reading the subject entries (right column), the dates, and the names of the parties in the messages, you can decide whether you want to read any messages posted to the list. When you post a message to a list, you should specify whether it is private or available to the public.

File Actions: Capture, Download, and Upload

The Files section of a bulletin board has as its primary purpose making space available for the sharing of software, graphics, program files, spreadsheet templates, and text documents. A BBS File menu has as its choices uploading (sending files from your computer to the bulletin board), downloading (receiving files from the BBS to your computer), or listing available files. If you choose either to download or to upload, the BBS software prompts you to select a communications protocol and to provide the name(s) of the file(s) you want to transfer.

Popular file transfer protocols include ASCII, Kermit, X-modem, Y-modem, and Z-modem. ASCII is used for files that contain only text characters—the kind you find on a manual typewriter keyboard. All other protocols may also be used to transfer text files but are designed for moving files containing program code. Program code may include formatting instructions in a word processor document, digitized graphics, or programming instructions for the computer. Kermit is one of the oldest protocols allowing personal computers to talk to larger mainframes. It is not the easiest to use. X-modem is an old standby. It moves data in small chunks and checks for errors along the way as the sending computer and receiving computer "compare notes" on the data moved.

While X-modem may move only one file at a time, both Y-modem and Z-modem have batch capabilities. That is, you can give the computer a list of files to send or receive at the outset, and the process continues unattended until the entire list is transferred. Y-modem moves files in bigger chunks than X-modem and is somewhat more efficient. Z-modem has the added feature of automated file transfer. If you have told the sending computer that you want to use Z-modem, the process starts automatically when you are done naming the files you want. With other file transfer protocols you have to go through a number of steps to actually start the transfer.

If the files you ask for would take longer than the time you are allotted on the bulletin board, you will receive a message similar to the one near the top of Figure 8-9. In this session, we asked for four files to be downloaded in a Y-modem batch routine. We were told that the fourth file would force us beyond the time limit we had allotted to us. Therefore, we downloaded only three files in the batch.

Many files are stored in a compressed format on bulletin board computers. The files are "packed" or "archived" using compression software. The files take less space on the BBS computer and also take less time to download or upload. In exchange for this convenience you must "unzip," or "unarchive," the file on your computer. You can tell whether a file is archived by the extension on the file name. Files are listed typically in the filename.ext format where the extension (ext) is generally three or fewer characters following the dot (period) after the main file name. If, for example, you download a file named "bbslist.zip," you know that it is archived and needs to be unzipped on a PC using the program PKUNZIP. Table 6-1 lists common file extensions and the environments with which they are associated.

Logging Sessions and Dumping Screens

One software trick to master before you get online long distance is that of "capturing" or "logging" or "saving" an online session. Many communications software packages allow you to save to a file all the text that passes your screen. In Red Ryder, "Capture Incoming Data To TEXT File" is the first item on the File menu (keyboard shortcut Apple-R). If you are using ProComm software or one of its clones, you can open a log file by pressing Alt-F1. (If you use the pull-down menus, it is "Toggle" a log file under the File menu.) Capturing text files or logging a session has many uses. It can be used much as a tape recorder is used to capture the precise wording of quotes during meetings and interviews. Logging a session is sometimes the easiest way to capture the information that passes your screen. A great advantage of session logging over tape recorders is that you finish with the text already in a computer file. As you are typing your story, you have no need to re-keyboard those choice quotes. You simply mark the quotes in your session file then copy the text to the file containing the story you are writing.

Related to session capturing is a process called doing "screen dumps." Assume for a moment you are just browsing through files and messages posted somewhere on the net and you happen onto some very useful information. You didn't have your session logging turned on when the "great stuff" hits your screen. But there it sits, staring at you. You could quickly take some notes or you could dump the screen to a capture file. On a Macintosh, you do this by holding down the "Shift" and "Apple" keys and pressing the "3" key. If you are using Windows, you accomplish the same end by holding down the "Alt" key and pressing the "Print Screen" key.

In the Mac environment, the result is that a picture of your Mac screen is dumped to a MacPaint file. The first file is placed on your desktop as "Screen 0," the second as "Screen 1," and so forth. (Some operating systems may save the files as "Picture 1.") These are graphic images and cannot be imported as text to the file you may be working on at the moment. If you prefer text, you can select text on your screen (by dragging your mouse over the text, for example), then through the Edit menu functions of copying and pasting, you can move text into the document you are presently composing.

In the Windows environment, you have the same options and problems. However, all screen dumps in Windows go to the clipboard. Every time you dump a screen to the clipboard, the screen image replaces whatever was previously on the clipboard. Therefore, to save what is on the clipboard, you need to go into another program (word processor, graphics program) and paste the clipboard image to a file. If it's text you want to save, it is better to highlight the text in question and copy it to your word processor, which you can have running in a window separate from the communications program. Stand-alone utilities as well as utilities that are part of other programs will capture Windows screens and write them to files. The Hijaak graphics conversion program has such a utility. Corel Draw is a suite of graphics programs that includes Corel Capture.

In the DOS environment, there are dozens of screen dump utilities, such as "SnapShot," that will capture text images, one right after another, and store them to files with a name you have designated. Subsequent dumps in SnapShot are numbered sequentially: 01, 02, and so forth. ProComm and other DOS-based communications programs have built-in text dump utilities. Other DOS-based utilities such as Inset, DOS Cap, and Frieze will capture graphic images of the DOS screen.

Bulletin Board Pricing

Many BBS systems operate free of charge. Others charge fees by the month, the year, the hour, or some combination of pricing schemes. Some ask for voluntary contributions. The Windmill Company in Lubbock, Texas, for example, charges $35 per year. Your membership on the Windmill BBS includes with it some limited Internet access. Membership on the Agape BBS is free. If you want Internet mail access from Agape, you pay by the message. Some local bulletin boards are linked to others in separate networks of bulletin boards. The oldest of these is FidoNet. Others include ILink, VBBSnet, WWIV, and RAnet. These "extended" bulletin boards allow people logged in to exchange messages with other people in geographically distant communities who are logged into their local board which is part of the Net. Some allow local BBS members to join conferences that include people from other geographic locations. Some provide at least e-mail access to the Internet. In Lubbock (a town of 187,000 people), there are 61 BBS systems enumerated on a frequently posted list of BBSes. Five of those list subscription fees, and three are private. More than a dozen indicate some type of affiliation with larger networks.

Each board develops its own personality, dictated largely by the sysop and, in part, by the members who sign on. Sometimes a board's name gives clues to the board's contents. Some boast of the thousands of software files they have available for download. Others tend to gather people interested in a particular issue or hobby. Some specialize in role-playing games. One gathers people of a particular religious persuasion. Another serves as a place where writers "convene" online. Still another bills itself as the center for people involved or interested in health concerns. The variety is as boundless as the human spirit.

The Uses for Journalists

Most local BBS systems will provide journalists little more than another place to meet people and to "talk" with them. National boards, reached through long distance calls, contain files with more hard news value. However, following correspondence on carefully selected local boards can be a way of measuring community pulse on issues. Just be sure you understand what section of the community you are measuring.

The main thrust at this stage of online learning is that you connect to several different BBS systems and explore what they have to offer. Read some of the messages to get the flavor of what each board sees as its mission. Log or capture some sessions; download a file or two. In short, get used to your communications software using local telephone calls. Then, when you must go long distance for a national BBS, you will have more certain footing from which to explore vast new territory.

The Treasures of (Inter)National BBSes

When you move beyond the neighborhood bulletin board to boards of regional and national scope, you attain new levels of information. Major government agencies run bulletin boards. Large non-profit organizations and special interest groups put up boards as a way to disburse their message and to communicate with their various publics. Few of them, however, have 1-800 phone numbers.

One that does is the United States Food and Drug Administration. You reach it by dialing 800-222-0185. Your parameters should be 7-E-1. When you are first connected, you might have to press the Enter key a few times to get the board to respond. This is not unusual. You will then see a menu of available choices from which you select the FDA BBS (choice 1 at this writing). Then press Enter. When you are asked to log in, type "bbs" (lower case) and press Enter. You will then be asked for your name in a typical BBS fashion. If your name is not in the FDA BBS data base, then you are asked if you would like to register. If your name is found, you are asked for a password. Once past all this, you are prompted to enter the topic area for your inquiry. If you don't know the topic area, type the command "topics," to get a list of acceptable topics. You can get help online by asking for it ("help" command), and one of the topics — Manual — retrieves an online user's manual for the FDA BBS. The board is a little difficult to get used to, but if your beat includes topics in which the FDA is involved, your time in learning the system could be worthwhile.

The grand master of all government bulletin boards is FedWorld, accessed by phoning 703-321-8020. FedWorld is an umbrella BBS operated by the National Technical Information Service (NTIS) under the U.S. Commerce Department. Through the FedWorld BBS, journalists have access not only to NTIS documents and data bases but also to dozens of other government agencies through the FedWorld GateWay system. When you choose the GateWay from FedWorld's menu system, you are taken to a menu with screens full of BBS listings.

The BBSes listed cover subjects ranging from agriculture to space exploration and from federal job opportunities to government computer systems security. The FedWorld system is described in Chapter 6.

Alternative Connections, Other Numbers

In some cases, agencies accessed through the FedWorld GateWay are also available directly. ALF, the National Agricultural Library's Forum is available at 301-504-5496. The U.S. Commerce Department's Economic Bulletin Board is available at 202-482-3870, and the Justice Department at 301-738-8895. Just as FedWorld is available by Internet Telnet connection, many of the same facilities accessed through FedWorld's GateWay are also available by Internet.

Other dial-up numbers of interest to journalists include:

- Cal Tech's Jet Propulsion Laboratory (818-354-1333), where there are GIF images and text files related to NASA space missions.
- Environmental Protection Agency Clean Up Board (301-589-8366), dedicated to reporting EPA cleanup activity.
- Strictly Business! BBS (614-538-9250) in Columbus, Ohio, which specializes in information for small business people.
- The WELL (415-332-6106) in San Francisco, which is a legendary big board with full Internet access.
- The World (617-739-9753) in Boston, which is another legendary big board with Internet access.

On your local boards watch for conferences and forums for writers. They often discuss matters of interest to journalists. There are forums and conference groups specifically dedicated to journalists on the Internet as well as in the dial-up world. For the dial-up connection for journalists, we need to visit one of the commercial online services.

Free-Nets

Many communities have in them a local "Free-Net." Cleveland, Ohio, was the first. Typically, Free-Nets are locally based networks usually initiated by volunteers with computing interests. Their purpose is manifold, but includes making online information more widely available to residents of their host communities. Local government information, community calendars, and places to chat about what's going on at home are among the fare on Free-Nets. But Free-Nets offer much more.

Foremost, Free-Nets provide their users at least some access to the larger world of networked computing. Behind the Free-Net concept is the mission of making telecommunications resources available to everyone. They are the products of National Public Telecommunication Network. Dialing into a Free-Net is much like dialing into any other BBS. You have a local number, and you gain access to the resources of the host system according to its rules. Free-Nets also have access to and are accessible from the Internet. Many Gopher (Chapter 7) and some Telnet (Chapter 6) sites offer access to Free-Nets.

Internet Relay Chat: Real Time Interaction

Although people on BBSes can be interacting with each other in almost real time, they do not necessarily have the feel of an interactive conversation. When you access a BBS message menu, you see a list of messages, and you choose the messages you want to read and respond to.

```
*** Numeric message: (4) irc.tamu.edu 2.8.14 oiws  biklmnopstv
*** Numeric message: (251) There are 2422 users and 828 invisible on 125
servers
*** Numeric message: (252) 87 operator(s) online
*** Numeric message: (254) 926 channels formed
*** Numeric message: (255) I have 61 clients and 1 servers
*** Numeric message: (375) - irc.tamu.edu Message of the Day -
*** Motd: - ================================================
*** Motd: -
*** Motd: -              Texas A&M Irc Server
*** Motd: -              Local Administration:
*** Motd: -
*** Motd: -       Lightning    jep8376@tamsun.tamu.edu
*** Motd: -       Brand        fubar@andromeda.tamu.edu
*** Motd: -
*** Motd: -       Address local questions/concerns to:
*** Motd: -                    irc@tamu.edu
*** Motd: - ================================================
*** Motd: -                 IRC ops:
*** Motd: -
*** Motd: -       Jazzie       b-epps@tamu.edu
*** Motd: -       dylan        michael@andromeda.tamu.edu
*** Motd: - ================================================
*** Numeric message: (376) End of /MOTD command.
```

Fig. 8-7: The welcome screen and Message of the Day from the IRC client at Texas A&M University. The screen reports the number of users (2,422), the number of active channels (926), operators (87), servers from the site (1), and clients (87).

Live, real time conversation is available elsewhere over the Internet through a service called Internet Relay Chat (IRC). Originally written by Jarkko Oikarinen in Finland in 1988, it has been used in more than sixty countries around the world. It is a multiuser chat system, where people convene on "channels" to talk in groups, publicly or privately. Channels are generally defined by the topics that are being discussed at that moment.

IRC has emerged as an interesting back channel of communication during several major, breaking news stories. In the first few hours following the Northridge earthquake in 1994, IRC was more reliable than telephone communications. During the police freeway pursuit and subsequent arrest of O.J. Simpson, Los Angeles residents, joined by fans and other interested folks, gathered in IRC channels like "#OJ" set up spontaneously to discuss the matter. When other, more traditional means of communication have been blocked or interrupted during the progress of a major news event, IRC has proven to be a viable alternative.

But, you should be aware that Internet Relay Chat is also fraught with many shortcomings. IRC clients are not as widely distributed as some other Internet tools. Conversation can be difficult to follow, especially in active channels when many people are chatting simultaneously. IRC forces

```
*** Signoff: doc
(APNews) Michale Jordan is going to play for Chicago WhiteSox?
*** Change: moo-man has left this Channel
*** Change: m80 has joined this Channel (#earthquake)
*** Change: serra has left this Channel
(APNews) BBC on 15.260mHz.
(Corax) I've been relaying this to several bbs talk channels in the UK. They
say thanks, to all the news guys.
*** Signoff: abb3w
(Taner) APNews:  KhZ
(Corax) *xanaduu* has san bernardino been affected?  i dont know exactly
where it is
(KNBC_News) thanx
(Corax) +in relation to the quake and the damage
*** Change: VisionC has left this Channel
(Newswire) Many victims of the Southern California earthquake may
(Taner) kHz - not MHz
(Newswire) face staggering repair bills since they lack insurance that will
pay
(Newswire) for fixing their homes.
(Newswire)   People will be able to claim fire damage under standard
homeowner
(Newswire) policies, insurance experts said. But many residents will not be
(Newswire) covered if their homes collapsed or had other structural damage
due to
*** Signoff: bmca
(Newswire) the quake.
*** Change: GoldDrake has joined this Channel (#earthquake)
*** Change: hoyt has joined this Channel (#earthquake)
(Newswire)   Even those who bought special earthquake insurance may face
steep
(Newswire) bills, because earthquake insurance policies typically require
(Newswire) customers to cover 5% to 10% of the damage themselves.
(Newswire)   Therefore, a couple with a $150,000 home, and quake insurance,
might
*** Signoff: ScurvyDog
*** Signoff: peacelady
(Newswire) have to pay for the first $15,000 of damage out of their own
pockets.
*** Change: pyd040 is now known as StarHawk
(Newswire)   ''I think there's quite a number of people who don't have the
[1;24r[24;1H[24;1H[1;23r[23;56H
*** Change: ellie has joined this Channel (#earthquake)
*** Change: DeadCupid has joined this Channel (#earthquake)
(Newswire) coverage,'' said Rock Jenkins, a spokesman for State Farm
Insurance,
(Newswire) the biggest provider of homeowners' insurance in California.
(Newswire)   The Insurance Information Institute estimates that 25% of all
```

Fig. 8-8: Text stream from the IRC channel #earthquake on the afternoon of Jan. 17, 1994. Each line of dialog is preceded by the sender's nickname in parenthesis. Channel status changes are preceded by a series of three asterisks.

people to communicate under assumed nicknames, which encourages artificial conversation and use of jargon in addition to complicating the process of verifying information.

Using IRC

Just as the World Wide Web and Web browsing software have captured the public's attention, a few flashy Web-based "chat zones" have helped fuel a Hollywood inspired image of life online. One of these sites may be found at http://www.theglobe.com/chat/chat.qry. However, Web-based chat sites are almost purely entertainment, and the site user does not have the same kind of control over the chat environment that one has with Internet Relay Chat.

When you launch Internet Relay Chat, you are greeted by your site's Message of the Day, which in IRC jargon is abbreviated simply "MOTD." The MOTD usually provides information about the site as well as current IRC traffic throughout the network. Figure 8-7 shows the MOTD at Texas A&M University's IRC client site. You are asked for a nickname or "handle" you want to be known as while you are using IRC. If you have a local client, you can make your nickname permanent so you don't have to fill it in each time.

Once you log onto an IRC client and enter a nickname, you may automatically start on an active channel called #chatzone or you may simply be staring at an inactive screen. All IRC channel names start with the # sign. All IRC commands are initiated with a slash mark. Most of the commands are logical.

To become a part of a chat session, you need to know the name of the channel. You can get a list of the different channels that are in use at that particular moment and the number of people talking on them. You do this by typing the "/list" command.

Don't do this if you are in a hurry. The greeting screen in Figure 8-7 reports 926 active channels. If you enter the "/list" command with no qualifying description, hundreds of channels will scroll past your screen. You can pause the scrolling by typing Ctrl-S and restart the scrolling by typing Ctrl-Q, but you are going to have a long scroll regardless.

Instead, you could do a search for channels on your topic by using a key word and wild card marks. If the topic is "earthquake," you could give the command

/list *quake* <CR>

and hope to turn up the channel. You might try other key word combinations to find a relevant channel.

You join a conversation by issuing the command "/join" followed by #(channel name). When you first join a channel, IRC announces that you have joined to everyone else on the channel and gives you a list of the nicknames of all those currently on the channel.

IRC can support both public and private conversations. When you are participating in a public conversation, everything you write is seen immediately by everybody who is participating on that channel. The action can be fast and furious—and the incoming discussion text randomly mixed—if a lot of people have a lot to say at the same time.

The conversation on most IRC channels is pretty mundane, not the stuff of which news is composed. Several people typically are online getting to know each other. In many ways it is like a party line telephone conversation without the $2 per minute charge and frequently with an international flavor. So, in many cases, while it may be fun for participants, it may not be an important tool for journalists.

But, when a major news story breaks, IRC can be very useful. In the same way that people run to the telephone to spread information about breaking news, some people now log onto IRC to chat. Moreover, the Internet was designed to withstand physical disruptions to any one part of the network and still continue to function. Therefore, even if the long distance telephone network is overburdened with calls or down for some other reason, IRC may still be functioning.

That was the case on January 17, 1994, when the Northridge earthquake hit. The command to join the #earthquake discussion on that day was

/join #earthquake <CR>

One hundred-sixty people were listed as participants in the #earthquake channel. If everyone who had joined #earthquake tried to chat at once, the resulting cacophony would have defeated all human communication processes. Less than a dozen—most affiliated with news organizations—had posting privileges.

As it was, much of the discussion was interrupted by reports of channel traffic—people entering and leaving the channel. Case Study 2 in Chapter 9 discusses "#earthquake" chat from the day of the Northridge quake. The conversation was dominated by "Newswire" reporting on the insurance uncertainties quake victims would be facing. Two or three paragraphs of the Newswire statement were interrupted repeatedly both by channel traffic reporting and by others authorized to use the channel for chat.

Even with fewer than twelve people allowed to chat, the conversation was hard to follow, especially when scores of other folks were drifting in and out of the channel. Still, IRC provided an alternative tool for reporters not on the scene in Los Angeles.

Moreover, during coup attempts and other major political upheavals, government officials may easily take over traditional means of mass communication such as broadcast stations. But it is very difficult to shut down the computer communications infrastructure in an entire country on short notice. During the demonstrations in Beijing in 1989, Chinese officials had no problem pulling the plug on CNN. Information still flowed out of the country via fax machines, however. IRC now can function in much the same way.

IRC Access

As with other Internet services, users of IRC run a client program that connects to a server somewhere in the Internet. IRC is most convenient if you have a local client. To see if you do, type IRC at the system prompt. If you do not have a local client installed, you should try to cajole your systems people to install one. As with most Internet client programs, the software for the client is available in the public domain.

There are several public access sites for IRC, but they tend to be crowded and can be unreliable from time to time. To reach a public access IRC client, you can Telnet to the address. You must include the port number in the Telnet address. If you don't, you will not be able to log onto the remote computer. Here are addresses of some public access clients:

- sci.dixie.edu 6677.
- exuokmas.ecn.uoknor.edu 6677.
- obelix.wu-wien.ac.at 6996.
- irc.tuzvo.sk 6668.
- irc.nsysu.edu.tw 6668.
- tiger.itc.univie.ac.at 6668.

Public access sites allow a very limited number of users. For example, sci.dixie.edu (at the Dixie College Center for Excellence in Southern Utah) will allow only eight users at any one time. Of the systems listed, irc.tuzvo.sk allows the most public access users at any one time—thirty-two—but is not a great site either. It is located in Slovakia; not only is the message of the day in Slovakian, but communication is very slow.

The first two addresses in the list are in the United States. Obelix.wu-wien.ac.at and tiger.itc.unvie.ac.at are in Austria, and irc.nsysu.edu.tw is in Taiwan.

The Potential of MUDs

Another Internet application with potential as a real-time interviewing tool was originally developed as a game program. The Multi-User Dungeon, or MUD, and its variations (MOOs, MUSHes, MUCKs) are role-playing games in which two or more participants in the same "room" together may interact with each other in many ways, including carrying on conversations. MUD software lends itself to interviewing. Here's how MUDs typically work.

When planning to use a MUD you will usually connect via Telnet (Chapter 6). Table 8-1 lists the addresses of a few MUDs available on the Internet using the Telnet protocol.

But, making the connection may be a little trickier than standard Telnet usage. Each Internet application has its own "port" of entry to a computer. The standard port for Gopher, for example, is 70. When an application is supposed to call on that standard port you do not have to include the port number in the URL. The standard Telnet access port is 23. But, because

MUDs are usually located at other ports, you must specify the port number when you open the location in Telnet. For example, to access MIT's MediaMOO from a VMS Telnet client, one might enter the command Telnet purple-crayon.media.mit.edu /port=8888. In other clients, you may specify the port in other ways. QVTNet's Terminal (Telnet) client has a box labeled "port" in which you can specify non-standard ports. In still other packages you might designate the port by simply adding a space and the port number to the end of the address. You should ask your instructor which method is appropriate for your situation.

Participating in a MUD

When you connect to a MediaMOO, the welcome screen provides enough information to get you started. After you log onto a MUD, typically you are taken to a "reception room" where there may be many other people. If others are there, and they are carrying on a conversation, you will see the text of their chatter. This can be confusing at first. Most MUD veterans are friendly and tolerant toward newcomers.

Each MUD will have something of its own personality, and among the various MUDs is a variety of different command dialects. Some commands might have to be preceded by the "@" sign, other require no special formatting. Table 8-2 lists some common MOO commands. You can usually get help in MUDs by typing in the command "help."

Thousands of people from all parts of the globe log onto MUDs to carry on conversations, to work in shared environments, and to play games interactively. When you "join" a MUD, you usually assume a character and, within limits, choose your character traits (text in Figure 8-2 suggests some of the character traits). You then move from place to place in the MUD where you may look around, pick up and take objects with you, buy and sell things, engage in conversation and/or battle (see Figure 8-3 for an encounter between two characters in one MUD). In some role-playing MUDs you may join tribes and unite with other characters inhabiting the MUD.

In practice, each site takes on its own personality. Until recently, all were text-based. More MUDs are becoming accessible through the World Wide Web, and some experiments are already underway with graphically based MUDs. Current information about MUDs may be found in the FAQ document posted regularly to the news group (Chapter 7) rec.games.mud.announce. This will often include a complete listing of MUDs. The newsgroup rec.games.mud.misc also carries active discussions about MUDs. You can also retrieve the FAQ by anonymous ftp (Chapter 6) from ftp.math.okstate.edu:/pub/muds/misc/mud-faq. Key word searches in Veronica (Chapter 4) or any of the World Wide Web search engines (Chapters 3 and 9) will also reveal a wealth of material on MUDs. A Gopher site with help information, FAQs, and links to several MUDs can be found at gopher://actlab.rtf.utexas.edu. Choose item 10, "Virtual Environments." You definitely should read the MUD FAQ before you begin to use MUDs as a reporting tool.

MUD for Journalists

While MUD software was originally conceived in an entertainment environment, many college writing instructors have found MUDs to be helpful teaching tools. In the same way, a journalist who masters MUD software may have at his or her command a powerful interviewing tool. By creating and controlling virtual rooms on MUD servers, the journalist can "close the door" on unwanted visitors and conduct real-time interviews with sources scattered throughout the world. Similarly, press conferences with significant figures could be "attended" via MUD software by reporters from throughout the world.

MUDs, IRC, and Journalism

MUDs and Internet Relay Chat are fun to use. They are methods of communicating with people around the world about topics of interest. By talking to people, journalists can get interesting ideas for stories as well as interesting leads to information.

But you have to keep in mind that, just because someone is computer savvy enough to be participating in a MUD or an IRC channel, does not mean he or she knows anything factual about the focal issue of a news story. Many MUDs and IRC channels are filled with rumors and mistakes, particularly about current affairs. Information gathered there has to be carefully checked out and verified.

The information gathered by using MUDS and IRC is even less trustworthy than that found in news groups. Everyone participating is using a nickname. Being anonymous is part of the fun; it lowers inhibitions and often increases sociability. But once people assume another identity, you have no way to verify whether they are telling you the truth or acting out a role. You should verify the facts elsewhere before reporting information obtained through IRC or MUDs.

Chapter

9

Search Strategies & Case Studies

In May 1996, A ValuJet DC-9 airplane bound for Atlanta plunged into the Florida Everglades shortly after taking off from Miami International Airport. All 110 people died; the bodies of many were never recovered.

Investigations revealed that the Federal Aviation Administration had completed a probe into the operation of this new, discount airline. The investigation had detailed at least 100 problems ranging from poor record keeping to inadequate maintenance inspections. The public also learned that a series of mishaps involving ValuJet planes not been highly publicized because nobody was injured.

The crash intensified the scrutiny into ValuJet. On June 17, under public and governmental pressure, the airline suspended operation. The message for many—ValuJet had been operating in an unsafe fashion, and the FAA had failed in its duty to protect the flying public.

The ValuJet episode shocked millions of people. But, if they had been reading their newspaper, the people of Cleveland should not have been surprised. The Cleveland *Plain Dealer* had published a story in April about ValuJet's safety problems and the FAA's efforts to keep them secret. Beth Marchak, *Plain Dealer* Washington Bureau chief, reported to the Computer Assisted Research & Reporting List (CARR-L) that the story could not have been published without extensive use of computer-based tools and information.

Using a computer data base, problems could be tracked plane by plane. A computerized registration list allowed reporters to identify who owned and leased which planes. A key pilot was located via a computerized list of pilots. Though standard telephone directory assistance operators could not locate his telephone number, it was found on a computerized data base of telephone numbers. The FAA's Web pages provided information that helped journalists determine the regulations involved in the agency's investigation of ValuJet. Finally, reporters gleaned key data from ValuJet's Web page, which contained the company's annual report and other details.

The net result—the story asserted that ValuJet was using inexperienced pilots and improperly trained flight attendants. Moreover, there were serious maintenance problems that had been kept quiet following an engine failure which had taken place the previous year, injuring a flight attendant. Readers in Cleveland, and others who read newspapers that receive the Newhouse News Service (which circulated the story), knew about the problems of ValuJet a month before the tragic crash. The ValuJet episode reflects the dynamic application of computer-based technology to reporting. Without the computer-mediated tools, the *Plain Dealer* reporters working on the story would have faced a much more difficult time accessing the information they needed. As Marchak reported, in pursuing the story she had talked to several very pleasant public affairs officials. They just would not tell her much about the details she wanted to know.

New online tools will change the practice of journalism. But, the more things change, the more they will remain the same. The essence of contemporary journalism—collecting information about events, people, and trends; placing that information within an appropriate context, then crafting an accurate and interesting story—should remain constant. However, as the sources for information multiply and the channels through which reporters can communicate with people grow, the potential contexts within which information can be understood will increase and journalists will have to work smarter and more efficiently to successfully prepare their stories.

This chapter will:

- suggest an overall strategy for using computer-based network tools to strengthen reporting.
- provide suggestions how to apply a sample of Internet tools to each part of the reporting process.
- offer some case studies in which network tools were used.
- close with some words of caution about online reporting.

The Reporting Process

Good reporters learn how to develop research strategies that will produce thorough, accurate information. They learn to dig, poke, prod and peruse and to pore over documents in courthouses, libraries, and other repositories. They learn to ask tough questions in interviews, to play one source of information against another, to do whatever it takes to shed light on the issue under examination.

But, they don't do so blindly. The best reporters relentlessly and systematically gather information.

The process of reporting a story can be broken into five steps. Every story starts with an **idea**. A reporter, an editor, a source or a reader has an idea that the public should be informed about a particular topic or issue. For example, Ralph Nader felt the American people should know about the safety performance of the General Motors Corvair. The result was his book, *Unsafe at Any Speed*, which placed automotive safety on the public agenda. Rachel Carson was concerned about the impact of DDT on the environment. *Silent Spring* and the contemporary environmental movement were the offspring of that concern.

The next step is **preliminary research**. Has the story already been written? Is the story worth pursuing and why? The preliminary research has several objectives. You want to identify potential sources of information, including experts and documentary records. And, you need to get an idea which people might already know about your topic and to get a sense of what they might not know but should. The preliminary research will also help you place the current aspects of your topic within the appropriate historical context and sequence of events.

The third step in the reporting process, particularly for enterprise reporting, is **self-education**. This process usually involves locating and studying books, articles, documents and reports—or sections of those types of publications—that have not yet received widespread publicity. To be effective news gatherers, reporters must fully understand the forces at play in the story.

For example, many topic areas have specialized vocabularies. Your self-education will allow you to learn the language you need to know to understand the area about which you are reporting. If you are a business reporter, you may need to understand terms such as "return on investment," "cash flow," and "amortization." If you don't, you will not be able to accurately report what is happening.

By doing homework, you will be able to formulate insightful questions for the people whom you will eventually interview. You will also be able to evaluate the information you receive via interviews. You will know who is not well informed, who is describing only part of the picture, and who you should trust.

Interviewing people is the fourth part of the process. By-and-large, journalists report on the activities of people. And, the heart of any news story is just that—a story. Telling stories generally requires reporters to communicate with people involved with the story directly to elicit the most appropriate, interesting information for the article.

Interviews—or interview-style exchanges—can take place in many different formats. The most information-rich setting for interviews is when the reporter can talk to the source privately, in person, and one-on-one. But, reporters also interview people at press conferences: via the telephone; by submitting questions via fax or e-mail; or by using video- or computer-based conferencing.

The final step in the reporting process is **checking the accuracy** of information. If reporters have questions about facts, they look for additional sources to verify or contradict the information they have. Some-times, they will check back with a source to be sure they correctly under-stood what they were told or what they read.

The five steps in the reporting process are not linear. Although jour-nalists may start with one idea for a story, as information is gathered the focus can change. In the mid-1980s, James Steele and Donald Barlett of *The Philadelphia Inquirer* wanted to learn what happened to people laid off from factory jobs. The finished project was an award-winning series about the policies that led to a growing gap between the rich and the poor in the United States during the presidency of Ronald Reagan.

As you gather information, you have to be ready to pursue new leads, you have to be ready to return to do more research, and you have to be prepared to talk to more people. During the Watergate investigation, law-yers from the special prosecutor's office, through an offhand question to a mid-ranking official, learned that President Richard Nixon had taped ev-ery conversation in the White House. His answer led to the information that eventually resulted in Nixon's resignation. Good reporters complete many iterations of those steps before they consider the story complete.

Of course, not every assignment requires the same kind of reporting. Many routine or ongoing stories do not require a reporter to read clips or access obscure documents. But, even stories for which reporters rely on a single source and stories that they already know quite a bit about can sometimes be improved through better reporting practices.

Online Tools and Reporting

Many journalists believe that conscientious reporting is the soul of good journalism. In the future, the methods reporters use to collect information will be one of the ways to distinguish journalists from other types of infor-mation professionals. Consequently, the ways in which you use the Internet and other electronic resources in reporting is very significant. Computer-based networks can help you in every aspect of reporting.

Perhaps the most important aspect of interesting journalism and the aspect most difficult to teach is generating good story ideas. Routine sto-ries are just that—routine. The best journalism takes place when report-ers pursue angles and leads that others have ignored. Typically, reporters get story ideas from the sources on their beat, from public relations pro-fessionals, friends, and elsewhere. Another avenue for generating ideas is reading about events elsewhere then finding a local angle for them.

While nobody can afford to subscribe to every newspaper or magazine in the world—or has the time to read them—the Internet allows reporters easy access to magazines, journals and publications that were hard to find or costly to receive in the past. In politics, for example, *Slate* magazine at

Fig. 9-1: The I/Spy Internet News Search tool (http://www.oneworld.net/ispy/) permits a meta-search of multiple news archives.

http://www.slate.com/ was the first magazine of political opinion to be initially launched on the Web. In addition to its own slant on events, *Slate* provides round-ups and digests of material that has appeared in other publications. Along the same lines, many national political reporters have long relied on the *National Journal* for inside information about the U.S. federal government. The *National Journal* has joined with ABC, *Newsweek*, the *Los Angeles Times*, and *The Washington Post* to form the Web site *PoliticsNow* at http://www.politicsnow.com/.

Research Tools

In an electronic version of a traditional activity, some companies have established services which send news items and press releases to reporters and editors. For example, Quadnet at http://www.vyne.com/ qnetwww/ carries science and technology, medical, environment, economics, business, and education news from universities, laboratories, technical centers, and professional societies. All material released by the agency is based on news developments and contains information not previously published in the general press. PR Newswire at http://

www.prnewswire.com/ distributes company press releases and information for both the media and investors. PR Newswire also owns Profnet, a service that connects journalists with academic experts from member colleges and universities. Profnet is accessed at http://www.vyne.com/profnet/. EurekaAlert, a news release service for science and health writers, is located at http://www.eurekalert.org/.

There are also several online sources for conducting preliminary research. Traditionally, for newspaper reporters, research has meant a trip to the clip morgue. In the case of reporters working for large media outlets, preliminary research consists of searching the Lexis-Nexis data base, a comprehensive, commercial online data base of news articles. For an overview of Lexis-Nexis visit http://www.lexis-nexis.com. Students connected to libraries which are part of the CARL system (see Chapter 6) may wish to look for the National News Index. The National News Index uses key word searches to locate articles published since 1989 in five newspapers, including *The Washington Post*, *The New York Times*, and *The Wall Street Journal*. The school library, however, must subscribe to the index.

Enterprising reporters typically conduct more extensive research simply by reviewing old newspaper clips. Newspaper articles are still the best place to begin preliminary research. While Lexis-Nexis and the National Newspaper Index provide extensive archives, more limited newspaper archives are available via the Web at the Reporter's Internet Guide, http://www.cfci.com/rig. You can conduct a meta-search of news archives at the I/Spy Internet News Search site at http://www.oneworld.net/ispy/ (Figure 9-1).

Search Engines

The World Wide Web and Gopher offer the best Internet resources for self-education once you have completed your preliminary research. There are several different methods for locating more in-depth information on the Web. The most obvious is to enter specific key words into several search engines. As noted in Chapter 4, among the most popular search engines are AltaVista (http://altavista.digital.com/), Infoseek (http://www.infoseek.com/), Lycos (http://www.lycos.com/), and Webcrawler (http://webcrawler.com/). There are "meta-engines" that search and combine the results from different individual search engines, such as Inktomi (http://inktomi.berkeley.edu/). For access to many search engines via one site, you can access http://www.search.com/ or http://pacific.discover.net/~dansyr/engines.html. You might also try one of the CUSI sites for a meta-search that gives options for finding documents, people, software, dictionaries, and more. One CUSI site is accessible at http://pubweb.nexor.co.uk/public/cusi/cusi.html.

Search engines, however, are blunt instruments. Often they will return a small subset of thousands of Web pages that contain your selected key words. While simple searches may lead you to the necessary information, you may find yourself reviewing many Web sites without locating what you need. To work more efficiently, you may want to take the time to learn how to use advanced searching techniques. Different search engines have different rules for advanced searches. For example, AltaVista offers an advanced search form in which you can indicate which key words are most significant and whether you can use the terms "and," "or," "not," "near," and "not" to help narrow your search. (This is known as a "Boolean search.") You can also use parenthesis and quotation marks to group phrases. In many cases, the best strategy is to learn the advanced techniques of two or three meta-search engines that each conduct the same simple searches on as many as twenty different search engines.

Virtual Libraries

As an alternative to using search engines for the self-education process, you may want to stop in at a "virtual library" related to the topic you are exploring. Virtual libraries are Web pages in which experts in the field have collected a wide range of related Internet resources. For example, there is a collection of international data bases concerning education at the Virtual Library-Education Databases at http://www.csu.edu.au/education/data base.html.

In addition to virtual libraries, there are many other information hubs. For example, an excellent starting point for social science statistics compiled by the United States government can be found at the White House's Social Science Briefing Room at http://www.whitehouse.gov/fsbr/ssbr.html. Economic statistics can be found at the Economics Briefing Room at http://www.whitehouse.gov/fsbr/esbr.html. A starting point for U.S. Congressional legislative information is http://thomas.loc.gov. The service is operated by the Library of Congress. An effective way to locate good starting points is to monitor relevant electronic mailing lists and Usenet news groups. You can also post a query to the lists or news groups when appropriate.

Finding People

The next step of your reporting journey is to identify human sources to interview. In many cases, you will find the names of people on the relevant Web pages you found. Many scientists and academics have created

Fig. 9-2: The FACSNET service for journalists (at http://www.facsnet.org/) contains an experts data base, background materials, Internet links, and several search tools.

personal Web pages describing their work and providing contact information. For example, a reporter was doing a story about research being conducted at a U.S. Army laboratory in New Hampshire. The work of most of the principal researchers and their contact information was posted on the laboratory's Web site, allowing the reporter to completely bypass the public information office. Larger agencies will sometimes allow access to a subset of their staff directories via the Web. Reviewing relevant Web sites is an outstanding way to identify sources who may be knowledgeable about your topic.

A second method for locating human sources is subscription to electronic mailing lists and Usenet news groups. People who post to these forums often include their contact information in what is called a signature file that is automatically attached to the end of their messages. The challenge is to identify lists and news groups that are discussing issues of interest to you. Use InReference at http://www.reference.com to search the archives of more than 16,000 Usenet news groups and approximately 1,000 publically-accessible electronic mailing lists. Another directory of electronic mailing lists and news groups is available at http://tile.net.

Although news groups and mailing lists present intriguing methods for reporters widening their circle of contacts, reporters have to be very careful about the way they use sources identified via news groups and mailing lists. Just because someone participates in a news group, he or she may not be a valid source for quotes about your topic. News group and mailing list participants may simply not be credible sources. Moreover, many participants in news groups and mailing lists may not wish to talk to reporters. They partake in these discussions for their own reasons and may not wish to have their views recorded in a different medium or public forum. If you contact them, they may refuse to be interviewed or to correspond electronically with you.

A third method of locating people to interview is through services such as Profnet, and FACSNET (Figure 9-2). Profnet is a service established by public information officers from colleges and universities across the United States. A reporter can send an e-mail message to a central location requesting an expert on a topic and Profnet responds with a relevant list. You can find out more about Profnet at http://www.vyne.com/profnet/. FACSNET's directory of news sources can be found under "Sources Online" at http://www.facsnet.org/. It is available to registered journalists.

After a story is written, diligent reporters and editors usually check the accuracy of the information to be published. E-mail is a convenient and efficient way to verify quotes. Obscure facts, such as court citations, can often be found via the Web.

In addition to the specific resources which can be applied to the reporting process, there are several other handy tools for journalists online. For example, there are several large data bases of telephone numbers, addresses, and e-mail addresses at places such as Switchboard (http://www.switchboard.com), the OKRA Database at http://okra.ucr.edu/okra and Ph Gateway at http://flaker.ncsa.uiuc.edu:8080.

Reference Sources

Once you have begun the writing process you may wish to use an electronic version of the *Oxford English Dictionary* at http://arts.uwaterloo.ca/ENGL/courses/engl210E/210e/assigns/2/html/kmoffat/sec _28.htm. *Barlett's Guide to Familiar Quotations* is available at http://www.columbia.edu/acis/bartleby/bartlett and Strunk and White's *The Elements of Style* is located at http://www.columbia.edu/acis/bartleby/strunk/. Finally, *Roget's Thesaurus* is at http://www.hti.umich.edu/dict/thes/. Because these sites have online searching mechanisms, they may be more convenient to use than their print equivalents.

This is just a small sample of online resources that can be directly applied to each step in the reporting and writing process. As you begin to work online, you can easily save your own set of favorite online resources found on the Web by saving them as bookmarks.

Case Studies

No matter how much potential the Internet and its online resources hold for journalism, the key is in their application. If the tools are inconvenient or hard to use, journalists and students working under deadline pressure simply will fall back to the methods with which they are most comfortable and familiar. The following section will provide three case studies in which three writers used online tools in reporting projects. In the first, Elliot King describes a project for the magazine he edits, *Scientific Computing & Automation* (SCA). In the second, Randy Reddick describes use of several Internet tools for developing stories on breaking news. In the final case, Mike Meiners provides several brief examples.

Case 1: The Emerging Bioinformatics Discipline

SCA is a monthly magazine with a readership of 72,000 which covers the use of new technology in scientific and engineering applications. In addition to King, there is only one other editor. Neither editor has a steady beat or ongoing contacts within a set universe of sources. In most cases, when an editor wishes to pursue a longer story, he may have only one or two leads with which to start.

Because *SCA* is a specialized magazine, what has been reported in the popular press is usually not of much help in developing new stories. Trends and developments are often reported in *Scientific Computing & Automation* months before they reach the general press. Furthermore, *SCA*'s readers demand a much greater level of detail than would be sufficient for a general reader.

Within these parameters, online tools have enabled the editors of *Scientific Computing & Automation* to pursue stories which they simply could not have pursued in the past. It has extended both the reach and the depth of the magazine.

Bioinformatics is a new scientific discipline still in what Jean Ward and Kathleen Hansen (in *Search Strategies in Mass Communication*) call the "discipline pioneering stage." As new computer-based automated processes are introduced in science to generate data, new methods have to be developed to process, store, retrieve, and analyze the data. In the scientific world, the term "informatics" has begun to be used to describe the merger of information science techniques with techniques in other scientific areas. The most common uses of the term are "bioinformatics" and "medical informatics," but there have also been references to "chemical informatics." And, sometimes, the term "informatics" is used standing alone.

In the spring of 1996, I decided to take an in-depth look at the state of the field. After I decided to tackle the project, I had to face certain constraints. First, I personally didn't know anyone associated with informatics. Second, I didn't know if there were any professional or research journals in the field and I did not have any articles in which the topic had been discussed. If I had not had access to online tools, I would not have had a starting point.

Grant Data Base Identifies Experts

My first step was a search of the CRISP data base at the National Institutes of Health. The CRISP data base is a Gopher service that provides a list of all the grants issued by the NIH to researchers for the past decade or so. Reporters can use a key word search using the name and addresses of the researchers and the duration and amount of the grant to access an abstract of the work. Although CRISP is a Gopher service, it is accessible via the NIH Web site at http://www.nih.gov/grants/.

The CRISP data base search returned several promising leads. It listed a grant for which Harold "Skip" Garner, of the University of Texas Southwestern Medical Center was identified as the principal investigator on a Human Genome Project informatics application. I had once talked to Skip Garner in reference to an earlier story I had written about lab automation, but Garner had left that post years before.

The CRISP search also turned up the name James Brinkley at the University of Washington. Brinkley was involved with an informatics problem associated with the Human Brain Project, an initiative about which I had never heard.

Finding Relevant Articles on the Net

While the CRISP search turned up some good leads, I still wanted to widen my net and learn more about informatics in general before I began interviewing experts. I used the AltaVista search engine at http://altavista.digital.com and found pointers to the Medical Informatics FAQ and an article titled "The Turning Point In Genome Research," authored by a person named Mark Boguski, which had appeared in the journal *Biochemical Sciences* and also a report of the Invitational Genome Informatics I: "Report of the Invitational DOE Workshop on Genome Informatics" which had taken place in 1993. The report included a list of participants in the workshop plus some identifying information.

The FAQ (Frequently Asked Questions document) had been developed by a Usenet news group concerned with medical informatics. It answered several basic questions about medical informatics and referenced experts and articles in the field. In fact, I learned that several universities, including Stanford, have degree programs in informatics.

Reading this material, I developed a working definition of the term. Informatics is an emerging discipline that has been defined as the study, invention, and implementation of structures and algorithms to improve communication, understanding, and management of scientific information.

Conducting Interviews

At this point, I began to work the telephone. After reading his grant abstract, I first called Skip Garner. Garner talked with me for more than an hour, providing key background both on his work and the field in general. At the end of the call, Garner offered to send a draft of a book chapter he had written titled "Can Informatics Keep Pace with Molecular Biology?" The book was not scheduled to be published for several months. Garner also provided the names of several additional people for me to call.

After reading the article found on the Web, my next call was to Mark Boguski at the National Center for Biotechnology Information. Boguski asked me to e-mail a list of questions prior to doing the interview so I could be better prepared. I did so, then conducted an extended telephone interview with Boguski, who turned out to be among the leaders in the emerging field of bioinformatics. After the call, Boguski sent by e-mail detailed statistics about the use of NCBI protein data bases—key informatics activities.

Boguski also recommended that I talk to several other key players in the field, including Lincoln Stein at MIT's Whitehead Human Genome Research Center and Frank Manion at the Fox Chase Cancer Research Center. I had once talked to Manion before, thus had rediscovered another good resource.

I knew I was well on my way to a good story about bioinformatics. But, what about other aspects of informatics? Using the information I found in the medical informatics FAQ, I subscribed to Medinf-L, a medical informatics mailing list, and I began to monitor the sci.med.informatics Usenet news group. Although, in the end, I did not follow up on any of the contacts from those lists, by monitoring them I was better able to understand the type of questions under discussion.

I also learned about Edward Shortliffe, the author of one of the standard textbooks on medical informatics. Shortliffe headed the medical informatics program at Stanford University. Using a Web search engine with Shortliffe as the keyword, I found the program's Web page, which, in addition to describing Shortliffe's work, referenced journals in the field, including the Journal of the American Medical Informatics Association and Computers and Biomedical Research.

Repeating the Process

Reading further, I then returned to my list of grant abstracts obtained via CRISP and called James Brinkley at the University of

Washington to learn more about the Human Brain Project. I found that the Human Brain Project was exceedingly ambitious and that informatics was at its core.

Brinkley had a personal Web page and maintained a Web page for the project as well. At this point, I began to aggressively work the Web, following links from page to page, identifying interesting work and appropriate researchers with whom to talk. I also found that most of the Human Genome Centers in the country had their own Web pages.

I found information about Frank Manion at the Web page for the Fox Chase Cancer Research Center and information about Lincoln Stein at the Whitehead Institute's Web page. I called Stein, only to have Stein's voice mail message inform me that Stein would be in France for the next two weeks. Two weeks would take me past my deadline.

So, I sent Stein e-mail describing the project. Stein agreed to respond to e-mail questions. I sent a dozen long and intricate questions. Stein responded with a thoughtful set of answers that did not seem stilted or canned. They were not "official" statements, but represented the thinking of a central player.

I continued the reporting process off and on for several days—searching linked Web sites for new leads, calling scientists, and monitoring the discussion lists and news groups. I then wrote a 5,000 word story about the emerging discipline of informatics. Whenever I had a question about my material, I would send e-mail to the appropriate source for clarification. In the final analysis, within two weeks I progressed from having an intriguing idea to producing a definitive story about an emerging scientific discipline that promises to have a considerable impact in many scientific and engineering areas in the future. I had been able to identify and interview a half dozen of the leading pioneers in the field. I had also been able to incorporate information from highly specialized scientific journals, from a book that would not be published for another six months, and from research that was currently underway—research in which the Federal government had invested hundreds of thousands of dollars.

Most important, the article met the needs of the readers of *Scientific Computing & Automation*. They had been alerted to an important new trend in their field.

Case 2: The Northridge Earthquake of 1994

At 4:31 a.m. on Monday, January 17, 1994, the ground in California's San Fernando Valley shook with a violence that produced the most costly natural disaster in U.S. history. An earthquake registering 6.7

on the Richter scale jolted a densely populated suburb northwest of Los Angeles. Apartment buildings collapsed. Water mains and gas lines broke. Sections of the freeway buckled and fires erupted throughout the valley. In all, fifty-seven people died and 20,000 lost their homes in the Northridge earthquake.

The quake was a major news story. But, in the predawn hours, there was no way to know how serious the quake was. News people and public safety officials at the scene had difficulty sizing up the damage. Complicating matters, electrical power and telecommunications networks had been interrupted, making communication with the rest of the world slow and erratic. People in Los Angeles knew little about what had really happened. People not in L.A. knew far less.

Within half an hour of the initial shock, Los Angeles television stations were on the air with reports of significant damage, at least in isolated areas. But, details were slow in coming and updates were sporadic.

I am based in Texas and decided to see if I could use the Internet as an alternative source of information. I only faced one problem, where to begin.

Locating Official Information

I started my search using Veronica and Jughead, search tools described in Chapter 7. I also knew that there were several Gopher projects offering subject-oriented searchable lists of Internet resources. One of these is "Gopher Jewels," a list of Gopher servers that maintain archives and pointers to other archives focused upon specialty topics. Ironically, the Gopher site which contains the "live" version of Gopher Jewels is located at the University of Southern California (cwis.usc.edu) and was knocked off the network for five hours following the earthquake.

A static version of the Gopher Jewels list—that is, one that lists the resources but does not automatically log you onto different servers—at Rice University contained the address of a Gopher server at the Oklahoma Geological Survey open station (wealaka.okgeosurvey1.gov). I then connected to other seismic sites outside Oklahoma, hoping to find information about the events in California.

My first choice, the USGS's U.S. National Earthquake Information Gopher in Golden, Colorado, proved fruitless. The files were several days to several weeks old. One of the "outside Oklahoma" sites listed on the Oklahoma Gopher was the Earthquake Information Gopher at the University of California at Berkeley. I selected that Gopher, which had a menu item titled "California OES Earthquake Program." I had been a reporter in California earlier in my career and I knew that OES is an acronym for the state's Office of Emergency Services. But, even reporters without an understanding of the acronym had only to select the menu item to group its meaning. The OES program offers the option to Telnet to the OES Emergency Digital Information Services (EDIS).

Operated by the governor's Office of Emergency Services, EDIS is a simple Telnet (Chapter 5) site. On January 17, it offered a menu of the fourteen latest messages from EDIS. Each message is numbered and one line of information about the message shows its headline, select code, the date and time the message was posted, and the source. A line across the bottom of the screen instructs the user to either enter a message number or leave the line blank to exit. When I first logged on, half the messages were more than three days old or indicated that they were system tests rather than newsworthy information.

But, the latest message on the screen, number 0393, had the headline "Urgent News Release." It had been posted on January 17 at 5:25 a.m., fifty-four minutes after the quake had struck. I knew I was in business.

The first message posted to the EDIS site on January 17 gave minimal quake statistics and ended with a plea and a promise to the media. It asked that the media not telephone OES at that time and promised to provide additional information as soon as it was available.

OES kept its promise. It provided updated information approximately every twelve minutes for the first six hours following the quake. Morning postings included information from Caltrans (the state's highway department) listing highway closures and damage as well as Red Cross relief efforts, disaster declarations, the activities of the Federal Emergency Management Agency (FEMA), reports on structural damage and evacuations, the locations of relief shelters, and the number of deaths. Press releases and media advisories were regularly posted. There were reports of oil spills, a spill of hydrochloric acid, and a derailed train spilling 5,000 gallons of sulfuric acid. The postings contained accounts of the U.S. Air Force flying surveillance missions, the California Conservation Corps assembling resource lists, National Guard deployments, and public safety officials coming from neighboring counties.

From this one site, I was able to obtain "official" information from several government agencies including the Federal Emergency Management Agency, Caltrans, the office of the Governor of California, and several public utilities, as well as the Red Cross and other groups on the scene. I was able to get information via the Internet that would take other reporters much more time to track down by telephone. Or they would have to attend endless press conferences, if they could get to the scene themselves.

Live Sources

But, I wanted to get more than just documentary sources. At the time, I knew of three discussion lists catering to journalists: Journet, CARR-L and NIT-Chron (see appendix for addresses). While official sources were busy gathering official information, reporters were hard at work as well. At 7:54 a.m., a woman from Pasadena posted a message about the quake to CARR-L. She attached her e-mail address and she consented to be interviewed.

As time passed, more people began to post to the discussion list and reporters began to share sources of information they had found on the network. In the three days after the temblor first struck, more than twenty messages were posted to the journalists' CARR-L list directing people to Internet resources relevant to the earthquake, including Quake-L, an established list that focuses on earthquake information.

At 9:35 a.m. on the first day, Adam Gaffin of Framingham, Massachusetts, posted a notice that an Internet Relay Chat (see Chapter 9) channel called #Earthquake had been established to share news about the quake. Actually, two channels were set up; one to distribute news and the other to discuss events.

The IRC #Earthquake channel was dominated by people representing news agencies in the Los Angeles area including the television stations KNBC and KTLA, as well as AP News. On a very active channel, IRC is often hard to follow because every incoming message interrupts what is being displayed on the screen.

In addition to IRC, the participants in three network news groups, la.general, alt.current-events.la-quake, and alt.california, began sharing information about the quake. On the day of the quake Kurt Foss of Madison, Wisconsin, noticed that Calvin Ogawa had posted a notice in alt.california five days earlier, observing, "a swarm of minor earthquakes, ranging from 2.0 to 4.0 (on the Richter scale)" in the Los Angeles area concentrated over three days. Ogawa predicted in his network message, "I think we're in for a sizable one, if not the big one." The Los Angeles Times ran a story about the prediction on January 19, two days after the quake occurred.

Background Information for Context

The final piece of the puzzle was background information. How significant were the events at Northridge? To answer that question, I used an Archie search to look for files with relevant earthquake information on FTP servers. The search returned "hits" at twelve different host computers bearing eighteen files as well as four directories with the word "earthquake" in the name. In this group I found historical information about earthquakes.

I also conducted a Veronica search of Gopher servers. This search identified 1,095 leads, including the USGS U.S. National Earthquake Information Service Gopher in Golden, Colorado. One file contained information about the most destructive earthquakes in the world; another outlined the ten largest quakes in the U.S. (both including and not including earthquakes in Alaska). A third classified earthquakes by magnitude. There were also several documents with general information about earthquakes of interest to the general reader as well as maps, graphs, and technical data.

In the final analysis, the Internet proved to be a very productive resource for news about this breaking story. Even though I was in Lubbock, Texas, I was able to get all the "hard" data provided by official sources in a timely fashion without relying on a wire service or uncertain telephone communications. Moreover, the accurate information could be "pasted" into a story without having to transcribe it. Furthermore, I was able to access background information and even communicate with some people who were present at the scene.

On the other hand, a "virtual" press conference is not the same as a real press conference. I was not able to ask official questions or to probe for information that may have been of interest to me. Also, the number of individuals with whom I could communicate directly was limited. That limited the amount of information which could be used to set the scene or describe the actual events.

Case 3: Using the Net on a Daily Basis

Mike Meiners, of the *Fort Lauderdale Sun-Sentinel* in Florida says he "always" uses a handful of sites in researching his stories. Among them are the U.S. Census site (http://www.census.gov/); the EDGAR data base at the Securities and Exchange Commission page; the "How Far Is It" distance locator site (http://www.indo.com/distance/); the JOSHUA page for Florida courts opinions (http://justice.courts.state.fl.us/courts/); and the Online Sunshine page for the Florida Legislature (http://www.leg.state.fl.us/).

During the 1996 general elections, Meiners reports "using the Florida Secretary of State's website for the Division of Elections to calculate how much (money) is being spent on the penny sugar tax referendum on the upcoming ballot. It is a searchable data base, highly effective, and accurate."

He also observes "when the preliminary FBI Uniform Crime Reports came out, we went to the FBI Internet Web site (http://www.fbi.gov/) to download the crime statistics, then we got population figures from the Census Web site (http://www.census.gov/). (We) downloaded both sets of stats into a spreadsheet program and, with a minimum of manipulation, located crime rankings for all cities over 100,000 population. This was a same-day deadline story that took about four hours total. (With paper figures and a calulator it would be nearly impossible.)"

Some Cautionary Words

Both larger case studies as well as the shorter examples demonstrate that the Internet and other online resources aid reporting both for breaking news and enterprise articles. The new resources allow reporters to tackle assignments that would have been impossible in the past. As the use and availability of online information grows, the constraints time and place impose on reporters is diminishing.

But, online resources are only one arrow among others in the reporter's quiver. It cannot replace the standard tools used by reporters, particularly, one-on-one interviews with human sources. It is through the one-on-one interview that people's stories come alive.

For example, Ben Barnes operates a computer bulletin board for people with AIDS based in Chicago. To prepare the story, it was not difficult to access the board to describe it. Also, he answered several questions via e-mail. But, only in a telephone interview did information about his partner who had passed away come to the fore. Only in a telephone interview could you feel his pain and sympathy for AIDS patients confined to hospital beds who have no visitors. Only at that point could you fully understand his passion to establish a way for them to communicate with one another and with people who care about them.

While extremely useful, at this point using online resources will only take you so far in the reporting process. Online resources can stimulate story ideas. They will help you educate yourself about a topic. They can be used to prepare you for interviews and can aid you in checking your facts. But, in the end, reporters still have to develop their own story ideas then talk to people, one-on-one, to get the whole story. Despite online access to information, people remain the heart and soul of good journalism. And, it is the interactions of reporters with their sources that produces the most compelling stories.

Chapter

10

Law, Ethics, and the Internet

In the spring of 1994, reporter Brock Meeks read a notice on the Internet from a company named Electronic Postal Service. Meeks said the company offered people money for receiving electronic mail, promising that people who signed up could earn between $200 and $500 a year and would receive full Internet access as well. Meeks, at the time a reporter for *Communications Daily* and editor and publisher of his own Internet news wire (*CyberWire Dispatch*), asked for more information. Meeks says the information did not come, but he later received a mailing from a company named Suarez Corporation Industries offering him a business opportunity, which the company claimed could generate from $30,000 to $1 million per year.

Investigating, Meeks discovered that the Electronic Postal Service (EPS) was an account registered to Suarez Corporation Industries. Moreover, Meeks said, federal and state agencies had brought suits against Suarez for their direct mail practices. Meeks wrote a story in *CyberWire Dispatch* expressing his disapproval of Suarez's business practices.

Suarez Industries then sued Meeks for defamation. It alleged that the article disparaged the company's products and interfered with its ability to develop EPS. Suarez filed the suit in Ohio, where it is headquartered. Meeks was based in Washington, D.C. Meeks was not the first person to be sued for libel based on information circulated on the Internet, but his case was well publicized. While the case was eventually settled with no admission of libel, Meeks faced more than $25,000 in legal fees—fees for which he was obligated personally because he wrote the story for his own news wire.

The Internet and computer networks in general are not outside the boundaries that generally govern speech and communications media in America. But, precisely how the Internet will be regulated is still being debated. Computer communication networks, including the Internet represent new media for expression. Because messages are usually written, computer-based communication functions much the same as print media. Because information can be widely distributed via networks providing one-to-many communication, conceptually it also functions to some degree in the manner of cable television. Because some messages appear to be private and because the federal government has played a large role in establishing the network infrastructure, the Internet itself can be seen as something akin to the post office or to the telephone system before it was deregulated. Because information can appear on people's computers in their homes without their having requested it, some computer networks resemble broadcast networks. And, because children can access and use computer-based networks relatively freely, these new media may face added scrutiny from the courts, which have a special mandate to protect children from certain categories of speech, including indecent language.

Ithiel de Sola Pool noted in his book *Technologies of Freedom*, that different media are regulated differently depending on the environment which existed when they came to prominence. Despite the simple phrasing of the United States' First Amendment, television has a different level of First Amendment protection than print media. And, cable television is regulated still differently. Neither came to prominence until long after the First Amendment was written.

The regulatory landscape for computer-based communications is in the process of being charted. The legal and ethical rules are not yet established. For journalists, computer-based communications have several functions. Computer networks serve to gather and to report information. They are also vehicles for expression.

This chapter will:
- look at regulation concerning the Internet as a medium of expression relative to obscenity, libel and copyright issues.
- review three areas in which the Internet is used as a tool for reporting—confidentiality, freedom of information, and open meeting laws.
- touch on other issues involving free speech and computer-based communication.
- examine some of the ethical dilemmas reporters using electronic communications resources may face.

The objective of this chapter is not to issue definitive legal or ethical opinions. Those will be worked out in practice and in court. Instead, it is intended to raise some of the key questions journalists, lawyers, publishers, students, and citizens confront as they incorporate this new communication media into their daily work routines. The law cited in this chapter is primarily law as it exists in the United States of America, in many ways the most liberal nation regarding journalistic freedom. The principles discussed apply as well—if not more fervently—to journalists in other nations.

Communications Decency Act

In February 1996, as part of a sweeping reform of the telecommunications industry, the United States Congress passed the Communications Decency Act. Drawing from language used to regulate television broadcasting, the bill banned the use of the Internet to transmit or display "indecent" or "patently offensive" material.

The legislation set off a storm of controversy. The proponents of the bill argued that there was a need to safeguard children from sexually explicit material readily available via the Internet. Outside cyberspace, they argued, there are laws to restrain the display of sexually graphic pictures in public places and the selling of pornography to children.

Opponents countered that the public must be able to use the Internet to access any information they wanted. Because users must proactively search for and request what they want to appear on their screen, the proposed regulations would not only prevent children from getting the questionable material, but adults as well would be denied access to information to which they were legally entitled. Material that was perfectly legal in print would be banned from the Internet. As one attorney put it, Congress "cannot ban 'indecent' speech among adults and cannot do so on the Internet as well." Opponents also argued that the law was unenforceable and that parents, rather than the government, should be responsible for controlling their children's access to undesirable material.

To challenge the law, a coalition of thirty-seven organizations joined a law suit. The coalition included online information services such as CompuServe and America OnLine, Internet service providers such as Netcom, computer companies, including Apple Computer and Microsoft, civil liberty organizations, and professional groups, including the Society of Professional Journalists and the American Society of Newspaper Editors. In two separate U.S. District Court decisions, federal judges ruled that the law was unconstitutional.

A three-judge federal panel in Philadelphia held that the Internet should have the broadest possible free speech protections along the lines afforded to newspapers and to people speaking in a public square. Any effort to restrict the content which people could communicate via the Internet would have a devastating effect on the First Amendment, the judges contended. A federal panel in San Francisco agreed.

Though journalists and free speech advocates saw the ruling as a great victory, the battle has not ended. The U.S. Department of Justice as appealed the case to the U.S. Supreme Court, which could issue the definitive decision regarding free speech and cyberspace. But, if the Supreme Court opts not to hear the appeal, the District Court decisions are considered authoritative.

Libel Considerations

While the Internet might enjoy the same First Amendment protection as print and speech itself, that does not mean anybody can say whatever he or she wishes online. As with print and broadcast media, there are still restraints against libel, copyright and misappropriation violations, obscene speech, and privacy violations.

Libel laws are perhaps the most significant for journalists. The overwhelming majority of news reports name people. Sometimes published information contains false information that may damage reputations of people. Libel laws specify the criteria defining when journalists can be punished for publishing false information that may hurt other people.

In the 1964 landmark *New York Times* v. *Sullivan* ruling, the U.S. Supreme Court ruled that the news media could not be punished for libel for reporting false information about public officials unless plaintiffs demonstrated that the journalists had acted with "actual malice." The court defined actual malice as a reckless disregard for the truth. The court reasoned that American democracy depended in part on a vigorous press, but a vigorous press was bound to make mistakes from time to time. Therefore, the press needed "breathing room" in which it could make mistakes without being punished.

Since then, the court has issued a series of rulings in which it refined the Sullivan decision. In *Sullivan* and in subsequent cases the court has maintained separate libel standards for public versus private figures. In *Gertz* v. *Robert Welch Inc.* (1973), it ruled that the *Sullivan* standard applied to public figures who had thrust themselves into the forefront of public controversies or had involuntarily been thrust to the forefront. The *Sullivan* standard did not apply to private figures who had neither thrust themselves nor had been thrust into the public arena. For private people, the states are free to develop their own standards for libel as long as they do not impose liability without fault.

In the 1989 *Harte-Hanks Communications* v. *Connaughton* decision, the court opined that the media exhibited "actual malice" if the reporters or editors most likely knew that the information they planned to publish was false, and they deliberately avoided acquiring the knowledge that would have confirmed the probable falsity of the information. In 1990, the court decided, in *Milkovich* v. *Lorain Journal Co.*, that "opinion" did not necessarily fall into a separate category regarding First Amendment protection. If an opinion column contained information that was demonstrably false and damaging to a person's reputation, the reporter and publication or broadcast company could be punished for libel.

Finally, in 1977, the Second Circuit Court of Appeals decided in *Edwards* v. *Audubon Society* that reporters and publications could not be punished for libel if they published attributed information from sources which they believed were reliable and credible, even if that information ultimately proved to be false and harmful.

The rules of libel, of course, apply to all journalists. But, reporters using the Internet and other electronic communication networks have to be particularly sensitive to potential problems. The first potential pitfall is the notion of a public figure.

What Is a Public Figure?

In some ways, computer-based discussion lists and network news groups are new types of public forums—forums in which individuals can be as vocal as they choose. Unlike other types of public forums, people on computer networks do not need a particular expertise to be recognized by people with authority, such as the moderator of a public meeting, to express their views.

As you monitor discussion lists and news groups looking for leads or sources of information, the names of people who regularly participate may quickly become very familiar to you, more familiar than perhaps other well-known individuals. People who aggressively post to an online discussion may become a source or a subject of a story for you.

It is not clear, however, that people become public figures simply because they are active in online discussion groups. From one vantage point they have clearly thrust themselves into public view (at least regarding the issues they are discussing). From another perspective, they have not. Legally, it is still not even clear whether the Internet should be considered a public forum.

The status of commercial information services such as Prodigy and CompuServe is even murkier. Because being active online may not make a person a public figure, reporters should not believe they are protected by the *Sullivan* rule if they choose to report on people they have encountered online.

Does Net Culture Encourage Libel?

The question about who is a public figure is more vexing because of the developing culture of the computer networks themselves. In many online discussions, despite admonitions against it, many participants will "flame" (violently disagree with) other people's messages, using intemperate, hostile, and vituperative terms. The majority of news groups (Chapter 7) are unmoderated. That means anyone can post anything. Moreover, from time to time, "flames" may be reposted to other discussion lists, to news groups, or may even be stored in data bases.

While people who "flame" others may believe they are exercising their right to free speech, what they post could be libelous. That is, the flames could consist of verifiably false information that damages the reputation of the person who has been flamed. Unless there are very compelling reasons, reporters generally should not look at flames as useable, legitimate information.

In most cases, reporters looking for information will monitor the discussion lists and news groups looking for leads then contact people privately. Nevertheless, they should be aware that almost all individuals participating in those discussions should be treated as if they are private individuals for the purposes of libel. Because different states have different libel standards for private individuals, reporters must be even more careful to avoid reporting damaging, false information.

The best defense against accusations of libel in the United States is provable truth. Reporters should treat information they find online, particularly information about people, as critically as they treat information they receive from other sources. Veteran computer users have a long-standing rule of thumb: garbage in = garbage out. That applies to information found on the Internet and other places as well.

Copyright

Copyright law is often poorly understood by journalists. In short, copyright law is intended to give holders of the copyright the exclusive right of use to what they have created. Generally, that copyright covers the expression of an idea via one of several media. The United States Copyright Act of 1976 created seven categories of authorship, including: literary works; musical works; dramatic works; sound recordings; audiovisual works; pantomime and choreographies; and pictorial, graphic and sculptural works. International copyright treaties extend similar guarantees across national boundaries. An infringement of copyright is judged by three factors: the originality of the work, the proof of access to the copyrighted work, and the similarities of the works compared.

Works falling into most of the categories outlined by the Copyright Act can be distributed via computer networks. Consequently, copyright laws are important for journalists in three areas. First, what are the restrictions on the use in their stories of information they have found online? Second, what are the copyright issues involved in creating a Web site? Finally, what rights do journalists have to their own work which may be distributed by a publisher online either via the Web or through an electronic data base?

Using Information Found Online

Because most journalists attribute the information they publish to a source, the key questions for reporters when they wish to use information they have found or received online is how much of the material they have found can be quoted verbatim and how much of the work can they use in general? A common scenario for online journalists occurs when they see an interesting message in a network news group or discussion list and want to quote it directly, crediting the source. Many journalists see news groups and discussion lists as analogous to public meetings. If people speak during business sessions of a public agency at a public meeting, of course, reporters can quote them.

But, postings to discussion groups are not spoken words; they are original works of authorship fixed in a tangible medium of expression—in this case electronic—which can be "perceived, reproduced or communicated either directly or with the aid of a device," to use language close to that of the copyright statute. Consequently, when someone posts something to a list or news group, that posting is presumed to have copyright protection. The person who holds the copyright legally controls how that posting can be used. If the person does not want you to quote the posting, he or she legally may be able to prevent you from doing so.

Copyright infringement is not the only danger you may face in using material you find published via computer-based networks. If you do not directly quote information you find electronically but only use the facts contained, you may be able to avoid copyright infringement. But, you may still be guilty of what is called misappropriation.

Misappropriation

Misappropriation is the legal expression of the notion that people should not be allowed to compete unfairly by using the work or property of others, particularly if they claim the purloined work is their own. The 1918 Supreme Court case *International News Service* v. *Associated Press* is a classic example of misappropriation.

William Randolph Hearst, who owned the International News Service (INS), admitted that he pirated stories from the Associated Press using a variety of tactics. Sometimes INS editors would rewrite the stories—sometimes they wouldn't—before transmitting them to its clients. Hearst claimed that, because AP did not copyright the story (the copyright law was somewhat different then), and nobody can copyright the news itself, the information was in the public domain. The Supreme Court decided that, although AP did not have copyright protection, the INS actions unfairly interfered with AP's operation at precisely the moment when it would reap the profit from efforts.

Misappropriation could emerge as a significant issue for people using online services. On the Internet, for example, many people now publish their own "news services." There are many, perhaps hundreds, of electronic journals circulating; and some print magazines are publishing electronic versions on computer networks. If journalists use these news wires and journals as sources of information, they have to be very careful about how they report the information. It is very easy, and tempting, to download information in an electronic form and cut and paste it into an article. That could put the reporter at risk of claims of infringement or misappropriation. Brock Meeks, for example, has complained that mainstream publications have used, without attribution, stories he has broken in the *CyberWire Dispatch*.

The Fair Use Doctrine

Copyright laws and the risk of misappropriation, however, do not mean you can never quote information from the Internet. The 1976 U.S. copyright law also included provisions for what is known as "fair use" of copyrighted material. The fair use provisions allow others to use portions of copyrighted material without the permission of the copyright holder under certain conditions. The criteria by which fair use is evaluated include the purpose and character of the use, including whether the material is used either for non-profit educational purposes or for-profit ventures; the nature of the copyrighted work itself; the amount of material used relative to the total amount of material; and the effect of the use upon the market value of the copyrighted work. Perhaps the two most important criteria are the nature of the copyrighted work itself and the effect of the use on the market value of the material.

In one episode, *Nation* magazine published an excerpt of the memoirs of former President Gerald Ford without the permission of Harper & Row, who held the copyright. In the 1984 case *Harper & Row* v. *Nation Inc.*, the U.S. Supreme Court observed that a critical element of the work is whether it is published or not. The scope of fair use is considerably more narrow for unpublished works.

In 1991, the Second Circuit Court of Appeals underscored the importance of protecting a creator's right to control the first public appearance of the expression of a work in *Wright* v. *Warner Books Inc.* Nevertheless, it allowed Warner Books to publish a biography of novelist Richard Wright, even though it included small portions of his letters and journals stored at the Yale University library and not yet published. Because posting something on a discussion list that may be read by thousands of people is like publishing, the scope of fair use for material found in electronic sources is broader than for things like unpublished personal letters. Electronic messages that have been publicly circulated are probably open for fair use.

A Work's Market Value

The second criterion that should help protect journalists if they choose to quote from news groups or discussion lists is the impact on the potential market value of the material. In *Salinger* v. *Random House* (1987), the Second Circuit Court of Appeals decided that biographer Ian Hamilton's use of unpublished letters in a biography of the novelist J.D. Salinger was not allowed because, in part, appearing in Hamilton's book could have an impact on the future commercial value of the letters. The panel ruled, however, that the biographer could use the factual content of the letters.

This ruling is significant because most of the postings on discussion lists and news groups probably have no future market value. News group postings often are not archived at all; they simply vanish. Consequently, journalists usually will not have to worry about hurting the market value of the postings they quote from electronic sources.

Nevertheless, if you want to quote material directly from the electronic sources, you should keep these limitations in mind. Nearly all of the information you find via electronic sources has copyright protection. Electronic journals, news wires and electronic versions of print material have the same copyright protection as material that has been traditionally published. You should also work under the assumption that information posted to news groups and discussion lists is copyrighted.

Therefore, you should limit the amount of material you quote directly as much as possible, particularly if you think that information either has not been published (you have been forwarded a copy of a private e-mail message, for example) or if you think the material may have market value in the future. In general, for published material, including material published electronically, fair use allows for the verbatim quoting of no more than 300 words of work and those 300 words can total no more than 20 percent of the total work. (In other words, you can't quote a 200-word poem entirely and claim fair use protection). The best alternative is to secure the permission of the creator of the work you wish to quote.

Some observers believe the need to secure permission from copyright holders to use specific material can have a chilling effect on robust debate in America. Nevertheless, in *Harper & Row* v. *Nation Inc.,* the Supreme Court specifically ruled out a First Amendment defense for copyright infringement. In that decision, the Court declared that *Nation's* interest in reporting the news as quickly as possible did not outweigh President Ford's right to control the first publication of his memoirs.

Copyright and Web Sites

Journalists must keep in mind that, if copyrighted material is posted to a computer bulletin board or Web site, the copyright itself has not been affected. A journalist cannot use material posted online with impunity. Furthermore, people who are creating Web sites cannot freely use material from other Web sites. Access providers to the Internet may also be at risk if copyrighted material is posted on a computer for which they provide access to the Internet.

In a well publicized case in 1995, the holders of the copyrights to the published and unpublished works of the founder of the Church of Scientology, L. Ron Hubbard, sued Dennis Erlich, a former minister of Scientology and now a vocal critic, for publishing portions of the writings in the Usenet news group alt.religion.scientology. Erlich used Netcom to gain access to Usenet. The copyright holders sued Erlich as well as Netcom after they refused to act on notification of copyright violation.

The plaintiff's arguments were that, because Netcom maintained the system which copied and distributed the works in question throughout the Internet worldwide, it was equally responsible for the copyright violation along with the person who had posted the material and the owner of the BBS on which it first appeared. Netcom responded that, while it maintained the system, the plaintiff's theory would make the operator of every Usenet server in the world liable for the copyright infringement.

In a preliminary ruling in the Fall of 1995, a northern California court indicated that it did not believe that Netcom could be held responsible for direct liability, but perhaps could be guilty of contributory libel for not acting after it was notified of the infringement. The court's opinion, however, was at odds with the Working Group on Intellectual Property Rights, a federal committee reviewing the issues of property rights in relationship to the National Information Infrastructure, which has proposed a stricter standard.

In the same case, the court reflected on people who simply read unauthorized copyrighted material online. The court argued that browsing the Internet is the functional equivalent of reading and is consequently fair use—much the same way as when a person browses through a book then decides not to buy it.

Overall, the issue of the responsibilities of Internet access providers and others concerning copyright infringement is not clear. Legislation has been introduced in the United States Congress which would add legal burdens to technology managers monitoring material on the Internet. Simon and Schuster and other publishers reportedly are carefully monitoring the Internet for copyright violations related to the books they have published.

It is clear, however, that people cannot post copyrighted information on their Web sites without permission. They can, however, insert pointers from their pages to other Web sites containing copyrighted material, allowing their viewers easy access to material.

Copyright Protects Creators

On one hand, journalists and Web site creators have to be careful about using copyrighted materials in an unauthorized fashion. On the other hand, copyright protects their work from being distributed online without their permission. For example, in 1993, eleven writers sued the New York Times Co., Time, Inc., the *Atlantic Monthly*, Lexis-Nexis and others for illegally sublicensing their articles to electronic data bases. Lexis-Nexis provides electronic archives of the articles of a wide range of newspapers and magazines. The publications contended that they had the right to provide the material to the data bases without compensating the authors.

In the Spring of 1996, *Atlantic Monthly* reached a settlement on the suit in which it agreed to pay the authors for the use of their material and to negotiate for electronic rights in the future. *Harper's* magazine, *The Washington Post* and *New Yorker* magazine pay for electronic rights and to additionally compensate authors whose material had been used.

Journalists and authors must carefully scrutinize the contracts and agreements they sign with publishers. If they do not sign over the electronic rights to their work, they retain those rights. If their articles then appear online or in an electronic data base, they probably have the right to additional compensation.

Confidential Privilege

Journalists working online must also be aware that they are working in a new medium. Some of the protection they may enjoy using traditional methods may not apply when they are online. Two of the most important ways in which online communication differs from other media is in the confidentiality of the information journalists gather and store electronically and in the emergence of speech codes governing online behavior in some settings.

Reporters have long fought to establish the principle that they can keep confidential the information they gather and the names of the sources from whom they gather it. The reasoning is that, without that protection, sources may not be willing to share with reporters important information that the public should know. The U.S. Supreme Court, however, has not accepted journalists' arguments about the need for a shield from law enforcement. In *Branzberg* v. *Hayes* (1972), the court decided 5–4 that the First Amendment did not absolve journalists from their responsibilities for testifying before grand juries and responding to relevant questions. Since then, some states have passed shield laws to limit the way law enforcement officials can force journalists to disclose information; some state courts have recognized a limited privilege for reporters based on the First Amendment; and several United States Circuit courts have acknowledged that information gathered by reporters should have some limited protection under specific circumstances. Still, there is no federal shield law rooted in the First Amendment. Nor has Congress chosen to pass a federal shield law.

The lack of a shield law could be more problematic for journalists working online. Typically, if police believe that a reporter has information relevant to a case, they subpoena the reporter to testify and to produce her notebooks. If need be, the police will issue a search warrant and physically gather notebooks and other information. In those types of situations, journalists working with what was known to be sensitive information could take precautions against being forced to disclose it. They may not tell their editors the names of their sources. They may hide their notebooks or not write down important facts. And, they can take a principled position and refuse to testify when called before the grand jury or into court. Several reporters have gone to jail rather than disclose confidential information. In many cases, their news organizations have supported them legally and financially in their efforts.

Online journalists do not have the same type of control over their information; nor can they necessarily count on the support of the computer system or company providing online access. By definition, online journalists initially gather information in an electronic format. At some point, that information is stored electronically on a hard disk or tape. As Oliver North (former National Security Council aide to President Ronald Reagan) found out, just because you delete something from a hard drive does not mean the information has been removed. When you do delete something, the information itself does not disappear until new information is written over it. Several software programs can retrieve deleted files.

Law enforcement officials know that computer hard drives can still retain information that the user intended to delete. Hard drives are now subpoenaed in the course of criminal investigations. Law enforcement officials will often confiscate the entire hard drive with all the information on it.

Consequently, if you capture or store sensitive information that you do not wish to disclose, you should not store it at any time on a hard drive. Moreover, if you store sensitive information on a hard drive that is shared with other users, you are putting all of the information on that drive at risk. A law enforcement agency could conceivably confiscate the entire computer and there would be little that an individual reporter could do about it.

People accessing the Internet through a university based connection could not rely on the support of the university if law enforcement agencies demanded the information. A university might be disinclined to lose an entire hard drive full of information employed by many users just to support your interpretation of the demands of a free press.

Of course, many reporters never are asked to surrender confidential information to law enforcement agencies because it is relevant to a criminal or civil proceeding. But, this extreme case raises a more common and troubling issue for online journalists. The information stored on a shared hard drive is not private or secure. In almost all cases, if you are accessing electronic information through a network, the system administrator can gain access to your files and can monitor your e-mail traffic. You have to conduct yourself accordingly.

And, while people who use the Internet like to believe that they also own it and should be able to establish the rules which cover its use, they don't and can't. The computers that are linked through the network are each owned by an organization or person. Those owners have the right to establish rules that govern their use. For example, Lawrence Livermore National Laboratory discharged workers for using its computer system to access pornographic sites on the Internet. Moreover, companies like America OnLine have made it clear they won't protect the confidentiality of their subscribers in the case of criminal and perhaps civil investigations. Journalists should be fully aware of the rules governing use of the computer systems they use and be careful not to violate them. Nor should journalists necessarily expect that Internet access providers will defend their free speech rights vigorously should a dispute arise.

Speech Codes

In fact, owners of computer-based communications networks have to be sensitive to more than just free speech concerns in controlling what is posted on their computers. In the fall of 1994, Santa Rosa Junior College reached a settlement with the U.S. Department of Education in which the college agreed to pay three students $15,000 to settle sex-discrimination charges related to men-only and women-only online computer conferences conducted by the school.

The students charged that the single-sex conferences violated a federal law that prohibits sex discrimination in schools that receive federal funds. The computer bulletin board, which was launched by a professor of journalism and hosted more than 100 online conferences, was seen as an educational activity of the school and, therefore, subject to what are known as Title IX regulations.

Federal investigators found that derogatory remarks about two women posted on the men-only conference were a form of sexual harassment creating a hostile educational environment. The Department of Education's Office of Civil Rights argued that computer bulletin boards do not enjoy the same level of First Amendment protection as the campus newspaper. The office has proposed banning comments that harass or denigrate people on the basis of sex or race.

The school's lawyer argued that the online conference should have been protected by the First Amendment. Nevertheless, the college felt compelled to settle the case.

Along the same lines, commercial services such as Prodigy and CompuServe are owned by companies that reserve the right to define the limits of free discussion enjoyed by those using those services. For example, Prodigy has policies in place to forbid the use of hate speech and other types of offensive speech. For many years NSFnet, long the major backbone network of the Internet, had rules forbidding commercial use of its networks. At one point in Winter of 1996, under pressure from the government of Germany, CompuServe banned its 4.3 million subscribers from accessing 200 sex-related data bases around the world. Colleges and universities can also restrict their users' access to controversial Usenet news groups and, perhaps, Web sites as well.

Open Meetings and Freedom of Information

Journalists are not the only community group taking advantage of computer-based communications networks. Public officials and government agencies are also incorporating new technology into their work. Their activities raise two vital concerns for journalists. First, "Are open meeting laws being circumvented through the use of computer networks?" Second, "How much of the information collected by governments should be available to journalists in an electronic format and how much should that information cost?"

Since the mid-1970s, many states have passed what are called Sunshine or Open Meeting laws. The purpose of these laws is to ensure that public business is conducted in the open where the public can see and hear what happens. Except under specified conditions, members of many school boards, local government commissions and other agencies cannot conduct official business without first notifying and inviting the public to observe or participate. As new forms of communication become available, the definitions both of meeting and public access to meetings have come under pressure. Can officials "meet" online or via a video conference to conduct business? Does inviting the public to a video or online conference fulfill the spirit and letter of the open meeting laws?

Sunshine laws vary from jurisdiction to jurisdiction. Journalists must be on guard to ensure that agencies do not try to use new communication technology to conduct the public business in a covert or hidden fashion.

Along these lines, public access to government computer files has been a significant issue for several years. The question has three important aspects.

1. Are electronic records considered "records" under freedom of information laws and therefore they must be made available on request?
2. Must government agencies provide information to journalists and the public in an electronic format?
3. How much can government agencies charge for access to electronic information? Can agencies give exclusive rights to information to private data providers who, in turn, can charge whatever the market will bear for the data, even if the pricing makes it prohibitive for smaller publications and individuals to purchase?

Once again, these questions are being decided at all levels of government. Journalists must stay aware of the deliberations that will resolve them as they could have profound influence on the practice of journalism.

Access for Online Journalists

As the number of people publishing online increases, the issue has emerged concerning who constitutes a "legitimate" journalist and thus should be allowed entry to locations such as the press gallery in the United States Congress and other restricted venues. The question of access frequently dogs journalists working in a new medium. For example, newspapers tried to bar radio reporters from certain locations in the 1930s. And, television cameras are routinely banned from criminal and civil courts, although newspaper reporters are allowed in. In most places, judges have broad discretion when it comes to televising, or even photographing, trials.

In February 1996, Vigdor Schreibman, the publisher of the Federal Information News Service (FINS), was denied admission to the United States Senate and House press galleries. FINS is published only online and is regularly read, according to Schreibman, by thousands of people. A subscription costs $2.95 a year, but the newsletter can be read free—and has been posted to different news group discussion sites.

According to the head of the Congressional periodical gallery, who is a working journalist, Schreibman was rejected because his publication was more of a hobby than a commercial venture. And, while representatives of online publications such as those created by *National Journal* will undoubtedly be recognized as legitimate journalists, the proliferation of online journalism will raise the question how to make distinctions. As Alan Fram, the Associated Press correspondent who heads the executive committee of the daily press gallery for Congress, remarked to *The Wall Street Journal*, "If we are going to admit such critters, how do we avoid opening the barn door to anyone with a home page."

Obscenity and Other Free Speech Issues

As participants in the robust debate protected by the First Amendment, journalists should also be aware of free speech issues that may not have a direct impact on the way they do their jobs. They include the ability of one jurisdiction to impose its standards for speech in another jurisdiction and the ability networks give journalists to circumvent international press law. As in other media, obscenity serves as the flash point of one locality imposing its standards on another. In its pivotal ruling in *Miller* v. *California* (1974), the Supreme Court decided that local community standards should be used to evaluate whether material was obscene.

In the summer of 1994, the city of Memphis won a decision against a computer bulletin board operator in the San Francisco Bay area for distributing obscene pictures. Law enforcement officials had actively requested that the material on the bulletin board be sent to them. The court ruled that because people had to subscribe to access the pornographic material, the operators of the bulletin board should have known that their material could not be distributed in Memphis.

In the same way that computer networks may be avenues for circumventing restrictions on the distribution of pornography, they may also provide ways to circumvent national press laws in other countries. As we reported about the Karla Homulka case, Canadians used network news groups to spread information about a grizzly murder case, even though the judge in the case had imposed a news blackout.

In many cases, people will be applauded for circumventing press laws. They will be seen as defying the heavy hand of censorship. But, people who do violate those press laws could have to pay a heavy price. The judge in the Karla Homulka case threatened to shut down specific computers suspected as the vehicle for violating his gag order. Journalists who receive information that has been distributed in violation of national press laws must keep in mind that somebody may have to pay a price for making that information available. It should not be published frivolously.

Online Ethics

Consider this scenario: You are walking along a road and you come across a knapsack. You stop, pick up a book that has partially fallen out of the knapsack, and open it. The first page states that the information is to be read and used only by people who have purchased the book.

At that point, is it unethical to read on, if only to see if you can find the name and address of the person who owns the knapsack? If, in looking for the person's name, you read something which could be of value to you, is it wrong to use that information? If you read the entire book then return it to the knapsack and leave, have you stolen anything?

As you use online information, you will likely come across information that was not intended for your eyes. As a reporter, you may join a list without the other list members knowing the focus of your interest. They may think the discussion is just among specialists in a narrowly defined area. A private e-mail message might be posted or forwarded mistakenly or maliciously to a discussion list. Navigating through the maze of computers on the network, you may find a back door to a commercial data base open only to those with paid subscriptions. In other words, from time to time, you will find a knapsack with an open book on the road.

Online journalism promises to open a whole new arena for discussions of media ethics. And, the ethical boundaries, what journalists morally should or should not do online, will only be worked out over time as more journalists use electronic services and more journalists debate their use. Nevertheless, all journalists should adhere to certain ethical guidelines.

First, journalists should almost always identify themselves as such if they plan to use information from discussion lists or network news groups. In most cases, journalists have the ethical obligation to allow people to choose to go on the record or not. Using hidden cameras is very controversial in standard journalism. To lurk on a discussion list then quote people who did not know that what they wrote would be used in a different context is as deceptive as posing or going undercover to report a story. While, from time to time, in traditional journalism the benefit of posing to reveal a significant social wrong may outweigh the deception involved, that probably will not be the case in most instances in online journalism. In almost all cases, journalists have an obligation to let the people with whom they interact know that they are talking to a reporter.

Second, journalists must identify the source of their information in their reporting. Attribution is an essential element of journalism. If you don't know definitively who the source of information is, you must be very careful if you choose to use it. Widely published journalism codes of ethics frequently warn that journalists should verify all information. At the same time, you should not claim credit for information that somebody has published on a network without crediting that source.

Third, journalists have to respect the limitations of the information they gather online. Online information should be treated in the same way as information gathered through any other technique.

While the three operational rules outlined above can help steer journalists to the right decision, they will not, and cannot, cover every situation. For example, was Daniel Ellsberg justified in stealing the Pentagon Papers in the early 1970s? Those papers laid out in vivid detail the way the United States government had misled and lied to the American people about its policies in Vietnam. Were *The New York Times* and *The Washington Post* justified in publishing that information, even though the information was both classified and stolen? Whatever you feel, Ellsberg could not have passed the Pentagon Papers along to *The New York Times* and *The Washington Post* as easily if photocopying—a new communications technology at that time—had not been invented.

Like photocopying—and radio and television before it—computer-based networks are a new communications technology. Legal and ethical controversies will only be decided in action, as people like you try to decide the correct course of action in the complex situations that will arise in the future.

Chapter **11**

The New News Media

In 1991, Skip Bayless lost his job as a sports columnist when the Dallas *Times-Herald* shut down. The day after the newspaper closed, listeners called into his five-day-a-week sports radio show and said they would pay him if he would continue to write the column and fax it to them. He agreed and began to publish his column as part of a newsletter which was faxed and e-mailed to around 25,000 readers. His column also began to appear on a World Wide Web site where it was accessed approximately 7,500 times a day.

The shuttering of daily newspapers have been a steady feature in journalism for at least the last two decades. When the *Houston Post* closed down in 1995, Lisa Bass lost her job as a copy editor as did her husband Frank, a Pulitzer Prize-winning reporter. While she was looking for a job, she taught herself HTML programming and created a Web site for ex-Houston Post employees. She dubbed her site the Toasted Posties (http:// rampages.onramp.net/~basses/toast2.htm).

The page was noticed by a reporter from *The Wall Street Journal* who contacted her. This led to Bass's husband being offered a job in the *Journal's* Houston bureau. Bass found work at a suburban daily as a features editor. She also continued to design Web sites.

Michael Kinsley has long been a star of inside-the-Beltway Washington punditry. A former Washington columnist and then editor of *The New Republic*, Kinsley's face became recognizable nationally as Pat Buchanen's liberal adversary on the show Crossfire on Cable News Network. But in 1996, Kinsley suddenly left CNN and Washington D.C. He was named editor of *Slate,* a new online magazine about politics and culture, funded by the Microsoft Corporation.

Slate is far from Microsoft's only venture into what can only be called journalism. When it launched its online Microsoft Network in August of 1995, the software giant established a large editorial operation to supply news to the service. In 1996, it set up a joint venture with NBC, creating

MSNBC, a 24-hour interactive cable news channel intended to compete with CNN and Fox's new 24-hour cable news venture.

New technology creates new vehicles to disseminate news. The great expansions of newspapers in America in both the 1830s and the 1880s was made possible in part by improvements in papermaking and printing technology. Color photography contributed to a huge expansion of general interest magazines like *Life* and *Look* in the 1940s and 1950s. In those years, the movie newsreel was an important news medium. And, of course, both radio and television have emerged as important news media.

As well as a useful tool for reporters, the Internet, and particularly the World Wide Web, is emerging as a significant new medium for news. Companies large and small are scrambling to establish a presence on the Web. Publishing on the Web ranges from the lonely crusading writers in the best tradition of pamphleteers like Thomas Paine to the largest media conglomerates in the world like Time-Warner.

This chapter will:

- explain why the Web as a publishing medium has exploded.
- look at a range of news media initiatives on the Web.
- consider the challenges posed by online publishing.
- describe the opportunity Web publishing offers journalists.

Why Online Publishing Has Exploded

Online publishing represents one of the most dramatic adoptions of new media technology in history. Compared to the penny press revolutions of the 1830s and the 1880s, or even the spread of radio in the late 1920s and early 1930s and television in the early 1950s, more people have gained access to the World Wide Web in a shorter period of time than have adopted any new media technology in previous history.

The concept for the Web was first outlined in the late 1980s. By the mid-1990s, tens of millions of people had access to the Web via their schools, places of work and at home, though all who have access do not necessarily avail themselves of the opportunity.

As important as the growth of a potential audience has been the ability for very small publishers, and even individuals, to become online publishers. With television, for example, during most of the 1950s and mid-1960s, many locations received only two or three channels. The introduction of UHF broadcasting increased that number to enable viewers in large cities to receive seven to ten stations.

Cable further increased the availability of programming. But, by the mid-1990s, even state-of-the-art cable systems offered only about seventy-five channels. So, while cable television has developed a mass audience, only a relatively small number of companies develop programming for television. The cost to produce professional quality television programming is just too high for many companies or organizations to fund the venture.

To become a print publisher is also a risky venture. The cost of building circulation, printing the publication then distributing it means that, in most cases, only companies with experience, expertise and sufficiently deep pockets can afford to launch new ventures. And, most new magazines fail. No new daily newspapers have been established in the United States for many years.

The Web, however, has completely altered the publishing equation. First, because everybody with a Web browser can theoretically access any Web site (webmasters can close their sites to the public should they choose), even the smallest online publisher can potentially reach the entire international online audience. Moreover, small publishers can register their sites with search engines and directories, assisting people who may be interested in the information they have to find their pages.

Second, the cost of building and maintaining a simple Web page can be extremely low. Many Internet service providers routinely offer their subscribers space to create personal Web pages. And many service providers charge only nominal rates—as little as $125 a month— to host Web pages with up to 50 megabytes of information, which is substantial. In 1995, a complete professional Web site with its own direct access to the Internet, running on its own server, could be started for less than $30,000 the first year.

Economic Incentives

Adding to the incentive to explore Web publishing, the cost of distributing the information via the Web is fixed, no matter how much information is available on the Web site. To publish more information, newspapers and magazines have to print and distribute more copies, adding to the cost. With the Web, the distribution cost does not go up as you increase the amount of information available.

Given the economics of Web publishing, it is not surprising that all sorts of enterprises have been willing to experiment with this new medium. As they also were when radio was first introduced, daily newspapers have been ready to experiment with online publishing. By mid-1996, according to Steve Outing, an online newspaper columnist associated with *Editor & Publisher*, the weekly trade journal of the newspaper industry, there were 1,115 commercial newspaper online services. That figure represented an increase of more than 300 from the beginning of the year and a jump from 100 at the beginning of the previous year. In addition, about 200 college newspapers had online versions by the middle of 1996.

Fig. 11-1: One new media attention grabber is *HotWired*, one of the more ambitious and flamboyant publishing projects on the Internet. This "e-zine" (electronic magazine) is accessible at http://www.hotwired.com/.

At the time of Outing's report, there were nearly 400 U.S. dailies (of approximately 1,700 daily newspapers in total) with online services. The vast majority of those services were World Wide Web sites. There were a nearly 220 U.S. weekly newspapers online as well.

To see updated statistics, visit *Editor & Publisher's* data base of online newspapers at its home page http://www.mediainfo.com/. *Editor & Publisher's* vice president of new media reported in mid-1996 that the company was receiving information about five to ten new online ventures daily. College and commercial newspapers can be accessed at http://www.newslink.org/. The Ecola newsstand has links to nearly 500 online newspapers and magazines at http://www.ecola.com/news/ and regularly adds new sites.

Newspapers are not the only traditional publishing media which have plugged in online. Radio stations, television networks and television stations are also plugging in. Scores of affiliates of National Public Radio, for example, have created Web sites. Links to those stations can be found at the National Public Radio home page at http://www.npr.org/. Links to public television stations can be found at http://www.pbs.org/. Other networks, such as CBS, also provide links to their affiliates.

But, perhaps the greatest stampede to the Internet has been by magazine publishers. Not only have Time, Inc., Hearst and other major magazine publishers invested heavily in developing Web sites, many small, entrepreneurial online magazines, often called e-zines (or just zines), have been launched. Perhaps the first Web-based magazine to capture widespread public attention was *HotWired* (http://www.hotwired.com/), the Web venture of *Wired* magazine, which, in the mid-1990s attempted to serve as the fresh, sassy voice of the online community.

Though the traditional media's attention focused on *HotWired,* the Web is alive with magazine-style publishing activity. When a research team led by Kathleen L. Endres and Richard Caplan entered the word "zine" into the Yahoo search directory in early 1996, they found the term listed in 1,146 categories. Ultimately, they sampled every tenth zine they found, building a data base of more than 500 zines.

People Are Reading Online

While nobody knows exactly how many people use the World Wide Web, it is clear that the Web and online publications are being read. Nando.net, a pioneering online venture of the *News & Observer* in Raleigh, North Carolina, reported that on the week of October 3, 1996, they received more than 8 million accesses.

Each access does not represent a reader. Depending on how the page is constructed, a single user may represent 25 to 100 accesses per session. But, even assuming an average of 100 accesses per user session, the statistics indicate that the online publication is accessed by more than 80,000 users a week. And, the figure could easily be two or three times that number.

The response to online publications has been strong enough that some are now charging for people to subscribe. *The Wall Street Journal* pioneered the effort to charge people to access online publications. In less than a month, it had signed up 30,000 paying customers, who paid either $29 or $49 for an annual subscription. Less than 40 percent of the subscribers to the Web site also subscribed to the print version of the *Journal*. The site was being visited by 32,000 to 40,000 people daily, the *Journal* reported.

Media which attracts readers also attracts advertisers, who then may fund ongoing growth for the media. In 1995, researchers estimated that companies spent approximately $42 million for advertising on the Web. In 1996, reliable sources indicated that advertising revenues could jump more than 700 percent to $312 million. And, the growth rate of online advertising could continue that upward trend for several years.

In addition to promising increased advertising revenue and potentially serving as an alternate source of subscribers, Web publishing also offers media companies access to new readers. A survey partially funded by *Parade* magazine, the Sunday newspaper supplement, conducted to analyze the attitudes of American teenagers about newspapers and online information sources, found that while 35 percent of teenagers between thirteen to seventeen never picked up a newspaper in a given week, 78 percent indicated that online information was fairly or very important in their lives. Online sources are rapidly growing as a familiar way to deliver information.

The Pioneering Ventures

Despite the widespread activity, online publishing, particularly on the Web, is still in its infancy. In fact, some pundits argue that the industry is still in its pre-history because a lot of the technology that will help the Web develop its own distinctive character is still under development.

As you learned in Chapter 4, many Web browsers still need additional "plug-ins" to play back delayed or real-time audio or video. Most browsers also do not yet automatically support multimedia material, fixed format documents (such as those demanding a PDF viewer), or three dimensional images (which are developed under VRML or Virtual Reality Modeling Language). As these types of tools become more available, the content of Web publishing will change significantly.

But, the browser is not the only technology which will improve. Java, Visual Basic, and ActiveX programming tools will allow Web developers to create new kinds of media and information applications to be delivered over the Web. The hype around Java and ActiveX (which allows developers to send small computer programs through the web from server to the client where they perform their tasks) began to build in 1996. But the potential of these tools has not yet been realized.

Finally, the infrastructure of the underlying telecommunications network will be upgraded as well. As information can move more quickly from server to client, new types of media content will be developed.

Although the best is clearly yet to come, current Web publishing ventures are extremely interesting. In this section, a sampling of different Web publishing concepts will be reviewed.

Newspaper Ventures: Large, Medium, and Small

The New York Times (http://www.nytimes.com/) has made an aggressive foray on the Web. Its publisher, Arthur Sulzberger Jr., has joked that he plans to deliver the news through whatever medium is appropriate, including "mind meld," he told an audience sponsored by the Columbia Graduate School of Journalism.

In ads that have run in the print edition of the newspaper, the *Times* asserts that it is trying to go beyond the print version of the newspaper to build an online community with the venture, which is named *CyberTimes*. Although the opening page has *The New York Times* classic look and a late news update, the Web page does go beyond the print version.

For example, Rich Meislin, senior editor for information and technology, has collected a nice set of related Internet sites for both the politics and the business sections of *CyberTimes*. During the 1996 presidential campaign, the political section included links to the White House, Congress, the Democratic and Republican parties, the Libertarian Party, Ross Perot's Reform Party, Ralph Nader's Green Party, and the Natural Law Party. There are also links to special interest groups, including the National Right to Life Coalition and the National Abortion and Reproductive Rights Action League. There is also a history of The American Presidency supplied by Grolier Online.

The Use of Competitors

The Business Links section reveals a trend that the Web may facilitate — the acknowledgement that many people rely on many sources of information, including several different newspapers. Through *The New York Times*, readers can get to *The Wall Street Journal*, *Barron's Online*, *Business Week*, *Money* magazine, and many others sources of information that are viewed as competitors in the traditional print world. It is hard to imagine a story in the pages of the *Times* telling its readers to now refer to *Business Week* for more information. But *CyberTimes* provides the functional equivalent.

In another twist, news stories on *CyberTimes* often supply audio clips as well. When a fire at Rockefeller Center in New York injured a dozen people, the story in *CyberTimes* included an audio clip from New York City's mayor, Rudolph Giuliani.

Finally, the page has what is called Web specials—information that apparently has been developed specifically for *CyberTimes*. In the fall of 1996, there were Web specials celebrating the 100th anniversary of *The New York Times* magazine and a gallery of 360 degree photography.

Radio Supplements

The *Christian Science Monitor* (http://csmonitor.com/) has been a respected national newspaper for most of the 20th century. More recently, it has also

Fig. 11-2: One of the more aggressive initiatives in online publishing is that of *The Nando Times,* a product of the *Raleigh News & Observer* in North Carolina. *The Nando Times* is available at http://www.nando.net/.

initiated an extensive radio operation, Monitor Radio, which competes in tone, format, and approach with National Public Radio. Its Web site combines aspects of both operations.

On the home page, a user can find the breaking news from the newspaper, hourly radio newscasts and a daily radio show. The audio portion of the page can be heard in real time. A typical feature may include a short question and answer about a pressing issue of the day or a political commentary. For example, after the first presidential debate in 1996, when Republican candidate Bob Dole invited television viewers to visit his home page, the *Christian Science Monitor* Web site carried a short audio clip of an interview with an expert discussing the impact of the Internet on the political campaign.

Another feature of the *Monitor* home page—a feature which can be found on many media Web sites—is a set of forums in which readers can post their views on a set of topics. After the vice presidential debates, for example, Web visitors could discuss the relative merits of each candidate's performance. Most of the comments were paeans to Vice President Al Gore's performance.

In addition, the Monitor Web page supplies an archive to articles printed in the newspaper since 1980, a feature titled the "President's Inbox," which includes links to material about a specific issue on the President's agenda at that moment, updated headlines from the Associated Press, and a crossword puzzle.

The Raleigh *News & Observer* (http://www.nando.net/) and the *San Jose Mercury News* (http://www.sjmercury.com/) are both mid-sized newspapers which were among the first newspapers to aggressively launch online initiatives. The founder of the *News & Observer's Nando Times* later went on to establish a company to make tools for programming for the Internet. Serving the Silicon Valley, the *San Jose Mercury News' Mercury Center* is an online showcase for Knight Ridder, a large media company— it owns the *The Miami Herald* and *The Philadelphia Inquirer* among other newspapers—which has invested heavily in new media technology.

Broadened Coverage

Both the *Nando Times* and the *Mercury Center* have used the Web to broaden their news coverage. For example, on a random day, the *Nando Times* had a story about an effort of composers in Romania to prevent their songs from being used in the election campaign and another about the support artists in India were giving to a painter who faced criminal charges for presenting a Hindu goddess in the nude. The *Nando Times* also carries a wide range of columnists and op-ed writers in its "Voices" section.

The *Mercury Center* supplied in-depth coverage of the Seybold Conference, an insiders' conference about multimedia publishing. The Seybold Conference was the type of event which used to pose a problem for daily newspapers. It was of deep interest to a small subsection of the readership. The Web page could satisfy the needs of industry insiders without stealing valuable news space for material of a more general interest.

The Arizona Daily Star's StarNet (http://www.azstarnet.com) has taken another approach to broadening its news coverage. In its News Links section, stories written by the newspaper's reporters are linked to related information. For example, a story about the legal troubles of Arizona governor Fife Symington was linked to a section which included the full 23-count indictment charging him with criminal wrongdoing, a profile of the governor, an archive of past stories, and other links to information about Symington.

On a lighter note, a notice about a promising new jazz singer, Kitty Margolis, who was scheduled to perform in Tucson during the weekend,

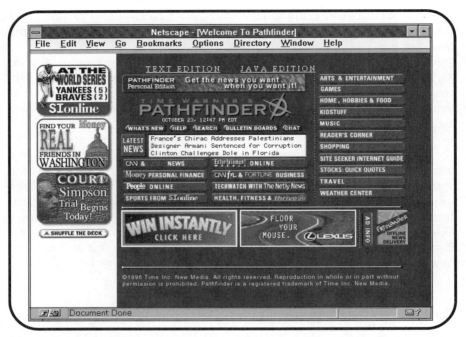

Fig. 11-3: The Pathfinder site serves as a gateway for the online offerings of Time Inc. magazines. The site resides at http://www.pathfinder.com/.

was linked to her home page. And, a story about the death of the designer of the G.I. Joe doll was linked to the Hasbro toy company's home page which displayed the entire G.I. Joe line.

The use of links to Web sites like Hasbro's has sparked a debate among some journalists. They question whether their news stories should be connected to Web sites which are essentially advertising and marketing ventures. It is an interesting question which surely will be the subject of ongoing debate as online reporting and publishing develops.

Magazines Climb Online

Unlike online newspapers, which have been primarily funded by existing newspaper companies, the Web has been a place of experimentation both for existing magazine companies and start-up ventures. The form, format and rhythm of Web publishing, which still depends primarily on text, graphics, and periodic updates, compares closely to traditional magazine publishing routines.

There are several differences in print and online magazines, though. Unlike their print counterparts, Web magazines can be "published" incrementally as different sections are updated or changed. A weekly or monthly magazine may be changed virtually every day or even several times a day. Moreover, magazines can experiment with different types of information such as audio and video. Finally, since print magazines generally carry longer articles than newspapers, online magazine publishers seem to have been bolder in experimenting with new methods of gathering and reporting information.

Time Inc. has launched one of the first and most ambitious online efforts in *Pathfinder* at http://pathfinder.com. *Pathfinder* serves as the central home page for four Time Inc. magazines including *People*, *Money*, *Sports Illustrated* and *Entertainment Weekly*. The page also promotes *CNN Online* and *CNNfn* (a financial news service created in conjunction with *Fortune* magazine), as well as maintaining a link to *AllPolitics*, a political news service created by several major media players.

The presentation of *Pathfinder* is almost like a television set with twelve or fifteen channels running at the same time. A viewer can choose any channel to watch or in which to participate. The site has chat rooms for real-time, live interaction and bulletin boards through which readers can express their opinions. You can also send letters to the editors of different Time Inc. publications.

Pathfinder is an indication that Time, Inc. is attempting to fully embrace the Web as a new medium. In an online issue of *Entertainment Weekly*, *EW* writer Ty Burr wrote a witty review of the Web sites of the major movie studios, of course with links to the sites themselves. There was also an article about the online buzz for Christian Bale, who starred in the movie "Little Women." The article noted that there was four times as much talk about Bale on America OnLine than about Mel Gibson. The article supplied links both to Bale's home page and a Usenet news group discussion.

Developing Unique Style

Like their print counterparts, the Time Inc. magazines are developing their own style and approach online. But entrepreneurial ventures are also pioneering new approaches to magazine publishing online. Like *Pathfinder*, *HotWired*, the online version of *Wired* magazine (http://www.hotwired.com), is actually a collection of several different Web sites joined together by a common home page. Both the print and online versions are intended to be significant for more than the content which they contain. Their crews hope to define and project the attitude of the emerging Net culture.

Consequently, the *HotWired* site incorporates most of the cutting edge tools available on the Web. A floating tool bar which allows you to easily

Fig. 11-4: *Slate,* at http://www.slate.com, is a weekly Internet publication dedicated to traditional journalistic practices with commentary, analysis, and thoughtful writing.

move from one part of the site to another pops up automatically when you visit the page. The tool bar has been written using Java, a promising new computer language for Web developers (your browser must be "Java-enabled" for it to work). Motion video and real time audio are incorporated in several places in the page.

Among the sections that *HotWired* offers is HotBot, a search engine that has indexed 54 million online documents. Its Netizen section is supposed to contribute to public life online. An online version of the print magazine is available as well as nine other distinct information areas. Although all the sections are accessible through the main *HotWired* URL, they also have their own distinct URLs as well. For example, HotBot is located at http://www.hotbot.com/. Netizen is at http://www.hotwired.com/. You can also have a daily version of *HotWired* sent to you via e-mail.

Among the more ambitious, *HotWired* is only one of several very distinct online magazines which have emerged on the Web. Other very stylish, sophisticated, and intriguing new online publications include *Feed* (http://www.feedmag.com), *Salon* (http://www.salon1999.com), *Word*"(http://www.word.com) and *Slate* (http://www.slate.com/). These online magazines are pioneering new ways to present journalism.

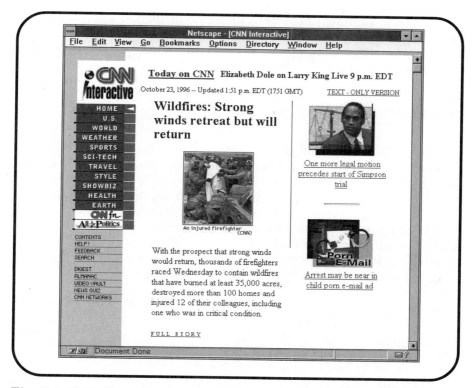

Fig. 11-5: Cable News Network has the most trafficked news site on the Internet with its *CNN Interactive* site at http://www.cnn.com/.

For example, although many Web sites allow users to respond or engage in dialogue, *Feed* incorporates the readers' commentary into the articles themselves. Once it held a round table of experts on the future of journalism. Comments and responses from readers, and the participants rejoinders to the comments, were printed in a column to the left of the primary article. *Salon* has made space on its hard disk available to folks such as political consultant James Carville and humorist Harry Shearer.

When Dick Morris, a top political consultant to President Clinton, was exposed consorting with a prostitute on the day before Clinton's acceptance speech at the Democratic National Convention, Carville was featured prominently on television urging viewers not to make too much of the scandal. In his column in *Salon,* however, Carville allowed that he really didn't like Morris much.

Slate is an interesting example of the way the Web can be used profitably by politically oriented opinion publications. For the past several election cycles, newspapers have taken to publishing "truth boxes" about political advertising run by candidates for different offices. The commentary is pretty standard—the ad is partially, but not entirely, true. In *Slate,* consultant Robert Schrum also analyzes political advertising in a section titled Varnish Remover. But, the reader can watch and listen to the ad while reading the commentary. And, clips from a recording accompany a music review.

Television, Radio, and the Web

While it is not hard for publishers working within a traditional print model to see the potential of online media products, the scenario is different for radio and television journalism. First, the economics of production and distribution are far different for broadcasting from that of print. In most cases, producing a professional television show is much more costly than a print product—why bother with smaller Web projects that will probably not attract as great an audience? Second, the distribution infrastructure for broadcasting is largely in place. Broadcasting more hours of programming does not affect the bottom line in the same way that increasing the print run of a magazine would.

As significantly, television and radio deal in high-quality video and audio. The network infrastructure is not yet in place to easily distribute that type of programming. It is simply not yet really feasible to watch a half-hour of high quality video or audio via the Web. So, while it is innovative for a print publisher to include a 15-second video clip with an article, the same combination can be seen as a step backward for a television broadcaster, whose entire broadcast consists of video.

Despite the different parameters, television and radio networks such as Cable News Network, National Public Radio, and CBS are all experimenting with products on the Web, as are individual radio and television stations. Not surprisingly, CNN is running one of the most aggressive online ventures, *CNN Interactive* at http://www.cnn.com/.

In addition to an ongoing breaking news service, *CNN Interactive* links readers to sections that deal with different areas of programming covered by CNN including U.S. and world news, weather, sports, entertainment, science, technology, and fashion. The home page also links to two related services, *CNNfn,* a business news-oriented Web site created in conjunction with *Fortune* magazine and *AllPolitics,* a Web site for political news, which is also a joint venture with Time Inc. and other news organizations.

The *AllPolitics* page demonstrates nice features with which the Web can liven up news coverage. After the vice presidential debates in 1996, *AllPolitics* provided a full transcript of the debate, highlight clips, and a poll for Web visitors to record who they thought won. Moreover, there was a contest for people to try to win a free T-shirt. And, for people who were really interested, there was an interactive, online game in which people could make their own strategic decisions guiding the campaigns of different presidential candidates.

The *AllPolitics* Web site significantly increased the potential for interaction among users.

Many broadcasting efforts on the Web can be categorized in one of three ways. Like *AllPolitics,* there are attempts to increase interaction. WJHU in Baltimore, Maryland (http://www.wjhu.org) invites listeners to respond to its talk show hosts via its Web site. Second, there are attempts to archive information. At the National Public Radio Web page (http://www.npr.org), for example, viewers can access transcripts and sound clips of past programs as well as to listen to its hourly news update. Finally, broadcasters use Web sites to distribute their schedules. WCPO, the ABC affiliate in Cincinnati, maintains a programming schedule as well as offering news capsules, transcripts and an archive of its investigative journalism at its Web site.

New Journalism on the Web

Although large and small companies have embraced the Web, perhaps the most intriguing element of this new medium is the potential for a single journalist to create a site that could make a difference. In the tradition of Thomas Paine, I.F. Stone, George Seldes and other pamphleteers and newsletter writers, a single person can publish on the Web, and perhaps make a difference.

"The Consortium" (http://www.delve.com/consort.html) bills itself as the Internet's first investigative zine. Published by Robert Barry, a former reporter for the Associated Press, *Newsweek,* and PBS Frontline, the Consortium for Independent Journalism was established in November 1995.

Stories covered by The Consortium include the reports that the U.S. Army's School of the Americas taught torture and assassination techniques to military officers from Latin America—a practice later renounced by U.S. Secretary of Defense William Perry. It has also published an interesting account of former Iranian president Abolhassan Bani-Sadr's allegations that the Ayatollah Khomeini had negotiated with a representative of then Republican presidential candidate Ronald Reagan about the release of American hostages in Iran prior to the 1980 U.S. presidential elections.

New Media Challenges

In the middle of the presidential campaign in 1996, a reporter for *HotWired* wrote a column concerning President Clinton's ethics. The piece had a link to a Web site which purported to detail Clinton's ethical failings. A White House staffer called to cry foul and the editors of *HotWired* agreed. They removed the offending link.

Publishing on the World Wide Web allows journalists to combine different kinds of information in new and different ways. But, not every combination may be appropriate. Should movie critics link their reviews to sites designed to promote the movie Web sites. Should political correspondents link their stories to the Web sites created by different political campaigns, candidates, or office holders? Can journalists vouch for the credibility of the information on other sites which may be related to stories on which they have worked? Should they be required to verify all the information on linked sites?

The criteria for linking sites points to a second challenge for online journalism. How can journalists maintain the difference between online ventures which offer legitimate journalism and sites which are basically geared for marketing and promotion?

The issue and problem of clearly delineating journalism from advertising and public relations in media products has a long history. In the early penny press, advertising material was published in the news columns in exactly the same format as news items. In the early 1900s, reporters would sometimes freelance as publicity agents and place laudatory articles in the news columns of their newspapers. With the explosion in the number of cable television channels, infomercials—paid advertising which looks like a television show—have become popular.

Currently, in most cases, advertising and non-advertising is clearly marked in each traditional medium. On the World Wide Web, the potential to blur the differences between news and advertising and public relations is clear. With hyperlinking, journalists can easily connect a news report to a promotional or advertising site. Exactly where a journalist should draw the line in integrating links into stories is not clear.

A third challenge the new news media presents journalists is the issue of convergence. In the past, different news media have had slightly different mandates and have jockeyed to find their own niches. For example, most radio news consists largely—though not entirely—as an hourly headline service. Television reports news stories that fit primarily into half-hour or hour formats. And, as the public increasingly received breaking news via broadcast, newspapers have offered more news analysis and trend stories. Each medium reports news in ways that utilize the technological strength of the media.

The Web combines attributes of the existing media with Web-specific characteristics such as interactivity and the ability to easily archive information. The convergence of different media on the Web presents a challenge to journalists to learn how each medium can be used most effectively.

At the same time, as the media converge in this new medium, will—for the first time—one medium completely lose its audience over time? Historically, one of the most notable features of communication has been that a new communications medium has never eliminated an older one (if you view facsimile as an updated version of the telegraph). After all, people still gather regularly for face-to-face meetings. Will computer-mediated communication be the first to drive an older medium from the news field?

Of all the media mergers which have taken place, online publishing has more examples of news operations with expertise in one media collaborating with operations with expertise in another. At some point, perhaps one of the underlying components will no longer be needed.

Or will online publishing develop its own voice, conventions and formats? Will publishing on the Web find its own niche in the news arena, leaving other niches to other forms? It generally takes a period of time for a new medium to find its form. The current form of the newspaper, for example, emerged in the late 1800s, after mass newspapers had been around for more than fifty years. In the early days of television, newscasts consisted of people reading the newspaper on the air. Only after videotape became widely available did television journalism truly create its own idiom.

In most cases, online journalism still consists of combining elements common in other media. News media on the Web has not yet developed a style or voice of its own. Perhaps it won't until tools like the Java and ActiveX programming languages have had time to develop.

Finally, convergence poses another serious problem for journalism. If virtually anyone can publish online, what makes one site "news" or "journalism" and another site "entertainment" or "advertising?" Since the form is still in flux, what characteristics identify and distinguish the work of journalists and journalism from other content producers on the Web?

For example, before Microsoft launched its Microsoft Network online, it assembled a large news room to create news content to distribute. A few of the journalists working for Microsoft then tried to join one of the online discussion lists created for use by working journalists. The attempt set off a fire storm. Were journalists working for Microsoft legitimate or not? Would Microsoft Network news be real news or not? Viewed another way, what is the point of reporting about a professional football game online if viewers can go directly to the National Football League's Web site for scores and highlights?

The Prospects for Journalism

In the news media, technological change has always led to great challenges. It also leads to great opportunity. With the emergence of the World Wide Web, journalist have an entirely new medium in which to practice their craft and their art, a medium unfettered by many of the constraints of other news media. The investment needed to launch a new daily newspaper are so great few ever try. While there has been an explosion of news programming on television, it is mainly financed by large networks or television stations.

The World Wide Web is the first international communication medium which can be successfully used by companies of all sizes and individuals as well. And, the Web is still at its infancy. The opportunities it offers journalists seem to be virtually limitless.

With the Web, journalists are only limited by their own initiative, creativity and desire. Like television in the 1950s and 1960s, new forms for journalism are being developed. And, like television from that period, when people look back at the online world today, undoubtedly they will see a golden age.

Starting Places for Journalists

Theoretically, you could start anywhere on the World Wide Web and find anything else on the Web *if*: 1) you had enough time, and 2) the Web "sat still" long enough. Neither condition prevails. Nor is news static. Online directories and key word search engines can help journalists find what they need, when they need it, to build background information and to set stories in the proper context. Here are a few carefully selected sites designed to get you started.

Key Word Search Engines

Different devices employ diverse net search strategies (robot vs. human) and offer various search refinements.

Yahoo—http://www.yahoo.com | Key word searching as well as subject-oriented browsing.

TradeWave Galaxy—http://galaxy.einet.net | Key word searching as well as subject-oriented browsing. Search Web, Gopher, Hytelnet at once. Links to other search tools and reference materials.

Tile.net—http://www.tile.net/ | Does key word searching for ftp sites, mail lists, and news groups.

Deja News—http://dejanews.com/forms/dnquery.html | Search for information posted in news groups. Several filter options.

InfoSeek—http://www2.infoseek.com | Annotated search results. In addition to key word, has subject catalogs. Can search web, news groups, e-mail addresses, and more.

Lycos—http://lycos.cs.cmu.edu | Search for title of documents, headings, links, key words. Note: rights to this engine recently sold.

Web Crawler—http://webcrawler.com | Searches by document title and content.

Opentext—http://www.opentext.com/omw/f-omw.html | Allows

weighted search, has "Power Search" option, Japanese Index, search for words or phrase.

Alta Vista—http://altavista.digital.com | Some 50 million pages indexed, has helpful "Advanced Search" options. Very powerful system, but must use advanced tools.

All-in One Search Page—http://www.albany.net/allinone/ | The name says it: Links to search & browsing sites from many different perspectives.

CUSI—http://Web.nexor.co.uk/public/cusi/cusi.html | One form allows search of several Web engines for documents, people, and more.

Veronica—Searches from many Gopher sites including Library of Congress (marvel.loc.gov), University of Minnesota (gopher.tc.umn.edu:70/1), and Washington & Lee (liberty.uc.wlu.edu).

General Directories

Directory sites or subject catalogs in Gopherspace and Webspace follow predetermined subject trees. Pick a subject—or related subjects—and browse for relevant information. Can be quick.

See Yahoo & Galaxy above.

Internet Public Library—http://ipl.sils.umich.edu/ | This site has links to reference documents, net catalogs, and search engines.

Clearinghouse for Subject-Oriented Internet Resource Guides—http://www.lib.umich.edu/chhome.html or gopher://una.hh.lib.umich.edu:70/11/inetdirs.

Live Gopher Jewels—gopher://cwis.usc.edu | Choose "Other Gopher and Information Resources" from Root menu. This will take you to hot-linked Gopher Jewels.

Riceinfo—gopher://riceinfo.rice.edu/11%2FSubject | One of several great Gophers.

Whole Internet Catalog—http://gnn.com/wic/ | Links arranged by large and lesser topics.

Library of Congress— gopher://marvel.loc.gov or http://www.loc.gov | Far-reaching resources. Links to many federal and state government agency resources.

PEG (Peripatetic Eclectic Gopher)—gopher://peg.cwis.uci.edu:7000/ | Strong resources related to governent, politics, and medicine.

Hot Lists and Other Journalists' Resources

These are sites where journalists have gathered—for the benefit of other journalists—lists and catalogs of links to other sites deemed useful.

FACSNET—http://www.facsnet.org | A new service with many original documents including backgrounders and reporting tutorials. Includes beat-oriented Internet browsing resource.

Stovin Hayter's European Journalism list—http://www.demon.co.uk/eurojournalism/ | Has geographical and topical links to information of interest to journalists in Europe.

Julian Sher's Investigative Journalism—http://www.vir.com/~sher/julian.htm | Internet tutorials and links for journalists, story tips, media criticism, government links, strong Canadian resources.

Nikos Markovits' Journalistic Resources—http://www.it-kompetens.se/journ.html | Links to journalism organizations, research sites, media sites, other hotlists.

Casey's Internet Survival Guide—http://www.qns.com/~casey/ | Strong on U.S. government resources. Also has links to reference materials and to Internet search engines. A few humor links.

Launch Pad for Journalists—http://www.ccrc.wustl.edu/spj/resources.html | St. Louis, Missouri (USA) chapter of SPJ, has resource links organized by topic areas.

Makulowich's Virtual Journalism Library—http://www.cais.com/makulow/vlj.html | Links to trade organizations, other sites.

Avi Bass's NewsPlace for News and Sources—http://www.niu.edu/newsplace/ | Separate lists for media sites, for primary source material, and for Internet navigating help.

Professional Organizations

National Press Photographers' Association—http://sunsite.unc.edu/nppa | NPPA programs, publications, contests, member services, and related topics.

Society of Professional Journalists—http://town.hall.org/places/spj/ | Society mission statement, selected publications, current topics of interest, membership information, and various mailing lists.

Asian American Journalists' Association Web site—http://www.aaja.org/ | Organization goals, membership information, conferences, links to chapters.

Associate Press News Executives Council, California-Nevada division online presence—http://www.apnec.org/ |Conferences, seminars, links to other AP and Cal-Neva media sites.

California Journalism Online—http://www.ccnet.com/CSNE/ | Joint project of CSNE, CNPA, CFAC, and APNEC. Job listings, CNPA Bulletin, salary survey, links to U.S. newspapers and to Internet resources for journalists.

American Society of Journalists and Authors—http:// www.eskimo.com/~brucem/asja.htm | Information about ASJA, an organization promoting freelance nonfiction authors and journalists. Information on hiring freelance writers, as well as member information and events.

European Journalism Centre—http://www.euronet.nl/~ejc01/ | Focused on the European journalist, providing education and contacts. Links to a mission statement, selected publications, and event information.

Newspaper Association of America—http://www.infi.net/naa/ | Conference and events calendars, NAA publications and news, and links to newspaper sites.

National Conference of Editorial Writers—http://www.infi.net/ncew/ | Conference information, calendar, job bank, links to other resources, mailing lists, and discussion topics.

Organization of News Ombudsmen—http://www.infi.net/ono/ | Mission statement from the ONO, information about its members, and selected publications.

CompuServe Journalism Forum—http://www.jforum.org/ | Information about and registration for the CompuServe Journalism Forum. Journalism links.

Investigative Reporters and Editors—http://www.ire.org/ | Thorough listing of IRE publications, programs, activities, and special projects. Occasional pieces from IRE Journal.

New Directions for News—http://www.missouri.edu/~ndnwww/ | Institute dedicated to fostering "innovation to help newspapers better serve democratic society" and helping "journalists to adapt and survive this period of rapid change."

National Association of Broadcasters—http://www.nab.org/ | Information about the organization, press releases, events, and job listings.

National Association of Black Journalists—http://www.nabj.org/ | NABJ history and objectives, directory of chapters, and board of directors.

Poynter Institute for Media Studies— http://www.nando.net/prof/ poynter/home.html | The Poynter Institute Web site. This site provides links to a mission statement, announcements and activities, publications, and other files.

National Association of Science Writers—http://www.nasw.org/ | Information about the organization, membership information (and inducements to join the organization), links to member home pages, and information about the NASW job bank.

National Institute for Computer-Assisted Reporting—http:// www.nicar.org/ | Links to NICAR mission satement, publications, events, and mailing lists.

Radio-Television News Directors Association—http://www.rtnda.org/ rtnda/ | Describes RTNDA organizations, membership, conventions, research, and RTNDA activities. Provides links to "Journalism and Media Resources on the Internet."

Radio and Television News Directors Foundation—http:// www.rtndf.org/rtndf/ | Mission statement, a list of programs sponsored by RTNDF, staff listing, and links to radio and television news sources on the Internet.

Society of Environmental Journalists—http://www.sej.org/ | Annotated links to environment-related sites, basic information and mission statement from SEJ, and selected publications.

National Press Club—http://www.town.hall.org/places/npc/ home.html | Contains information about NPC services (including dining, etc.), publications, an events schedule, and research tools through the Eric Friedheim Library and News Information Center.

Minorities in Broadcasting Training Program—http:// www.webcom.com/mibtp | MBTP is a non-profit organization dedicated to placing multi-cultural trainees at television and radio stations across the United States.

Other Useful Sites

A few "jumping off" places containing exceptionally rich resources.

Awesome list—http://www.clark.net:80/pub/journalism/ awesome.html | John Makulowich's list of thirty-eight "truly awesome" and many more merely awesome net resources.

CARL—telnet//pac.carl.org or http://www.carl.org/ | Journal and magazine articles can be located here and faxed to you (for a fee). UnCover Data base.

FedWorld—http://www.fedworld.gov or telnet://fedworld.gov | U.S. Commerce Dept. gateway to 130+ Federal agencies.

City.Net—http://city.net | Links to city information worldwide. Mass transit maps.

MetroScope—http://isotropic.com/metro/scope.html | More cities information.

Choosing an Access Provider

Journalists may have Internet access from the office and students from school, but, for any number of reasons, either might benefit from a personal account providing a 24-hour Internet connection. In many regions of North America and the United Kingdom, Internet Service Providers (ISPs) offer unlimited dial-up access to the net for less than a typical cable television subscription.

While the challenge of the past was to find a service provider, the challenge today is to select from a myriad of choices. The purpose of this appendix is to describe different types of services, to suggest guidelines for choosing one, and to provide phone numbers for contacting a select few.

Commercial Hybrids vs. ISPs

Commercial hybrid online services such as America OnLine, CompuServe, Delphi, GEnie, and Prodigy have long passed e-mail to one another and thousands of other destinations via the Internet. By 1994, most had begun to offer to their subscribers other Internet-based services including access to Usenet news groups, Telnet, and, finally, World Wide Web access. One should understand that these companies have become Internet access providers second, and that their first business was to provide other services.

Commercial hybrids have always offered e-mail. They have provided various "forums" or "rooms" or "chat groups" for people to gather online and to share points of view on topics of mutual interest. They also have offered access to encyclopedias and other references to their subscribers as well as newspaper and wire service text, magazine content of varying kinds, and gateways to premium information services.

Internet access provided by these services has often had a premium cost attached to it, has been limited in its range, and has been plagued with slow performance. Even under the best of circumstances, they will charge you an hourly premium for any Internet access beyond a basic allowance for their accounts, typically five hours per month. It is very easy to use five hours a *week,* with only casual "cruising" of the Internet.

Dial-up access from ISPs dedicated to providing Internet connections is almost always more economical. ISPs offering flat rates for unlimited access abound. For the journalist seeking to mine the information riches on the Internet, unlimited, flat-rate service is the first criterion you should demand from an ISP offering dial-up access.

Shell Accounts, SLIP, and PPP

Dial-up access comes in two basic varieties: shell accounts and SLIP/PPP accounts. The shell account is less expensive (generally less than $10 per month), uses simple technology, and is text-based. Still, the shell account can provide access to many resources on the Internet. It's just that you don't see the graphics or hear the sounds on the more sophisticated World Wide Web pages as they are loaded into your computer. It is, however, possible to download graphics and audio and play them back later.

What you get with a shell account is space on and access to a Net-connected computer—typically a UNIX-based machine. This machine is your host. You use a simple communications program to dial into and "talk" with the host. When you log in, you see a system prompt, and you must type commands following each system prompt in order to make things happen. Pointing and clicking a mouse does not make things happen on the remote host for a shell account.

Most important, all the computing is done and all the programs are run on the distant computer that you have dialed into. The only thing that happens on your machine is that the communications program makes your computer emulate a dumb terminal, totally reliant on the host to do all the work of computing.

With SLIP (Serial Line Internet Protocol) and PPP (Point-to-Point Protocol) accounts, you run a dialer program that talks to the remote host and asks it to open a direct connection to the Internet. This allows you to run whichever programs you have selected on your machine. The most apparent difference is that you can use graphical World Wide Web browsers, and other client software that takes advantage of the built-in features of your computer's operating system. With Windows and Macintosh computers this means you have point-and-click convenience, the ability to copy-and-paste between windows or applications, and other system conveniences.

SLIP and PPP accounts generally come at a higher cost (anywhere from $99 per year to $30 per month in the United States) than shell accounts, but their flexibility, especially when it comes to using World Wide Web browsers, makes them worth a higher price. Many ISPs offer both shell and SLIP/PPP access for their flat fee. For journalists who are prone to travel much in their work, the added convenience of both SLIP/PPP and shell access can be a great boon. Consider the following circumstances.

I maintain a PPP account with a large ISP, for which I am charged a flat $19.95 U.S. per month. I also keep an account with CompuServe, one I have had for more than a decade. One of the reasons I chose my ISP is that it has local telephone access in more than 400 cities across the United States. Any major city I visit in the U.S. can be reached by PPP access.

When I am abroad, however, I still have local Internet access through the account's shell provision. I have this because CompuServe has local dial-up numbers worldwide. When I am in London or Geneva or Montreal or Mexico City I access CompuServe, which gives me the ability to Telnet back to my shell account then receive my e-mail. In that way I stay in touch with my editors, my colleagues, and my family wherever I am.

Weighing Price and Features

Some providers, especially commercial hybrids, such as CompuServe, will include a certain number of "free" hours with their basic monthly charge. Typically, this is five to ten hours per month, or one to two hours per week. Beyond the basic charge there is a surcharge for each minute you are connected. It is very easy to burn up one or two hours a day once you are connected to the Net. Five to ten hours of "free time" to just nose around might be all right for a start. But, if you are going to use the Internet on a regular basis to do research for news stories and other articles, then you should look for an account with "unlimited" access.

By "unlimited" access, we mean your provider does not care how many hours you are connected. Your monthly charge is the same whether you are on one hour per day or twenty. In selecting your access provider, you should specify that you plan to be online several hours per day and you want a "flat" rate.

Internet magazines such as *Internet World*, *Net Guide*, or *Boardwatch* carry advertising for ISPs. You might choose one of them, using the guidelines here described. The following lists may be of help.

Internet Service Providers

America Online	800-827-6364
Concentric Network	800-939-4262
EarthLink Network	800-395-8425
GNN	800-819-6112
IDT Internet	800-438-8996
NetCom	800-501-8649
Pipeline (PSINet)	800-379-8847
Primenet	800-463-8386
SpryNet	800-777-9638
UUNet	800-488-6383

All of these providers give some kind of "unlimited" PPP access for a flat monthly fee (some restrictions on hours may apply). All have points of presence in most major cities in the U.S. Many have some kind of 800 access for regions lacking a local number.

Other considerations in choosing an ISP might include the number of communities with local access, if you do a lot of traveling; whether the account also includes shell access; and, what kind of software and technical support are provided. Not all the providers listed here have presences outside the United States.

Commercial "Hybrid" Providers

CompuServe	800-848-8199
Delphi	800-695-4005
GEnie	800-638-9636
Microsoft Network	800-373-3676
Prodigy	800-776-3449

These services are long on support, almost always have local phone numbers, have low fees for basic service, offer immediate access to many virtual communities, and provide many other attractive services.

Glossary

alias — (n.) An e-mail address given as a substitute for a longer, less intuitive address. For example, a college may issue a student the address z4j28@pegasus.acs.ttu.edu. Through an alias utility, the student may get mail addressed simply to McCoy@ttu.edu.

anonymous FTP — (n.) A process allowing anyone with an FTP (File Transfer Protocol) client to access FTP servers and to retrieve files from that server. Under anonymous FTP, one typically logs in using the ID "anonymous" and one's e-mail address as the password.

Archie — (n.) A program that searches for files publicly accessible at anonymous FTP sites.

ASCII — (n.) An acronym for American Standard Code for Information Interchange, ASCII (or ascii) commonly refers to the set of characters used to represent text on paper. Distinguished from binary (q.v.), or computer instruction code. "Text" is sometimes used as a synonym. Most word processors allow you to save files in text (ascii) format. E-mail, by its nature, is communication carried in ascii format. Files that contain only text characters are called ascii files.

bandwidth — (n.) The capacity of a network to handle data traffic. "Bandwidth" is often used to imply that online communication is a limited resource which should not be wasted frivolously.

binary — (n., adj.) Computer code, distinguished from "text" or ascii. Binary files contain instructions that tell computers and computer peripherals such as printers how to do their work.

Boolean — (adj.) Applied to logic used in searching for information. Boolean logic uses terms such as "AND," "OR," and "NOT" to limit the results of information searches. A search for "defense AND policy NOT nuclear" would produce a list of files and directories containing both "defense" and "policy" in them but would eliminate from the list any such files or directories that contain the word "nuclear."

BPS (Bits Per Second) — The measure used to gauge the speed of a modem. The more bits per second a modem can transmit, the faster it is. Although slightly different, Baud rate is another term which refers to the speed of a modem.

BTW — Shorthand for "By The Way."

client — (n.) Name given to a computer or software program that negotiates with another computer (the "server") the delivery of files and information to the first computer. Sometimes used to describe the computer on which the software resides.

code — (n.) Programming instructions that tell computers (and computer peripherals) what to do. (v.) To write computer programs.

commercial information services — Commercial enterprise which provides information online for a fee. The largest consumer-oriented commercial information services are CompuServe and America OnLine. Many more services are in the planning stages. Most commercial information services also provide access to the Internet.

cyber — A combining form used generally to refer to the online world.

cyberspace — (n.) The collective environments or "places" created by computer networks. Term coined by William Gibson in the book *Neuromancer*.

data base — (n.) A body of facts, usually focused on a predefined topic, and gathered together in some computer. Organized into meaningful patterns, data (facts) in a data base becomes information.

discussion list — (n.) A method by which individuals can communicate easily with many people by using e-mail. People subscribe to discussion lists then automatically receive all messages other subscribers send to the list.

DNS — (n.) Domain Name Server. A computer that uses a distributed data base to translate network address names (such as pegasus.acs.ttu.edu) into numeric Internet Protocol addresses (such as 129.118.2.52) and vice versa.

domain — (n.) A naming system given to Internet nodes, or subnetworks connected to the Internet. All computers belonging to the subnetwork share the same domain name when they are linked to the Internet. A university typically has several large computers and many lesser computers under one domain. For example, "ttu.edu" is the domain for Texas Tech University. Host computers sharing that domain include UNIX machines named "Pegasus" and "Unicorn" and a VAX cluster under the generic name "TTACS."

download — (v.) To retrieve a file from a server or any other online computer.

e-mail — (n.) Electronic mail. Text messages sent across computer networks to digital mail boxes where they are retrieved and read at the leisure of the recipient.

emoticons — (n.) A grouped combination of keyboard symbols and text used to express emotions in computer communications. The best known is called a "smiley" and is formed using the keys colon, dash, and right parenthesis :-).

ethernet — A type of local area network.

e-zine — (n.) Electronic magazine. Refers to the content and the site of an online magazine product.

ethernet — (n.) A type of local area network (LAN) in which computers containing network cards are linked by cabling to other computers with similar cards.

FAQ — (n.) Acronym for "Frequently Asked Questions," commonly pronounced "fak." A text file that addresses common concerns about a given subject or topic.

file — (n.) A discreet, complete set of digital information containing such items as a text document, program instructions, graphic images, or data base resources. (v.) To cause information to be placed in computer storage.

firewall — (n.) A network security barrier designed to protect a local network from being accessed by unauthorized persons via the Internet. Typically, firewalls disable some of the Internet's packet sharing features to make outside access more difficult.

flame — (n., v.) Heated responses/insults directed at an individual who has posted something on the net to which the responder is reacting.

FTP — (n.) Acronym for File Transfer Protocol, a set of instructions for moving files across the network from one computer to another. Sometimes employed as if it were a verb (FTP'ed, FTP'ing): "I FTP'ed that program from Sunsite."

FWIW — Shorthand for "For What It's Worth."

FYI — Shorthand for "For Your Information."

gateway — (n.) An access point between networks or computer systems, a connection that allows computer systems to transfer data between normally incompatible applications or networks.

GIF — (n.) A graphics file specification popularized on the CompuServe network. GIF is an acronym for "Graphics Interchange Format." Widely used on the World Wide Web.

Gopher — (n.) An Internet program that organizes information into menu hierarchies. Gopher puts a uniform interface on network navigation, providing links to varied network resources scattered throughout the world and providing access to search tools for finding that information. Created at the University of Minnesota, where the school mascot is the Golden Gopher. (v.) To use Gopher client access network resources.

Gopher hole — (n.) Nickname given to a Gopher site and the collection of resources accessible from the site. Also called a "burrow."

Gopherspace — (n.) Aggregate of all resources available worldwide through Gopher servers. The cyberspace "places" occupied by Gopher servers and their resources.

home page — (n.) Applied to HTTP documents on the World Wide Web. Originally used to describe the page first loaded by a World Wide Web client program (browser) when it starts up. Has come to refer to the top page (welcome, or index page) of Web sites and to personal pages placed on web servers by many individuals.

host — (n.) A computer (system) offering network access, disk storage space, and client software to its account holders. Typically, the host is the computer where a person's electronic mail is received, stored, and processed. See also "client" and "site."

HTML — (n.) HyperText Markup Language, an ascii-based scripting language used to create documents served on the World Wide Web.

HTTP — (n.) HyperText Transfer Protocol, the network data communications specification used on the World Wide Web.

hypertext — (n.) A means of linking information.

IMHO — Shorthand for "In My Humble Opinion."

IMNSHO — Shorthand for "In My Not-So-Humble Opinion."

Internet Relay Chat (IRC) — (n.) Internet software that allows real-time interactive typed "conversations" among many participants.

Internet — (n.) The network of computer networks that use the TCP/IP communications protocol and can communicate with each other. Some people see the Internet as the prototype of the Information Superhighway.

list — (n.) In e-mail, all the people subscribed to a discussion group.

Listproc — (n.) A program for managing an e-mail discussion list. Very much like ListServ software.

ListServ — (n.) Software for managing an e-mail discussion list. ListServ takes messages sent to a list and distributes those messages to all who are subscribed. ListServ is also used to designate the machine on which the software resides.

lurk — (v.) To read, without posting, messages to a news group or an e-mail discussion list. Recommended behavior for people new to a list or group.

mirror — (n.) A computer site that provides the same resources as another, distant one. Set up to redirect network traffic away from especially popular, busy sites.

network — (n., v.) Computers linked in order to transfer information and share other resources. The act of so linking computers.

newbie — (n.) Term applied to persons new to a network or any one of its online communities.

news group — (n.) A discussion forum within the Usenet news system.

node — (n.) Term applied to a host computer (or computer system) for a subnetwork (LAN or WAN). The node is assigned a domain name and all other computers part of the system share that domain name.

packet — (n.) A discrete block of data carried over a network. The packet contains all or part of a text message (or a binary file), the addresses of the originating and destination computers, message assembly instructions, and error control information.

PC — (n.) Personal Computer. In this book it may mean a Macintosh, an IBM compatible, or any other machine that is yours to work with and on which you may run programs of your choice.

post — (v., n.) The act of sending a message to a discussion list or a news group. A message so sent.

PPP — (n.) Point-to-Point Protocol. A set of communications parameters that enables a computer to use TCP/IP over a standard voice telephone line and a high speed modem. PPP provides the computer the functionality of one directly connected to the Internet through a network card and cable.

program — (n.) A set of instructions written in binary code, telling a computer how to perform certain tasks. (v.) The act of writing such instructions.

protocol — (n.) A set of rules and procedures by which computers communicate.

RTFM — Shorthand for "Read the Manual." A curt response when somebody asks a question for which the answer is readily available elsewhere.

server — (n.) A machine on which resides software designed to deliver information across a network in a manner specifically recognized by a client. Also describes the software that delivers the information.

SIG — (n.) Acronym for "Special Interest Group," a virtual community of people who "meet" online to exchange information on a clearly defined topic of interest.

SLIP — (n.) Acronym for Serial Line Internet Protocol. A set of communications parameters that allows a computer to use TCP/IP over a standard voice telephone line using a high-speed modem. PPP provides the computer the functionality of one directly connected to the Internet through a network card and cable.

string — (n.) A series of characters tied together without interruption. A unique sequence of characters used to locate specific text is called a search string.

sysop — (n.) The systems operator, usually the owner, of a computer bulletin board. Sometimes used to identify the person who moderates a SIG on a larger system such as CompuServe or America OnLine.

system prompt — (n.) A character or string of characters that tell the computer user in a command line environment that the machine is waiting for a new command and that all non-system programs have terminated. In DOS, the system prompt is typically a "C:>"; in UNIX it often is "%"; in VMS it frequently is "$."

TCP/IP — (n.) Acronym for Transmission Control Protocol/Internet Protocol, the set of communications rules by which computers connected to the Internet talk to one another.

Telnet — (n.) an Internet application program that allows you to log onto another computer and to use programs available there.

terminal — (n.) A computer workstation composed of a monitor (VDT) for viewing computer output and a keyboard for talking to the computer or network. One of the most universally accepted terminals is the DEC VT100. Most personal computer communications programs allow the computer to emulate terminals such as VT100s so that the network host or server can understand what you type at your computer.

UNIX — (n.) A popular operating system used by computers more powerful than PCs. Server software is often based on computers running UNIX and many times people will log onto UNIX-based machines to access the Internet.

user name — (n.) A name assigned to an account holder by a system administrator. The user name is associated with a password in providing access to network computing resources.

virtual — (adj.) Having the quality of existing in effect, but not in reality. Network news groups are said to be virtual communities because they bring together many people who are united by common interests and goals.

virtual community — (n.) A term used to describe the collective presence of people who "come together" in an online setting to "chat" or exchange information on a topic of mutual interest. Used by Howard Rheingold as a title to a book about "life" on computer networks.

WAIS — (n.) Wide Area Information Servers allow for the indexing, identification and retrieval of information located on specific Internet computers. WAIS servers are accessed by WAIS client programs.

World Wide Web — (n.) allows for information located on many different computers to be linked through key terms. This approach is called Hypertext or Hypermedia. The Web is accessed through client programs such as Internet Explorer, Lynx, Mosaic, and Netscape.

Index

Interviewing
  e-mail and, 55–56
  in informatics
    research, 196
  MUDs and, 181–182
  in reporting process,
    187
Intranets, 21
Investigative Reporters
  and Editors
  organization. *See also*
  IRE-L
  Web reports from, 66
  Web site of, 76
IP. *See* Internet Protocol
  (IP)
IP number, 70. *See*
  Internet Protocol (IP)
IRC. *See* Internet Relay
  Chat (IRC)
IRE-L (Investigative
  Reporters and Editors
  List), 135
  subscribing to, 138
I/Spy Internet News
  Search tool, 189

Java programming
  language, 23, 226
Johns Hopkins
  University, role of e-
  mail in student
  shooting, 37
Johnson, Tom, 77
Journal do Brasil, 1–2
Journalism, on Web, 235
Journalists' Hotlists, 69
Journet, 200
JPEG format, 68, 80
Jpeg View (Mac), 68
Jughead search
  program, 85, 95–96,
  198

Kalnoskas, Aimee, 130
Kermit communication
  program, 101, 129, 165
  for bulletin board file
    transfers, 171

Keyboard commands.
  See Commands;
  Gopher
Key words
  for discussion list
    archives, 142
  for MUDs, 182–183
  for search engines,
    74–75
  in searches, 191
  in Usenet searches,
    156–157
  using with Archie, 131
Kiefer, Kara, 83
Kinsley, Michael, 221
Knight Ridder, online
  news from, 229
Knock-Knock feature, of
  Switchboard, 53–54

LANs. *See* Local area
  networks (LANs)
Law. *See* Ethical issues;
  Legal issues
Leads. *See* Story leads
Lee, Tim Beners, 24
Legal issues. *See also*
  Ethical issues; Libel
  confidentiality of
    information and
    sources, 213–215
  copyright, 208, 209–
    213
  copyright and
    discussion lists,
    141–142
  e-mail and, 42, 54
  and Internet, 203–204
  libel considerations,
    206–208
  misappropriation,
    209–210
  obscenity, 218
  speech codes, 215–216
Legislation. *See also*
  Legal issues;
  Regulation
  for Internet
    regulation, 205

Leutwyler, Kristin, 11
Lexis/Nexis system, 30,
  190
Libel, 206–208
  cases, 203
  definition of public
    figure and, 207
  Net culture, 207–208
Libraries, 33. *See also*
  Information online;
  Library of Congress
  CARL system, 190
  internetworking of,
    17–18
  virtual, 191
  World Wide Web
    Virtual Library, 75
Library of Congress, 33
  Gopher server at, 97,
    99–100
  virtual library and,
    191
Links
  ethics of, 235–236
  Web searches and, 70
  to Web sites, 229–230
"List of Active News
  Groups," 147
"List of Lists" document,
  address for obtaining,
  141
Listproc, 136, 138
Lists. *See also* Mailing
  lists
  discussion, 136–137
Listserv, 136. *See also*
  Discussion list
  addresses of relevant,
    140–141
  journalists uses of,
    158–159
  setting parameters for,
    138–139
"Live Gopher Jewels"
  site, 98
Local area networks
  (LANs), 13, 43
Local clients, 16
Local hosts, 15–16